Steven Zeeland

The Masculine Marine: Homoeroticism in the U.S. Marine Corps

Pre-publication
REVIEWS,
COMMENTARIES,
EVALUATIONS . . .

"**O**nce again Steven Zeeland is defining the cutting edge of sexual studies–for both scholars and general readers. Even sharper than his earlier military inquiries, *The Masculine Marine* guides us through the physical and psychic orifices of the modern Marine, challenging us and them to re-examine what makes a man masculine. The special treat Zeeland provides us in this book is his own fluid, alluring, personal narrative of how he came to know his Marine buddies, and how both he and they were changed by getting to know each other."

Frank Browning
Author, *A Queer Geography*
and *The Culture of Desire*

"**R**eading *The Masculine Marine* was a thorough pleasure. Through interviews, anecdotes, and speculation, Steven Zeeland introduces his readers to the gay male world of gender and desire in the military. Zeeland shows that the Marine 'masculinity' is wild territory. The hypermasculine Marine is not necessarily in conflict with intense desires for other men; on the contrary, the construction of Marine hypergender is in many ways the venue of gay male desire. This book not only furnishes enormously important and startling insights into male homoeroticism in Marine life, but it offers a way of understanding the construction of masculinity–a 'training' in masculinity that never pretends to know finally what masculinity is. Zeeland pursues the gendered meanings of homoeroticism, but never lets those meanings settle into simple formulae. Sexy, witty, smart, and shocking, this book weaves contemporary gay theory into excellent writing, and offers a view of Marine life that flies in the face of 'official' military renderings. In a time in which 'don't ask, don't tell' has inaugurated the heightening of official prurience into the lives of gay men, and homosexuality within the military is cast as a sign of public shame, Zeeland's book turns the tables. He tells the story of male homoeroticism in the military with shameless and compelling humor, insight, and courage, and forces us to rethink the image of the military as always and only an instrument of repression. This book will be key reading for anyone interested in gay writing, gays in the military, queer theory, and the construction of gender. It offers glimpses into a world that is rarely documented, and will make us all see how wonderfully common male homoeroticism is."

Judith Butler
Professor, Department of Rhetoric and Department of Comparative Literature, University of California, Berkeley; Author, *Gender Trouble* and *Bodies That Matter*

More pre-publication
REVIEWS, COMMENTARIES, EVALUATIONS . . .

"**S**teven Zeeland gives voice to men who have been robbed of their voices in the one-sided national 'debate' on gays in the military, and restores their humanity in the process. *The Masculine Marine* is a fascinating and candid look at the intimate lives and passions of a group of men played out against the homoerotic landscape that is the U.S. Marine Corps."

Susan Faludi
Author, *Backlash: The Undeclared War Against American Women*

"**N**ot a book about 'gays in the military' but a book about being young, male, American, and in love with masculinity in the nineties. Not a collection of interviews with jarheads but pure poetry about desire, identity, longing, and belonging, from men who are not supposed to dream. Zeeland's *The Masculine Marine* is a song of innocence and experience that speaks what should not be spoken in a world that doesn't want to listen."

Mark Simpson
Author, *Male Impersonators: Men Performing Masculinity*

"**C**ompelling reading. . . . The Marines' tales of erotic encounters and fantasies of submission undermine the stereotypes of masculinity so necessary to the conservative right's conception of the military and to their attacks on gay and lesbian liberation."

Jonathon Weinberg, PhD
Assistant Professor,
History of Art, Yale University;
Author, *Speaking for Vice*

The Masculine Marine
Homoeroticism
in the U.S. Marine Corps

HAWORTH Gay & Lesbian Studies
John P. De Cecco, PhD
Editor in Chief

The Masculine Marine
Homoeroticism in the U. S. Marine Corps

Steven Zeeland

Harrington Park Press
An Imprint of The Haworth Press, Inc.
New York • London

Published by

Harrington Park Press, an imprint of The Haworth Press, Inc., 10 Alice Street, Binghamton, NY 13904-1580

Depiction or mention of any person in this work should not be construed as an implication of said person's sexual orientation.

Names of, and some personal details about, active duty servicemembers depicted in this work have been changed or scrambled to protect their identities.

Cover designed by Marylouise E. Doyle.

Library of Congress Cataloging-in-Publication Data

Zeeland, Steven
    The masculine marine : homoeroticism in the U.S. Marine Corps / Steven Zeeland.
        p.   cm.
    ISBN 1-56023-874-7 (alk. paper).
    1. United States. Marine Corps–Gays. 2. Gays–United States–Identity. I. Title.
VE23.Z44 1996
306.76'6'088355–dc20   96-6803
                                                                                           CIP

CONTENTS

ABOUT THE AUTHOR

Steven Zeeland is the author of *Sailors and Sexual Identity: Crossing the Line Between "Straight" and "Gay" in the U. S. Navy* and *Barrack Buddies and Soldier Lovers*, both also published by The Haworth Press. He attended the University of Michigan at Ann Arbor and is a Research Associate at the Center for Research and Education in Sexuality (CERES) at San Francisco State University.

Prologue

Central to the pursuit of Marineness is an eroticization of the purposively elusive.

I was 22 when I discovered a taste for military men. My best friend Brent had joined the Army, and married. I had followed him to Germany intent on seeing him discharged—and divorced. The Army, more perverse than I could ever aspire to be, hired me to clerk for an on-base athletic goods store. After my first week of employment, I informed Brent that the soldiers who shopped there were ugly.

"What do you mean, 'ugly'?" he asked.

"You know," I answered. "*Häßlich*. Physically unattractive." I liked college boys, and I felt strongly that Brent must become one. GIs seemed to me unacceptably coarse and antithetically opposed to my left-wing Ann Arbor values.

The Army guys who shopped in the store *were* typically loud, sneering, and disgruntled. Their chief topic of conversation was the number of days remaining before they returned to "the world" or got out of the Army altogether. Their attitude toward military service was summed up by the many T-shirts and ball caps they commissioned us to emblazon with felt letters spelling FTA, for "Fuck the Army." (Later, it was precisely this rebel pose that I came to relish in soldiers—and, somewhat modified, in sailors).

Another element of my job description was to fit soldiers with the special insulated combat boots our store sold. One day, kneeling before an MP in battle dress uniform, I looked up at him and understood that (*swoon*) I had eroticized the lost love object-as-soldier.

Brent was gone, which only made me want him all the more. But now I had a few thousand Brents.

My fellow employees at the store included a lower middle-class New Hampshire mother-daughter team named Susan and Wendy. When her mom wasn't looking, Wendy, a senior at Frankfurt American High School, liked to flirt with the GIs, an activity I soon emulated. One day, an off-duty serviceman came in who immediately struck us both as different. He had about him a certain aura— serene, self-possessed, yet severe—like some kind of cultist. And he had about him the scent of sexual promise. The fiercely competitive Wendy beat me to the draw, and so got to do all the kneeling. As this enigmatic stranger, a guard at the consulate, left the store, she whispered to me in thrilled, reverential awe: "He's *a Marine*."

Ten years later, after my relocation to the States, I was visiting a bookstore in San Francisco's Haight called DEVIANT, and I was eyeing two very quiet, very handsome young men with severely cropped hair. When they left the store, I overheard one clerk ask another, "Do you think they were real Marines? Or just queens?" By then I could pronounce with authority: "They were both."

But even after I had come to *know* Marines, I was still sometimes liable to be suckered into mistaking a wanna-be for the real thing, and I was still unable to say just what a "real Marine" was.

One summer evening in the Clinton years finds me loitering, pretending to look at boring porn magazines at an adult bookstore near Marine Corps Recruit Depot (MCRD), San Diego. A man comes through the door sporting a "high and tight" haircut, scowling demeanor, hard-muscled body, and tight jeans outlining a thick bulging dick. He obtains change at the counter. *This is someone trying to look like a Marine*, I think. Or . . .? Studying his walk as he heads for the video booths, I decide I will try the handle to his door.

It is unlocked. I step in and sit down across from him in the spacious upholstered booth so thoughtfully required of peep shows by San Diego municipal codes. With studied impassiveness he stares at the screen, flicking past channels, pausing for long moments on images of "straight" sex. My heart is beating with excitement—and fear; he looks so mean and tough. (A caption to an illustration in the *Marine Battle Skills Training Handbook*: "Execute a heel stomp to your opponent's skull, ending the encounter."[1]) I reach over and lay my hand on the inside of his thigh. He looks me in the eye and curtly announces: "I just want to be sucked. Nothing else."

Beneath his jeans I find white discount store briefs hand-lettered with his last name. . . .

I have the nerve to ask him for a ride home. On the way there (I get him lost), I manage to pump from him some monosyllabic utterances. He is stationed at Camp Lejeune. He is in San Diego, for the first time since boot camp, to attend recruiter school. No, there are no adult bookstores where he lives in North Carolina. Downtown San Diego has changed a lot in ten years. Not as sleazy as he remembered. (His visit to the video arcade seems to have been inspired by nostalgia.) As we approach my neighborhood, Hillcrest, I comment on workers setting up barriers for the following day's lesbian and gay pride parade. He is silent. At my gate, I invite him to come up and watch some more videos. He says he has to go, but he does take my card.

Drinking bad watery beer the next afternoon with friends who, like me, have paid eight dollars for their pride, I am unnerved to spy my Marine in wraparound sunglasses chatting effusively with friends. Incensed at having been taken in, I march over and greet him with sarcasm. Politely, this man answers me with a voice, a style, and a story at odds with The Recruiter—it isn't him after all, only a civilian look-alike.

The following week I return to the video arcade. After I've waited several hours, The True Recruiter reappears. This time, as I kneel before him, he interrupts to ask of me, dreamily: "What did you want me to do over at your house? I kept *thinkin' about callin' you*. I kept *thinkin' about what we'd do*."

"Mmmm"—I clear my mouth—"we could go there now."

But he doesn't want to do that; he wants me to suggest something else I could do with him in the booth.

Exiting the bookstore, My Recruiter is at least a little more talkative than the last time. It turns out that he is probably going to fail recruiter school. Unsurprisingly, he is stoic about the prospect. Out of habit I begin to interview him, soliciting his opinion on the media hoopla over the rejected Marine Corps policy of barring young Marines from marrying.

He dismisses my inquiry: "Civilians just don't understand Marines."

We arrive in front of the Boll Weevil meat restaurant and bar and he excuses himself. "Got to go in and see my girlfriend." He offers that he will meet me at the same time and place next week.

He wasn't there. *That is why I still fantasize about him . . .*

This, I believe, illustrates a paradox that confronts me in writing this book: *The less I tell you about Marines, the more satisfied you may be.* A sailor friend asked of me, almost indignantly, "How could you even write a book about Marines? They're not like soldiers or sailors." It is, after all, a mythical, even mystical image that the Marine Corps propagates in order to maintain public favor, and to recruit young men ("and women"—authors of books on Marines usually add parenthetically or in footnotes) who will strive to fulfill the image. Marines are fundamentally different from common soldiers only to the extent that they believe in Marineness.

It would seem I am doomed to disappoint. If I am too successful in penetrating the Marine mystique, some readers will resent me for having cheated them of a cherished illusion (or will merely dismiss the book as unrepresentative of "real" Marines). If, on the other hand, I proffer only another soft-focus paean to the ineffable glory of "the" Marine—well, you probably will have already guessed that I won't be doing that.

It is not my purpose to embarrass or denigrate the Marine Corps— on the contrary. Although (or more probably because) I am a pacifistic ethical vegetarian, I have a great love of military men. This book is intended to celebrate the homoerotic lure of "the masculine Marine," even as it documents flaws and contradictions in that archetype. I believe this can be of use in subverting the force of manmade categories that trap us all: "straight" and "gay," "masculine" and "feminine," and ultimately "man" and "woman."

* * *

This book is the final volume of a series of interviews conducted with U.S. Armed Forces service members between 1990 and 1995. The first volume, *Barrack Buddies and Soldier Lovers*, recorded the voices of soldiers and airmen stationed in the former West Germany. The second, *Sailors and Sexual Identity: Crossing the Line Between "Straight" and "Gay" in the U.S. Navy*, is more closely related to this book. Both were authored in the same place (San Diego). They overlap in time, and reference some persons common to both. As before, I generally prefer to present stories rather than explain them. And I stubbornly persist in believing that a text can be both scholarly and salacious.

As befits Marines, I have endeavored to make this the leanest and most disciplined of my writings. I conducted multiple taped interviews with 21 Marines; the verbatim transcripts of conversations with nine Marines are included here. Some quotes from other interviews are referenced in the endnotes. My methodology has not changed: I befriended servicemen, sometimes in an intimate way, in part to win their trust so that I could ask them terribly personal questions, and in part just because I liked them. The interviews included here represent those Marines I learned the most from.

I am indebted to my senior editor, John P. DeCecco; my kind and generous publisher, Bill Cohen; my managing editor, Bill Palmer, who always found time in his busy schedule for me; the other good people at The Haworth Press, including Patricia Brown, Marylouise Doyle, Sarah Eldred, Lisa Franko, Peg Marr, Paula Patton, Margaret Tatich, and Susan Trzeciak; Jon-Paul Baumer; Frank Browning, who forgave my blondness and gave me good advice; Rolf Hardesty, who generously supplied me with materials from his archive of military erotica; David Lloyd; Sal Lucarello, Gene Nocon; pioneering sex writer, editor, and publisher Scott O'Hara; Mark Simpson, whose work and friendship inspired me to persevere when my spirits were flagging; pop culture archivist par excellence Bart Snowfleet; Wayne Stanley; my good Hillcrest neighbors David Alberts, Monica Brown, Mark Gabrish Conlan, Shawn DiNunzio and Austin Wallace; Steven Patrick Morrissey, who, along with Jeremy, Max, and Samantha, gave me reasons to live; and my unfailingly supportive friends Tom Adesko, Udo Boll, Thomas Hach, Heinz Kort, Sabine Schröder, Melvin, T. C. Merritt, Tom Purdy, Tom Ragusa, Hannelorre Schultes, Uwe Sohncke, Phillip Torrente, and Brian Younker.

Most especially, of course, I thank the Marines who so generously contributed to this book.

S.Z.
San Diego

Introduction:
Penetrating Marine Machismo

"He's never been with a fag, have you Butch?"

Half-Cherokee finished his beer with a provocative long suck.
"No, sir, and I ain't startin' now. Hell, in the Marines at Pendleton, they was selling their asses for ten bucks a throw—but
not yours truly! I was always saving up for a good broad. Like
you, Myra."

—Gore Vidal, *Myron*

To be a Marine is to be thought a man. Masculine. *Unquestionably*
heterosexual.

Constituting just 6 percent of the service, women in the Marine
Corps are called "woman Marines" and are barred from the military
occupational specialty that popularly defines the Marine: life-taking
rifleman.

"Gay Marines" would seem to be another oxymoron. Our heterosexual system demands that man and woman be "opposite sexes."[1]
Gay men are popularly conceived of as persons with the bodies of
men and the heterosexual desires of women—less than all-man, and
the opposite of Marines. One Marine publicly expressing his opposition to gay Marines wrote, "It makes my skin crawl to think you half
men are wearing a Man's [sic] uniform."[2]

Again and again in my work on this and my previous two books,
when I asked military men what a man should be, they could only
answer, "Not a woman." When I asked them, "What is masculine?"
they told me, "The opposite of feminine." I kept waiting for more,
something that would address the complicated mingling of "masculine" and "feminine" attributes I saw in even the butchest soldier boys
I lusted after. With a curious reluctance, my interviewees added that

1

masculine *could* mean "forceful," "projecting," and "well-built"—qualities, some of them remarked, that women sometimes surpassed men in exhibiting. At last I began to catch on: these men's initial simple answers said it all. "Masculine man" can *only* exist as the opposite of "feminine woman." Writes Judith Butler:

> One is one's gender to the extent that one is not the other gender, a formulation that presupposes and enforces that restriction of gender within that binary pair. . . . There is no gender identity behind the expressions of gender; that identity is performatively constituted by the very "expressions" that are said to be its results.[3]

Growing up, I was taught that masculinity was the *natural* expression of maleness, a fundamental *animal* quality that grew from the penis and testicles. But if this were true, why would males have to join the Marine Corps to become . . . male?

We know that this is the primary reason why young men enlist in the military, especially the Marine Corps. Says a former commandant of the Marine Corps:

> There is an inherent need in all males of the animal world to prove their masculinity or maleness. . . . The Marine Corps reputation, richly deserved, for physical toughness, courage, and its demands on mind and body, attracts those who want to prove their manliness. Here the search ends.[4]

But Marines are more complex than, say, fighting dogs. Marine masculinity is a cultural, historical, and personal *human invention*, and scrutiny of its display reveals deliciously perverse—and instructive—flaws and contradictions. Consider just a few of the problems pointed to by the Marines interviewed in this book: 1990s Marines devote attention to appearance so fastidious as to be called effeminate or narcissistic. In building up and exhibiting their hard-muscled bodies, Marines may be mistaken for gay gym queens. In striving to be "more man than a man can ever be," they may be called butch drag queens. And what about the strong sexual undercurrent rippling among men who exalt the masculine over the feminine and live and work in a "Spartan" environment? Even gays may discount sexual acts accompanying military bonding as mere "situational homosexuality" devoid of deeper emotional meaning.[5] But Marines, famously, risk and sacrifice their lives for the *love* of their brother Marines.[6]

That homoerotic bonding is the secret to an effective fighting force is old news. In ancient Greece, homosexuality was understood to augment, not weaken, military unit cohesion. Then, as today, some voices said that soldier-love should be platonic. But the Sacred Band of Thebes was an elite army of male-male *lovers.*[7] (Some have joked that the Marine Corps leadership had the Sacred Band in the back of their minds when, in 1993, they sought to bar Marines from marrying heterosexually.[8])

"Homosexual" is not the right noun, however, for the ancient Greek warrior. And, in his foreword to Jonathan Ned Katz's *The Invention of Heterosexuality*, Gore Vidal points out about heterosexuality that:

> The Greeks didn't know what it was. They knew about reproduction. They knew about lust and love. They knew about the intensity of sexual desire between men and men, women and women, but for them, Lesbos was just an island off the coast of Asia Minor while Sappho was your average Pulitzer Prize winning poet.[9]

In ancient Greece, it was considered normal and manly for a man to want to insert his penis in the anus or between the hairless thighs of a younger man or boy. The adult free man known to willingly permit a penis to enter him, however, was publicly disgraced for repudiating his penetrator privilege. Plutarch reported that "Those who enjoy playing the passive role we treat as the lowest of the low, and we have not the slightest degree of respect or affection for them."[10] Culturally distinct varieties of this warrior top-man ethos are said to have prevailed among the Japanese samurai,[11] the Vikings,[12] and among German militarists of the 1920s and 1930s.[13] In many macho cultures of the world today (in southern Europe, in northern Africa, in Central America), a man may have sex with other men and still be considered virile as long as he *stays on top.*[14]

How, then, are we to understand a popular belief among contemporary gays that United States Marines, when they engage in sex with other males, demonstrate a marked, consistent preference to play the "passive" role in anal intercourse? This idea, known to every one of the hundreds of self-identified gay sailors and Marines I have spoken with, is propagated by anecdotes,[15] jokes,[16] and erotica,[17] and has led to the formation of many clever theories that seek to explain such a seemingly shocking contradiction. For what could be more incongruous than the picture of the most macho of American fighting men—indeed, the most potent surviving icon of traditional masculinity (think of John Wayne in *The Sands of Iwo Jima*, or Clint Eastwood in *Heartbreak Ridge*)—wanting to *take it like a woman?*

One might reasonably question whether this claim is not motivated simply by a wish to discredit Marine masculinity, to say that, behind their macho facades, Marines are not really so tough after all. But when gay men recount instances of picking up studly, super-butch Marines only to get them home and have them (eventually) roll over, it is typically not with smug triumph, but with disappointment. Perhaps even more than Marines, the Marine-chaser wants to believe that to be a Marine is to be *all man*. So when sailor Trent says, "Most of the Marines I've encountered are bottoms," he adds ruefully, "It's a big turnoff for me. Most of the guys I pick up are normally pretty big, and I can't see me pumpin' their kitty."[18]

That plenty of Marines are in practice "exclusive tops" (that is, penetrators of their orifices of choice)—or at least "versatile'—is not the point. For the stereotype encapsulates an unsettling truth: all men, even the most "masculine," *can* be bottoms.

In *Male Impersonators: Men Performing Masculinity*, Mark Simpson writes that:

> The performance of masculinity in all its various rites, from football to war, has more to do with the anxiety a man has about the "hole" hidden between his legs than his phallus, the possession of which he is forever advertising. If, as Quentin Crisp has suggested, homosexuality is "the fatal flaw" in masculinity, then the anus is the fatal flaw in men, a physical flaw that admits the psychical one, one that they must constantly repudiate because their anus, much as they might like to pretend otherwise, is always with them.[19]

The first thing to strike the prurient observer about a seemingly physically representative embodiment of the stereotypical Marine is likely to be his ass, "the seat of a Marine's vanity."[20] Readers who doubt this crude generalization need only visit Oceanside, California[21] to see for themselves jarheads with *awesomely* muscular buttocks uncannily true to the gay caricature of Figure 12. Simpson, in his trenchant analysis of the pursuit of masculinity among soccer players, might just as easily be writing of Marines when he notes:

> All that running around produces a *physical* reassurance against the possibility of penetration: the famous footballer's arse. The swollen gluteus maximus and quadriceps are the strong, sturdy, vigilant "goalkeepers" of his rectum. But as ever, the disavowal contains within it the seeds of his failure: the overdeveloped legs and arses of footballers have the effect of drawing the spectator's eye to them, so that the male rectum, his "ass,". . . becomes the unacknowledged centre of attention.[22]

Camp Pendleton Marines do a great deal of running, forced march hill-climbing ("humping"), and leg-building exercises—activities that, according to one Marine bottom theorist, "make for itchy prostates."[23] Another theorist counters that the Marine Corps *attracts* men of a certain square, muscular "mesomorphic somatotype"—anatomically destined to serve as deluxe, voluptuous bottoms.[24] (One Marine I interviewed recalled his surprise at the number of recruits in his platoon who arrived at boot camp already in possession of Marine Corps bodies, and even USMC tattoos.)[25] But there are plenty of Marines with thin, wiry frames and nominal buttocks. Some of the drill instructors I observed at Marine Corps Recruit Depot, San Diego[26] were astonishingly slight of build (these, I was told, are often the meanest).

Theories that presume to explain "Marine sexuality" inevitably come paired with annoyingly contradictory counter-theories.

Recruit training can exert a powerful and lingering influence on all spheres of any service member's life. Marine Corps boot camp is longer and far more rigorous than that of the other branches. In the course of three months, recruits are supposed to be stripped of their individual civilian identities, reassembled as Marines, and taught to tightly bond as an elite "band of brothers." That Marines are different from members of the other regular forces ("harder," more serious, more professional, and more mysterious) is usually attributed to boot camp.

But men who join the Marine Corps are already different *before* they go to boot camp. They are the select targeted *few* who buy what the USMC (through television commercials and recruiter-salesmen, and in collusion with Hollywood iconography) is selling.[27] The Army, the Air Force, and the Navy entice with promises of cash for college, technical training, and travel.[28] The Marine Corps advertises a hard masculine image: *look like* the poster Marine in his dress blue uniform—and a hard masculine identity: *be* one of us, "the few, the proud, the Marines." Soldiers, sailors, or airmen are likely to say that they are "*in the*" Army, Navy, or Air Force. But a Marine will tell you that he *is* a Marine—with a capital "M." (Marine identity may not even be contingent on being in the Marine Corps, for it is said "Once a Marine, always a Marine.") A gay porn magazine piece on cruising Marines comments on this pitch:

> Here is an obvious appeal to elitism. It has its biggest pull on the boy who feels he has something to prove. The outcast, the jail-bird, the hillbilly poor. Also, the boy who's afraid he's queer, who thinks he'll be cured by a baptism of fire into manhood. I suspect that the brutality of Marine boot camp is one of the Corps' hidden selling points. . . . [Marine recruits] are never addressed as anything above the level of "shit maggots" until graduation day, when they are called Marines for the first time. To come out of such a program intact requires a fiercely independent mind. Grunts are not noted for fiercely independent minds. So after weeks of ego-smashing and pecking-order bootlicking, what the Corps turns out, often, is the most physically-fit masochists in the world. They have been submersed in a manhood mystique as thorough, as seductive, as any experienced by gay men.[29]

Alex, a Marine corporal interviewed in this book, confirms that some Marines eroticize the pain and humiliations of boot camp:

> There are times when I like to play the bottom, and there is a naturalness to it that I attribute to being in the Marine Corps. In the breakdown phase of recruit training, they totally debase you. The drill instructors talk down to you, call you "maggot"—they make you feel worthless, subhuman. They totally strip you of your identity, so as to build you back up as a Marine. Even outside of basic training, the Marine Corps still debases you. As a

Marine, you always strive to please your higher ups. There is a craving to serve, to win approval, or even love. . . .[30]

But the prospect of being abused in boot camp may itself attract young men to the Marine Corps. Of the Marines I talked to who told me that they had been physically struck by drill instructors (DIs), most said they felt that they deserved it; some offered that they would have felt disappointed had they not been hit. Corporal Jack even expressed the wish that boot camp would have been more like it was depicted in the movie *Full Metal Jacket*.[31]

A Freudian theory of Marine sexuality may find almost embarrassingly blunt support in some of these interviews. Alex entertained both patricidal and sexual fantasies of the DI-as-father. Corporal Ted (whose sexual preference is for women, though he sometimes dreams of men) seems to have joined the Marine Corps in hopes of winning love from his drifter dad. And First Lieutenant Frank, a bodybuilder who grew up as a fatherless sissy-boy, describes how his first fantasy of being anally penetrated occurred in boot camp with the top man a DI. Guilt about his desire for a man senior to him led Frank to abandon the fantasy in favor of imitating, of becoming like, the drill instructor. In this, he doubtless accomplished what every good Marine is supposed to (and put the lesson to excellent use in advancing his successful military career).

Major Luke describes his father as strong and very present, but, just like all of his family members, emotionally cold. An aviator, Luke tells us that, in flight school, when asked the hypothetical question whether they would rather vomit on a public conveyance or slam their fingers in a car door, Marines invariably state a preference to crush their fingers. (Navy men would rather throw up.) "Isolated pain, as opposed to public humiliation," is how Luke characterizes the choice. But there is a nagging suspicion that Marines see some *reward* in pain. (We have already seen how even a sailor may associate the pain of getting a tattoo with the masculinity of his father, equated with "putting yourself through pain to make yourself look good"[32]—another quality it may share with femininity.)

The authors of a 1971 book detailing boot camp abuses, *See Parris and Die*, say that:

Marines understand that young men join their ranks for a variety of personal reasons, some of which they may not understand themselves. It is significant to note that enlistments *rose* following publicity surrounding the McKeon "death march" of 1956 [a drill instructor-devised punishment in which seventy-five recruits were ordered to march in a swamp at night and six drowned].

According to these authors, the Marine Corps "satisfies the needs of the poorly adjusted late adolescent." Such teenage boys "are searching for the firm, dependable father figure they never had. In training they regress to a much younger stage of this dependency, in which their basic motivation is to please the father figure." A Navy psychologist is cited:

> The phallic aggressive imagery used by the Drill Instructor to spur his recruits onward may help them toward focusing their sexual drives appropriately, although it is unlikely that feelings of tenderness and compassion are thus inculcated. For the insecure and uncertain, the opportunity to fondle and sleep with his rifle must be a powerful contribution toward his masculine self-image.

To this, a second Navy psychologist responds:

> I agree with your concept of phallic aggressive imagery, but I think you underplay the latent homosexual relationship between the Drill Instructor and the recruit. This, incidentally, is part of many initiation rites. The initiate first has to accept the homosexual penetration by the adult before he is made a part of the adult group.[33]

The Marine Corps might well be compared with the male ritual cults of Papua New Guinea societies studied by anthropologist Gilbert Herdt, who believe that boys can only become warriors by being anally or orally infused with the semen of older men[34] (and by undergoing deprivations, torments, and tests of endurance surpassing even those demanded of Marines. The Sambia tribe drive sharp grasses up the noses of initiates; another tribe favors a "severe penis cutting" ritual.[35] On October 28, 1993, millions of U.S. viewers of ABC television's *Prime Time* watched videotaped footage of senior members of the Marine Corps' elite "silent drill team" in Yuma, Arizona, applying burning chemicals to the penises and anuses of initiates.[36] In their interviews in this book, Alex, Frank, and Jack describe the "blood stripe" ritual accompanying the promotion to corporal of enlisted Marines—painful blows to the thighs and upper arms, and metal pins driven into the collarbone.[37] It is the understanding of both the Sambia and the Marines that "Unless boys undergo the rigors of initiation, they will remain soft and weak"[38]). But in conferring gender identity, Sambia ritual homosexuality carefully preserves rank structure. The elder New Guinea tribesmen do not admit to letting initiates top them.

The first interview of this book begins with Corporal Keith, who sees himself as dominant and aggressive, describing how, patrolling an empty barracks one night on MP duty in Okinawa, he came upon two Marines having sex: a private first class topping a captain. Keith dates his first homosexual fantasies to this picture. A corporal, he fantasized about the private fucking him.

Is this a turnaround from the traditional warrior top?

* * *

In "The Gay Daddy" chapter of his book *Homos*, Leo Bersani analyzes, via Foucault, the reversibility of roles in sadomasochism. He suggests that:

> Perhaps inherent in the very exercise of power is the temptation of its renunciation—as if the excitement of a hyperbolic self-assertion, of an unthwarted mastery over the world, and more precisely, brutalization of the other, were inseparable from an impulse of self-dissolution. . . .[39]

In his earlier essay "Is the Rectum a Grave?" Bersani emphasized the persistence of the ancient Greeks' view that "*To be penetrated is to abdicate power.*"[40] The issue, Bersani says, is not about top/bottom, but inserter/insertee because "for the woman to get on top is just a way of letting her play the game of power for awhile, although . . . even on the bottom, the man can still concentrate his deceptively renounced aggressiveness in the thrusting movement of his penis."[41] Bersani theorizes that in fearing/desiring anal penetration, dominating masculine men ache for self-dissolution, "that is, female sexuality as a male body has in fantasy experienced it."[42] (Interestingly, Bersani has very little to say about sucking, an activity that nicely confuses the issue of who is the "active" and who is the "passive" party.)

However, some Marines I have known claim that Marines view being penetrated not at all as female, but as a *manly* test of endurance that, successfully withstood, leaves the bottom with *more* power. According to Captain Eric, "it takes a lot more masculinity to be a bottom than to be a top." He recites a favorite DI aphorism: "Pain is weakness leaving the body."

But stimulating the anus and prostate can provide physical ecstasy (which may make getting fucked not all that different from "submitting" to getting sucked). Eric concedes: "There's thirty seconds of pain and then it's pleasure. Speaking from my experience." Whatever other rewards some of them may be seeking, butch Marines, notorious for abnegating responsibility for their homosexual contacts, may take selfish, *lazy* pleasure in getting fucked. Yes, this is a pleasure that ordinary men are, like the ancient Greeks, supposed to repudiate in the interest of preserving their penetrator power. But Marines are not ordinary men. As Frank points out, having survived the hell of boot camp, Marines are fitted with an armor of supermasculinity that may allow them to play with the man-woman binarism secure in the belief that, whatever they do, they will always land back on top.

Sometimes, they may even come to see through the binarism.

* * *

I remember a group of sailors in the audience on "The Geraldo Show." After it was announced who and what I was, they kept on looking at me, they kept on wanting something. I could feel their eyes traveling up and down my surgically-constructed, hormonally-enhanced woman's body. What's the pull? What is it about a sexually-blended, gender-bended body that lights those flames? I know it gets me going!

—Kate Bornstein, *Gender Outlaw*[43]

Early on in *Homos*, Bersani (although he admits to no special knowledge of, or attraction to, military men; he points to a possible "continuity between a sexual preference for rough and uniformed trade, a sentimentalizing of the armed forces, and right-wing politics"[44]), tackles the subject of gay sailors and (with no transition) gay Marines. He concedes the point I tried to make in *Sailors and Sexual Identity*, in his words that "the homoeroticism inherent in military life . . . risks being exposed to those who would at once deny and enjoy it when self-confessed homos from within the ranks go public." But he argues that:

> Perhaps the most serious danger in gay Marines being open about their gayness is that they might begin, like some of their gay civilian brothers, to play at being Marines. Not that they would make fun of the Marines. On the contrary: they may find ways of being so Marine-like that they will no longer be "real" Marines. . . . In imagining what he presumably already is (both gay and a Marine), the gay Marine may learn the invaluable lesson that identity is not serious (as if what he is imitating never existed before it was imitated). Nothing is more inimical to military life than that lesson. . . . The military might lose them as they begin to move about in their roles, to voice and advertise their versatile (ever hardening and ever melting) masculinity in a context where masculinity is not supposed to move. The gay soldier letting out his gayness may begin to see its theatricalities as incompatible with the monolithic theatricality of military masculinity.[45]

Bersani is certainly correct to say that Marine masculinity is not supposed to *publicly* move. The Marine Corps (as opposed to the Navy, as Lieutenant Frank testifies) has no room for men who *advertise* sexual versatility. But in contrast to what Bersani imagines to be their civilian "gay brothers" in San Francisco and New York, gay Marines do not seem to come, over time, to view masculinity ironically. The gay Marines I have met are all *terribly* serious people. Keith's leatherman forays into the pages of *Drummer* magazine may or may not have conflicted with the Marine Corps' public image (though he perhaps threatened to become a parody of a "real" Marine, the Hollywood machismo that many Marines seek to emulate is itself parodic). But Keith continued to view both his Marineness and his "gayness" with a near *religious* solemnity—so much so that he undertook to have a custom tattoo designed featuring the Marine Corps anchor, globe, and eagle logo superimposed over a gay rainbow flag, and had it tattooed over his heart.[46]

And Marines do not have to adopt a gay identity in order to, at least privately, play with military masculinity. Alex tells us that his buddy Brian liked to wear nylons and nail polish, that his friend Shane confessed a fondness for his wife's vibrator, and that his gunnery sergeant regularly declaimed that being a Marine was "all an act."[47] Sergeant Wood, whose sexual preference is for women, says that Marines, out in the field, take pleasure in acting like "frivolous girls." In fact, perceived-straight Marines might often be at least a little freer to play with gender than their often humorlessly macho (because *still not masculine enough*) gay self-identified counterparts.

In a story for *The New Yorker*, Susan Faludi recounted her visit to a gay bar near The Citadel, an all-male Southern military college embroiled in controversy over whether to admit females. Her purpose was to collect stories about the hate crimes she assumed cadets must be committing against gay men. She discovered that there had been several bashings, but Faludi was surprised to learn something else from visiting the gay bar:

> "The proper terminology for The Citadel," a customer at the bar named Chris said, "is The Closet." Up and down the bar, heads bobbed in agreement. "They love faggots like me. . . . The cadets go for drag queens." Chris' observation was echoed in ensuing conversations in the bar. There are thousands of cadets, presumably, who have not dated drag queens, but . . . I could find only two drag queens, out of maybe a dozen, who did not tell me of dating a cadet—and that was only because these two found Citadel men "too emotional."

A drag queen called Tiffany told Faludi: "It's like all of us are female illusionists and they are male illusionists. A man in a uniform is kind of a dream. . . . For Halloween, you know what my cadet boyfriend wanted to dress as? A cadet."[48]

On the streets of Oceanside, transvestite prostitutes sell their bodies to Marines who know that they are not "real" women.[49] The conventional explanation is that such Marines are merely seeking a form of closeted gay sex. But isn't it possible that some of these men might, on some level, be yearning for at least momentary liberation from the straitjacket of gender itself?

Keith admits to being aroused by women who look like men; Alex is turned on by drag queens. In line at the San Diego airport, I was surprised to find myself enraptured by the "feminine" prettiness of a butch Marine in dress blues standing before me. Susan Sontag, in her famous "Notes on Camp," wrote that "the most refined form of sexual attractiveness (as well as the most refined form of sexual pleasure) consists in going against the grain of one's sex. What is most beautiful in virile men is something feminine; what is most beautiful in feminine women is something masculine."[50] But as Judith Butler points out—and this is terribly important—if:

> we dispense with the priority of "man" and "woman" as abiding substances, then it is no longer possible to subordinate dissonant gendered features as so many secondary and accidental character-istics of a gender ontology that is fundamentally intact. If the notion of an abiding substance is a fictive construction produced through the compulsory ordering of attributes into coherent gen-der sequences, then it seems that gender as substance, the viabil-ity of *man* and *woman* as nouns, is called into question by the dissonant play of attributes that fail to conform to sequential or causal models of intelligibility.[51]

("Common sense" answers that there are some obvious physical differences between men and women. But Butler and other feminists point to the seeming impossibility of considering sexed bodies inde-pendently of culturally mandated interpretations of what physical "differences" mean.[52])

So-called dumb jarheads may sometimes understand more of this than those who theorize or fantasize about them imagine. After ten years in the service, poster-Marine Frank admits to being "kinda lost" behind his super-butch Parris Island-built armor. Hard, unfeel-ing masculinity is, he has come to realize, "not a natural thing . . . but it's done so subconsciously that it seems innate."

Obviously, most Marines don't, won't, or can't talk about "gender ontology." But even the fabled Marine who recites the classic lie "Oh man, was I drunk last night" to excuse the fact that he has had sex with another man may be displaying not just his fear that what he has done will be called queer—that is, unmanly—but his recognition that *it is dishonest and unfair to call what he has done any significant departure from what anyone else might feel or do*. Maybe he recognizes as factitious the only socially accepted excuse for what is really only (like even the most "trangressive" imaginable human sexual acts) the mundane exercise of just another human potential.

The biggest problem for gay Marines is that in conceptualizing their desire as *other*, they may cut themselves off from physical and emotional closeness with Marines.[53] U.S. gay activists have campaigned for a policy that would allow service members to come out publicly with the proviso that they never actually engage in sex. The reverse might conceivably serve the Marine Corps better: continuing to ban declarations of gay identity (a potentially divisive distinction in what is supposed to be a secretly homoerotic environment) but eliminating penalties for sexual behavior that does, after all, sometimes accompany the tight bonding and brother-love the military so prizes. Maybe the Marine Corps is, in a rarified way, already "homosexual" enough.

But of course since there really is no essential difference between "homosexuals" and "heterosexuals," military men who subscribe to supposedly opposite sexual identities can, and do, effectively bond.

* * *

When I tell friends that I can no longer divide men up into gay and straight, they sometimes answer that I am overlooking an obvious distinction. "Straight men like *pussy*. Gay men like *dick!*" It bears repeating, however, that human sexuality is shaped not in the genitals, but in the mind. Even a disembodied penis penetrating a glory hole in a Camp Pendleton bowling alley men's room is always something more than *meat*,[54] and may mean something different to me than it does to you—and could mean something different still tomorrow.

In *The Invention of Heterosexuality*, historian Jonathon Ned Katz has documented how heterosexuality as we know it was invented to universalize man-on-top-of-woman sex as the only "natural" sex even when pursued not for procreation, but for recreation. He writes, "To be sure, a reproductive necessity, distinctions between the sexes, and eroticism among the sexes have been around for a long time. But sexual reproduction, sex difference, and sexual pleasure have been produced and combined in different social systems in radically different ways."[55] Our words "homosexual" and "heterosexual," Katz reminds us, are little more than one-hundred years old.

He quotes Gore Vidal:

> [T]here is no such thing as a homosexual or a heterosexual person. . . . Most people are a mixture of impulses if not practices, and what anyone does with a willing partner is of no social or cosmic significance. So why all the fuss? In order for a ruling class to rule, there must be arbitrary prohibitions. Of all prohibitions, sexual taboo is the most useful because sex involves everyone. . . . We have allowed our governors to divide the population into two teams. One team is good, godly, straight; the other is evil, sick, vicious.[56]

And he quotes James Baldwin, who sees the "Homosexual" as the creation of:

> the macho men—truck drivers, cops, football players—these people are far more complex than they want to realize. . . . They have needs which, for them, are literally inexpressible. They don't dare look into the mirror. And that is why they need faggots. They've created faggots in order to act out a sexual fantasy on the body of another man and not take any responsibility for it.[57]

Baldwin also observed that "It is quite impossible to write a worth-while novel about a Jew or a Gentile or a Homosexual, for people refuse, unhappily, to function in so neat and one-dimensional a fashion."[58] In my work, I have had to sacrifice much of my sexual fantasy attraction to archetypes of military masculinity for knowledge of some of the confusing, irreducibly complex persons the uniform dissembles. Upon closer acquaintance, the mystique lifts, leaving only someone known as Scott, Troy, Alex. (I have not been too unhappy with this exchange.)

Corporal Jack seems to have eroticized military men at the same time in life as I did—though from a polar political standpoint. This book concludes with him remarking:

> By actually joining the ranks I figured I would have greater insight into what makes Marines tick. . . . [But after four years,]

I'm not any closer to figuring out what they're about. For being as conformist as they appear, and despite the uniformity of their heritage, they are all very much unique. Surprisingly.

The trouble with all theories of sexuality, Marine or otherwise, is that they fail to account for the wonderful peculiarities of individual *becoming*. The sexuality of even the dullest, most conformist person in uniform is nuanced, always potentially "protean, and wholly fantastic."[59] As John DeCecco observes, "human beings have the almost irascible ability of synthesizing options into quite unanticipated choices."[60]

*   *   *

Marineness is like a religion; either you believe in it or you don't.

The special beauty I see in young Marines stems from the tremendous *earnestness* with which they strive to be hard men, from the contradiction of, as Jack puts it, the baby-faced killer.

Seemingly built into the pursuit of Marine masculinity are pleasure potentials that are most satisfying because they are forbidden and (supposed to be) secret. But there is pleasure in violating this taboo, too.

During my last months of work on this book, I kept returning to an enlisted men's club at one of the outer camps of Camp Pendleton. Here, on weekend nights, young Marines aged 18 and 19 enjoy a pause in grueling combat training, the opportunity to drink beer, and unabashedly celebrate the intimacy of their special bond. Sometimes I could not help an ironic "gay" smile as I watched them dance together, tenderly holding and hugging each other's Corps-built bodies (then loudly yelling). But the genuineness of their emotion was profoundly moving. I saw in these young men a purity of heart, a *faith* that repels mockery. And inquest.

Beside me, my companion Alex looked on at the embracing Marines sullenly. He felt, he told me, regret that he had traded the warm sense of intimacy he had felt (or thought he had felt, or wanted to feel) with other young Marines for the fast pleasure pursuits of being an out gay.

But far from being opposites, gay and Marine strivings can coincide in unexpected ways.

Corporal Keith:
The Devil Dog Yell

A hundred or so beautiful young men stand in line outside a crowded dance club bitching about the doorman and fussily adjusting each other's clothes. Everything about them suggests an obsessional devotion to appearance. Not a single moussed hair is out of place (you can tell they visit the salon weekly); "blouses" are tucked in just so. Many wear tight trousers and T-shirts chosen to flatter their taut-muscled bodies. You can tell they work out daily. A hundred or so colognes clash in the warm Southern California air blending into a sickly sweet aerial soup.

It is a half-hour wait to get inside. Cover for me, a nonmember, is four bucks. I am a little afraid that they won't let me in but they do, and I get in line to obtain a pitcher of bad watery beer for me and my companion, Alex.

Soundtrack: the ubiquitous thumping techno. A new song comes on and two men race past us to the dance floor, laughing and pointing at a third man as they mouth along the singer's stinging declamation: "Don't want no short/dick/man." The penis is the subject of messages on an assortment of T-shirts in the club; one shirt depicting a bulldog claims "It's not the size of the dog in the fight, it's the size of the fight in the dog." There are a few women here, but tonight men outnumber them ten to one.

"They are almost *unnaturally* good-looking, these boys," I think, studying their flashing eyes and teeth in the strobe light. Whatever their skin color, ethnicity, or physical type, they all have that same Leni Riefenstahl sculpted fascist-god quality. And they are all so *young*, mostly under 21. An International Male model type standing close to my left raises his nostrils when he sees me looking at him, but a slightly older man to my right is more to my taste: rugged, scowling, impassive. The rolled-up sleeve on his camouflage top exposes his bulging tattooed biceps. With studied insouciance he pretends not to see me as I stroll past him outside.

Country music twangs under the starry Western sky; a rock-ish song comes on about "strokin' it." Men with enormous belt buckles and Stetsons and revealingly tight Wranglers pose drinking beer straight from the pitcher. The rounded muscular ass on one swaggering cowboy compels me to follow him to the men's room.

There is a line to get at the trough. Between four and six men are accommodated; they are not averse to touching. I squeeze in along-side my cowboy who (I cannot help notice) makes no effort to conceal his (long, fat) penis. Appreciating my attention, and recip-rocating with a downward glance of his own, he grins, and reads aloud to me from the condom dispenser mounted on the wall before us: " 'Diff'rent colors!' "

" 'Different textures', " I add, and we both laugh. To his right, the boy with the bulldog shirt strides up and rips open his fly, unleash-ing his timid (but cute) pup as though it were a rottweiler. Someone in line behind him admonishes him to "Hurry the fuck up," threat-ening that otherwise he will *piss on his leg.* Comes the reply: "You can *piss in my ass.*"

Incredulous, I return to Alex and breathlessly enthuse: "I'm putting it in my will: When I die, pour my ashes, or at least the cremated bone fragments, in the piss trough of the Camp Pendleton Del Mar Enlisted Club."

Alex replies laconically, "I thought you'd have a good time."

On the way out, we observe two Marines in silhouette at the edge of the parking lot with their arms around each other, pissing together. . . .

The enlisted-club-as-gay-bar metaphor verges on the ridiculous when, later, at another smaller club 20 miles inside the remote interior of this vast, 124,000-acre base, I videotape and photograph uniformed Marine boots ecstatically gyrating and singing along to the Village People's "Y.M.C.A." (see Figure 1), reminding us that, as sexual theorist Judith Butler puts it, "gay is to straight *not* as copy is to original, but as copy is to copy."[1] A slow song comes on and two male-female couples dance, joined by a tangle of eight uniformed boots who hold and caress each other in the euphoric embrace of victorious football players—but for ten passionate min-utes or longer.

It has been two and a half years since my introduction to Camp Pendleton, my first interview with a Marine, and my first experience with a Marine Corps enlisted club.

Part One

Keith is a bulky, redheaded bulldog of a man from West Texas. His parents are retired U.S. Navy officers; his mom is a nurse, his dad is a Methodist preacher active in prison outreach. After our meeting at a San Diego dance club, Keith invited me to spend a night with him in his Camp Pendleton barracks.

It was an hour's drive north in heavy January rain to the sprawling base, home to 44,000 United States Marines. After passing a rainsoaked sentry at the main gate, we negotiated mile after winding mile between penumbral hills undulating spookily beyond the windshield wipers of Keith's Mitsubishi Eclipse, finally arriving at an isolated cinder block high-rise barracks with outside walkways, sort of a Marine Corps Motel 6. Keith is the lone occupant of an austere two-man cell; he shares a bathroom and shower with the adjoining room's occupant, his buddy Ted (subject of the following interview). Fans of the 1960s TV series *Gomer Pyle: U.S.M.C.* starring Jim Nabors may be comforted to know that elsewhere on the base some Marines still do live in open squad bay Quonset huts. An outside loudspeaker system played "Taps." Keith called me to the door to listen to damp coyotes howling in answer from the sodden hills.

Signing in as "Corporal Zeeland" at the chow hall the next morning, I was smug in my ability to pass as a Marine solely on the basis of my haircut and friends. Keith gave me a tour of the base and bought me a T-shirt at the mainside Exchange that said "MARINES JUST DO IT." We spent the afternoon off-base keeping dry inside the El Camino Real mall—prime Marine-watching territory. The plan for the evening was to pick up Ted from the base and drive him down to San Diego to get a new tattoo.

Back on Camp Pendleton it began to rain as I had never seen it rain before. Jokes about my newly adopted state sliding into the ocean suddenly made alarming sense. The road was increasingly carpeted with mud and fallen chaparral. I voiced concern to Keith that maybe we should just get the hell out of there. "Relax," he told me, "this is a Marine Corps base. No matter what, this road will stay open."

He was wrong. Too late did his Mitsubishi Amphibious Vehicle begin its return descent into the waters swirling on the Santa Margarita River flood plain that is part of Camp Pendleton—goaded forward by the intractable Keith even as its headlights disappeared underwater, to our surprise and relief emerging unscathed on the excruciatingly distant shore—only to be put through the same punishment in reverse as an MP stopped us with news that a dike had burst. The bridge ahead had been swept away by a 15-foot wall of rushing water, taking with it an historic mission chapel as well as 70 helicopters and fixed-wing aircraft. All alternate escape routes were likewise closed.

Trapped on Camp Pendleton! ("Corporal" Zeeland's smugness evaporated in what he imagined to be an atavistic Dutchman response to this, his first flash flood.)

I retired with Keith and Ted to an enlisted club where the three of us got drunk. The bar was half filled with studly young Marines, some good-humored about being stuck there, but others decidedly ornery. A fight broke out by the pool tables. Draining another plastic cup of Courvoisier I began to grow (more) self-conscious, wondering whether an untoward movement or stare might give my "queerness" away. But then, I considered, many of these Marines seemed to be staring at each other—and at me. I asked Keith why, and he said it was a challenge to see who would look away first.

A bar harboring only men with short hair engaged in a perpetual staredown contest? I snickered at the recognition. A video jukebox began to replay the same country lament for the nth time. I directed Keith to put in some quarters and select Madonna's "Erotica," wondering just how close to a gay bar I could make this. . . .

Keith: I'm twenty-six now. I was twenty-two when I figured out that I was gay. It was right after I got to Okinawa, Japan.

I'm a diesel mechanic. That's my MOS [military occupational specialty]. I was FAPped out [fleet assistance pool], which is a TAD-[temporary additional duty] type process. I was placed with the MPs. I was on duty one night doing a routine K-9 patrol through some empty barracks. I heard a voice say, "Yeah, fuck me," and shit like that. A male voice. I pulled out my forty-five, and I had my flashlight. I found them and they were fucking. The shock in their eyes—it was like spotlighting two deer. They were like, frozen in mid-stroke.

"Freeze! Please stay in the position you're at, do not move!" I told them, "If you do move, the dog will attack with no command!"

I had it locked and cocked. I was ready to fire if I had to. I was scared. I honestly didn't know what to expect. Even with the dog there—the dog can't take care of both people. I've never really wanted to shoot anybody. I was afraid of the dark, too.

I told them, "At this time, would you please very carefully get up. You go to this corner, you go to this corner." I asked to see ID cards. Well, the guy that was getting fucked was a captain. The other guy was a PFC.

Zeeland: The PFC was on top?

K: Yeah. The doggie-style position. PFC was hunkered over, he was kneeling with one leg up. He was getting after it!

I'm looking at ID cards, I put my weapon back in my holster. The officer is like, "What are you gonna fucking do about it?" I was a lance corporal at the time. I was real nervous. I kept looking at them, and staring at their ID cards.

Z: They were just standing there naked?

K: Yeah. Totally butt-fucking naked. The PFC is over here sweating his balls off, like, "Oh my God! I can't believe this guy found us!" And the officer, he's pissed. "What are you gonna do? Are you gonna turn us in?"

I said, "Okay. Sir, I'm giving your ID card back to you. PFC, okay." I said, "I didn't see none of this. Just put your clothes back on and get the fuck out of here. I don't want to ever see you again."

About two or three days later the Captain approached me. He said, "Excuse me lance corporal, I'd like to talk with you." I'm like, oh shit. Now what? He said, "If you ever need somebody to talk to, or you ever need anything, consider me a friend. You helped me, and I appreciate that." Then the PFC, I would see him at chow. Every time he'd sit down and say, "What's up?" I'd be very nervous. I'd be just sitting down to eat, but I'd get up. "Fuck this. I'm outta here."

But after that I kept thinking about it and thinking about it. I just had really—fantasies and shit like that. I kept wondering what it would be like.

Z: Who did you fantasize about?

K: I fantasized about watching them. I fantasized about fucking the captain, but to tell you the truth mostly I fantasized about the PFC. Uh-huh. Yeah. "Dude. It's cool! But I don't do that kind of stuff." So I laughed it off.

I never would approach that PFC. I wanted to so bad.

Well, I got back to the United States. I was stationed in Yuma, Arizona.

I had gone to—there's a bookstore there. Big cruising area. I was just there to check the place out. I had heard from people in Okinawa, straight friends, that this certain bookstore was the place to go if you liked looking at dirty books.

I was in there watching movies one night. I was watching straight films. I was getting bored. Then I was watching two guys do it. And I was remembering from back in Okinawa, what I had saw, and got so very aroused. I was rock hard. I was like, "Well, shit. You can't deny it when it's like this."

Well, guess what. That same night, who shows up? That PFC. He got stationed there. I told you I had a helluva story!

Yeah. Well. He said, "Don't I know you from somewhere? You're that MP, aren't you?" "That was just a FAP-type deal. I'm a diesel mechanic." "You stationed here?" "Yeah." "No shit. So am I." I said, "I got a lot of questions." He said, "Yeah, I figured you probably would." For some reason he could read me like a book.

His name is Michael. He was basically the one that helped me out. I was like, "What do you do? There's got to be more to it than just fucking up the ass." He said, "Well, yeah. Do you want to go back to the barracks?"

So I was in bed with him the first night. And even when—one thing that was stupid was, I always had a guilty conscience when I was a little kid jacking off. After I did it—enjoy myself—I would get upset. "Why did I do that?" I was very punishing to myself. Okay, so, it was four or five in the morning when we finished. We did everything and anything. And—I did not feel that guilt at all. I couldn't believe it. So much tension had been released. And I never had felt that much attraction to another guy in my life.

We kind of dated for a month or so. And we just figured out that we'd be better friends than anything. Mike told me straight out that he was gay. "Oh." "What are you?" "Well, I've never been with a woman before, so who knows what I am." 'Cause I didn't know.

He was from L.A. He took me out to all the clubs. There were other gay Marines I met through Michael that were on base. It was a clique. A tightly woven kind of thing. There were, like, ten of us.

Z: From the base in Arizona, but you would drive all the way to L.A.?

K: Mmm-hmm. [Pauses to spit out tobacco juice.] The first time I went up there was on my twenty-third birthday. I was dying to go. "Please take me places. I want to meet people." He took me there. I had a blast. "This is too much!" From them on I knew that I was gay. I didn't have to reproach myself no more because I had peace of mind with who I was.

November tenth [the Marine Corps birthday] some friends asked us to come out to this party. It was mostly all Marines that were gay, and we had our own Marine Corps ball. It was really neat. They had a cake-cutting ceremony. There were one or two Marine Corps officers there. It was well planned. After that they all said, "We're going down to West Hollywood." I'm like, "You've gotta be joking! In fucking uniform we're going to the fucking bar!"

"Yeah."

"Yeah. Okay." I'm like, what the fuck. No big deal. Fuck it, I'll go.

We went down there and went to this bar, and that's where I met my first lover. His name is Jim. He was twenty-two. It was basically a stare-down contest the whole night. "Somebody's going to have to talk. The worst thing he can do is tell me to get the fuck outta his face." So we started talking. He said, "I love your uniform." I said, "Thank you. What do you do?" He said, "I'm a cop."

"No shit!" LAPD. He'd just graduated three or four days before that. He was out there celebrating with all his friends.

I was trying to be a Marine, but I was very much attracted to this guy, and I couldn't keep my hands off of him. We got outside, and I was pretty much trashed. He said, "There's something I gotta do." He pushed me up against the wall and kissed me. I'd never had anybody be aggressive like that, and I kinda liked it.

He was in L.A. and I was in Arizona, but we were together every weekend. It was a four-hour drive. The phone bills! His parents knew of our relationship and they were very much open to it. They were impressed that I was a Marine. I was in my dress blue uniform in this guy's house, with his parents there.

Z: Did he dress up for you in his cop uniform?

K: Yeah. It was a fantasy-type thing. The handcuffs and all.

Z: Did you play around with that, sometimes?

K: Sometimes, yeah. It was kinda cool!

I loved Jim, very much. It's sometimes kind of hard to talk about it. . . .

Z: You were together for nine months, you said, until . . .

K: One of his friends said he was screwing around on me. I went to the other guy before I said anything to Jim about it. "I hope it was good, because you really fucked up my relationship." He said, "I'm sorry." I said, "There's no sorry about it; you did what you did. I hope it was good."

My parents knew that I was hurt real bad. They already knew that I was gay. When Jim and me were dating I made the mistake of telling my parents that I had a girlfriend. My mom kept acting like, "Oh my God, he's got a girlfriend!" They knew I never dated much in high school, so they were very excited for me. They kept asking me about it. Finally I told my mom, "You ask too many fucking questions." And I never, ever, talked that way to my mom. She's like, "There's something wrong." So they sat me down and said, "What's wrong?" I said, "Mom, Dad—" I broke down crying. I said, "I'm gay." My dad kind of laughed at me. I said, "Gee, thanks a lot." He said, "We always knew." Just the way I sometimes acted or associated with people. I was very withdrawn so they just assumed. I didn't like football or anything like that. From the time I was four years old until I came in the Marine Corps I did gymnastics. And tap dancing. That was another thing that made everybody think I was gay. I stopped when I was fifteen because I was tired of all the shit I took from people. I'd still probably be doing it today. In the little town I grew up in you didn't do stuff like that.

Z: It was considered a sissy thing?

K: Yeah.

Z: Did having been called that figure into your wanting to become a Marine?

K: Very much so. I was trying to prove to people that I am a man. I always tried to prove that to people.

I went to Texas A&M University for a semester. I was in the Corps Cadets. Mostly everybody gets a commission in the Army. They also have ROTC for Marines. We had a Marine Corps officer come and talk to us one day. I saw him in his dress blues. "I can't believe it; they're so awesome looking." Then I got to see a training film. After watching that, seeing how tough it really was: "That's exactly what I want to do." There were so many people not interested in it, "Fuck the Marines." But I said, "Damn. I want to do that. I've got to do that! Just to say I did it. And I want a pair of those dress blues."

So, I dropped out of college. I came home and told my parents I was joining the military. They were very upset. They knew I had been planning on getting a commission. My dad is a retired Navy officer, and my mom was also a Navy officer. That was a cardinal sin. "One of our kids can't be a common enlisted man." I told them, "I'm nineteen and I can do whatever I want." Mom and Dad are very different about that now.

"Well, at least he's doing something with his life. At least he can stand up for himself."

K: Marines are the elite. We are the crème de la crème. We are the hardest service branch in the United States. When you think of Marines, you think of a drill instructor. It's just like in the movies. They don't actually hit you anymore. Every now and then you'll still see it, but not as much as you would back in the early days. You're going to do what they say; it's not like they have to beat it into you. Most everybody wants to be there.

When you go to boot camp in the Navy you're considered a sailor from day one. You have to *earn* the title "Marine." It's not given to you. You're referred to as a "recruit." You don't even rate to be considered a private, because you're not a Marine yet. Being a Marine is a very sacred thing to me and most of my brothers. . . .

It's very tough getting through boot camp. If you didn't cry at least once in boot camp, I don't see how you made it. The biggest guy in the group cried.

I grew up a very sheltered person. Basically life was thrown at me. I wasn't prepared to be away from home. At night I'd have to cry myself to sleep because I was so worried about what was going on at home. I didn't spend enough time with my family before I left. I felt guilty.

Those drill instructors are mean. They are very mean. They're very professional; they're there to do a job. They're not there to be your friend. From the time you get off the bus and they say "You are at The Marine Corps Recruit Depot, San Diego, California. From now on the first and last word out of your mouth will be 'sir.' Do you understand?" "Sir yes sir!" Just the way they present themselves with the smokey, and the charlies—that's the green uniform—it puts the fear of God in you.

There were a lot of times I thought I wasn't going to make it. I got hurt at boot camp. I had to stay an extra two weeks. It was a very depressing experience for me because most of the people there were getting out. All the guys that you bond with—it's very, very, very close. You go in there as individuals, but you leave as one person. That's one thing they instill in you.

There's three different phases. The first is the breaking-down phase: ripping your civilian life away from you, taking everything away. That's enough to break everybody's spirit, and that's what they do. Then they rebuild you. And the person that comes out of that is awesome.

When I came in the Marine Corps I was the shortest person in the platoon. Only redhead in the battalion. So everybody fucked with me. I was well known throughout the entire battalion. My drill instructors told me, "If any other drill instructors fuck with you, you let me know." But I guess I was just a special case, because every drill instructor had their way with me.

Z: What do you think made them single you out?

K: I think they were just trying to make me more strong. I looked like I was fourteen years old. I was nineteen. I was more boyish-looking than the other guys in the platoon.

The drill instructors used to call me "faggot." It was either "backward ass country fuck"—because I had a real bad Southern accent—or "little redheaded faggot." "Hey faggot." "Private faggot." It really bothered me but it was also—fuck it, it's something that's gotta be done.

Z: Did they use the same word with other people?

K: No.

Z: You were the only one they called faggot?

K: Yeah. Because my voice was not very masculine. The first night, we were on the deck, and I was nervous. I was shaking. The junior DI, he says, "You're shaking so bad you're making me *hard*. I'm gonna bend you over and fuck you right now." I was really scared. He's saying that right in front of God and everybody. And from then on he called me faggot. . . .

K: When you first get there, they take all your civilian clothes away from you. Then they give you the thirty-second haircut, which really hurts. We looked like we just got into Auschwitz [see Figure 3]. The people I had gone with—it took me a week to recognize all of them.

Just being away from home was hard. I was talking with this one guy. We were talking about home. We were at sick call. We had just gotten a brand new pair of boots, and we had been out on the "grinder," which is what we called the place where we marched, the parade deck. We'd been marching all afternoon, and I had developed a sore on the back of my heel. He said he'd gotten a letter from home. He was saying his little sister— they'd never really gotten along—but she wrote and said she loved him and missed him. And he broke down. And just seeing him cry made me cry too. It made me think of my family. We were like two little kids, just bawling. And all these other people were looking at us. I didn't care. We were hugging each other, "It's gonna be okay. It's gonna be all right."

There's a certain area where we used to run out behind the airport. That's another bad thing about going to boot camp here in San Diego. You'd be on fire watch late at night, you and three other people roving throughout the squad bay, and you can look out the windows and see the skyline of San Diego and these jets. And when one of those jets takes off, you're looking up like, God. . . . And the drill instructors—"Oh, what are we fucking lookin' at? Aw, we wanna go home? [Makes waving gesture.] Goodbye! Goodbye!" They had to aggravate us, so, "Well, I don't really wanna look at the jets."

Eventually you get to the point where you got enough other stuff on your mind that you just don't think about [home]. You've got your inspections: How am I gonna do on my PFT [Physical Fitness Test]? How am I gonna look in my uniform?

They always give you an hour of free time before you turn in. And it's basically time to shit/shower/shave. That's basically the only time you can make a sitting head call. A head call is to go to the urinal. But you had to request to make a sitting head call.

Z: Were there any partitions in the heads?

K: There are partitions, but they're open, so you're basically looking at the guy across from you.

Z: Was that hard to get used to?

K: No, not really. Then the showers were just these big columns with these spigots. So everybody and anybody, it was just get in there, shower up and lather down, and get out. Just make sure you're clean because before you go to sleep at night they have health inspections. See how well you cleaned.

Every night before we went to bed they made us drink a full canteen of water. That was a torture. We could not use the head an hour after we went to bed. They made us drink this water, then sometime in the night you'd have to get up. If you didn't, you'd piss in the rack. They call it water discipline. One drill instructor we had, he used to make us drink a full canteen of water before we went to chow. God forbid if you tried to eat a lot. We're not talking just leisurely drinking, we're talking chugging an entire canteen. And you're thinking, "I'll get over on this motherfucker." He made you hold it upside down over your head. And they would check to make sure it was completely full. And if you did try to get over and they found out, they would make you drink the rest of that water, then they would make you go back and get another full canteen of water. And then after chow we'd come back and he'd make us drink an entire canteen of water again. People would be puking. He'd say, "Oh, you want to puke on my quarterdeck? Good. Start field day." Field day is a term for cleaning your area.

The worst thing they could do to you, besides hit you, was to put you in the sand pit for five or ten minutes and make you do all kinds of calisthenics at a very fast pace. I had one drill instructor who liked to make a square in the sand. He would make you fill up that square with sweat. And it wasn't just for disciplinary action. They would do it for spite. "Get up here now! *I don't like you!* Get on my fucking quarterdeck!" But everything they do is for a reason. It's building you up somehow. Building up muscles you thought you never had.

Z: Did anybody hit you?

K: Yeah. [Pause.] We were at RFTD, Recruit Field Training Division, at Camp Pendleton. For some reason, I pissed off a drill instructor to the point that he—I don't remember exactly what I did, but I did something wrong, and he slapped me upside the head. "When I tell you to do some-thing, I expect you to fucking do it!" I'll never forget that experience in my life. First time I'd ever been hit like that. Open handed, WHAP! across the head, when I wasn't expecting it at all, standing straight at attention. "Oh, you're gonna flinch now, huh?" So he hits me again. He hit me three times. "What are you gonna do? Are you gonna cry? Are you a little pussy?"

I could have reported him. But I was so scared. There's a network. They could lie their way out of it. I felt they wouldn't believe me. So I never said anything. In fact, I haven't told very many people about that. It was very scary. [Pause.] I don't like to talk about it. It's not no big deal. But I'll never forget that day.

You never forget your drill instructors, either. Staff Sergeant D, I'll remember him as long as I live. He always told me, "You'll never make it. Just give up. Why are you even here?" The more he did that, the more it pissed me off. But you think, "Fuck this, I can do it. I *will* do it."

Z: Tell me about your life after your break-up with Jim.

K: I thought Jim and me had a very honest relationship. Always put everything on the table and talk about it. I had never opened myself up to somebody like that. I gave him everything I had. And just got my heart stomped into the ground. I never expected I would cry over some guy! I've always been an emotional person. I get choked up about a lot of different things. Especially about being a Marine. The Marine Corps hymn brings tears to my eyes. But yeah, I loved Jim very much.

I went back to Okinawa for two years. I had a lot of time to think. I basically tortured myself. Rosy palm and her five sisters just don't do it. Most all the people I met it was just basically friendship. I was still so afraid that I—I wanted to meet people, very much so. I was very attracted to most of the people I met. And most of them wanted to go to bed with me. But I said no, I can't afford to do this to myself, or to you.

Z: Where did you go to meet other gay guys?

K: Camp Hansen was a cruisy area because most of the grunts went there.

Z: Why did that make it cruisy?

K: Because hell, there's only so many things you can do. There's not a whole hell of a lot of American women. And not everybody's into Oriental women. And I think there was a lot of straight guys having gay sex.

Z: What makes you think that?

K: [Laughs.] I just do.

One time—We're in the field. Most of the time when we weren't doing mechanical work, we were supporting the grunts by just driving trucks around and doing shit like that. And one particular unit from Hawaii, they had some pretty weird motherfuckers in the group. And they decided—It was probably about six or seven o'clock in the evening, and it was still light enough outside so that you could see what was going on. These grunts were talking about having an over-the-line contest. Being the naïve person that I was, I asked, "What the fuck are we talking about here?" "You wanna be in it?" "No, I just wanna know what it is." "Well, we'll let you judge." The other guys are like, "Yeah, let him judge."

What they did is, they drew a line—one old boy took his boot and made a line in the mud—

Z: Right by the tents?

K: No, this is farther out away. Basically in the middle of this jungle. Lots of shrubbery. There's five of us, four of them and one of me. Three lance corporals and a corporal. One guy was eighteen, the other guys were like nineteen or twenty. Just a really rough crowd, guys I wouldn't want to associate with. They drew the line in the mud, and they stood about two or three feet back. Each one of them would do this by themselves.

Z: Do what?

K: Jerk off!

Z: One after the other?

K: Yeah. They had a little place were they stood. They were standing behind the line. I had to stand in front of the line. And the object of the game was to get it over the line. Whoever got it farthest over the line was the winner. And all the rest of the guys would watch them do this.

Z: They weren't staring, though, were they?

K: Yeah they were! They were most definitely staring. One guy took at least fifteen minutes. He was really enjoying himself. And they were telling him, "Yeah, you can do it!" and all this kind of shit. "Yeah, shoot it!" Honest to God, I thought the whole group was gay. I don't know because to this day I haven't ever seen one of them again. [Laughs.] But yeah, they were coaching each other like, yeah, do it this certain way. "Fuckin' go for it dude! *Arrr!*" And that was another thing, soon as they got ready to bust a nut, they had to give out a devil dog yell. "*Arrr!*" Supposedly that was to help trajectory.

The first two guys, they didn't even make it to the line so they were disqualified. Basically just all over the hand, and they were [makes wiping motion] on their cammies and shit. One guy made it halfway to the line, but the corporal won it; he made it just over the line. I'm out here in the middle of the jungle with these fucking grunts, watching my back, making sure—'cause I was not out. I don't even know why I did it. It's just one of those things.

Z: They didn't touch each other, or jerk themselves off while they were watching?
K: Uh-uh. No.
Z: Did you fantasize about this experience afterwards?
K: Not really. It was just like: not a big fucking deal. It was wild; it was stupid.
Z: Do you think they did this regularly?
K: I honestly think they did it every time they went to the field. 'Cause there was other people that talked about over the line contests, too. Other people in this unit. You get a lot of crazy grunts together, they do shit like that. We weren't drinking or anything, but they were just so fucking bored. There wasn't nothin' else for them to do.[2]

A few months ago I was at my last command. It was a very slow day. There really wasn't a whole hell of a lot going on. Had a lance corporal that was in the shop and he was trying to get out of the Marine Corps. I don't think he was gay. He was so fucking bored. Picture this: sitting on the top step of a five-ton truck, legs hanging over the side, he's leaning back with one hand behind him. He's in coveralls. He takes his—the coveralls have two zippers on them. You can either zip them from the bottom or from the top. So he zips open from the bottom—I happened to be sitting right there. From my little office I can peek around the corner and watch without him noticing, and where he was, there was only one way into this area anyway so if somebody would have been there there was no way he could have been caught. I don't know if he knew I was in my little office. He's over there jerking off. He enjoys himself thoroughly, and of course it's all over the deck. And then after that he goes and gets the lieutenant and fucking shows him what he did. "Sir, I'm so fucking bored I jerked off all over the deck." The lieutenant went high and to the right about it. "You're a sick individual. You definitely need help."

I thought it was awful bizarre.

Z: Tell me about your buddy Ted.
K: He's going through some emotional problems, and he opened up to me. And I told him, "If you need somebody to talk to, I'll be there for you."

He was pretty upset Wednesday. "What are you doing tonight?" "I'm going to San Diego. If you want to you can come along." Before, I had made a stupid comment that I had a brother who's gay. He said, "That's no big deal. I'm pretty much open about it." So I told him, "Look, I don't have a gay brother. I'm sorry I lied to you. There is a person that's gay, but it's not my brother. It's me." He kinda laughed. He said, "There's a lot of people coming out now because of the new President." I said, "I'm not going to say nothing to nobody. Do you have any qualms about being around me?" He said, "No." I said, "Don't worry about me. The only difference between me and you, if anything, is you like girls and I like guys. Have you ever been to a gay bar before?" "No." "I promised that I would take you to San Diego tonight. I'm supposed to meet some friends there. Would you mind going with me?" "Sure." "We'll play pool, have a good time." Just get him away from the barracks, so he'd have somebody to be with.

He had a good time. I was really impressed. In fact, I took him out Friday to a different bar. It was really cool. He enjoyed himself, playing pool and talking. There were people that wanted him, but—can't do that.

Z: You explained that he was straight?

K: Yeah.

Z: How did he respond to them?

K: He didn't tell them. There was one guy that [laughs] kept bugging him. I said, "If anybody bugs you, let me know. I'll just tell them you're with me." And he says, "Let's do something a little bit different. Put your arm around me." I thought, "What?" He was very open to it. I was like, "Cool!" So I was holding him, and making it look like we were together, and this other guy finally got the hint. He left him alone, but then my other friends were like, "Who is this?" They knew I wasn't going out with anybody. "Just a friend of mine." I introduced him to all my friends. "He's good-looking!" There was one guy that was very attracted to him, but I said, "I'm sorry, he's straight."

"No way!"

Ted says, "Yeah, I am." And in fact when I took him to [a gay dance club] the other night, the same person asked, "What are you trying to do, convert him?" [Laughs.] But he just needed somebody to hang out with. He told me, "I could have anybody I want, male or female." Must be nice! But he's got a girlfriend he's going to get married to, so.

Yesterday, I took him to some tattoo shops.

Z: Do you have any tattoos?

K: Yes. I've got my dragon on my chest. And I've got my USMC tattoo; it's got a skull and a cowboy hat with a Confederate flag. At one time in my life, I was a cowboy 'cause I grew up on a ranch. That was my first tattoo. I got it right after I came in the Corps. My mother said, "I can't believe you've done that to your body." I said, "It's a piece of art." And that's the way I look at it.

Sometimes I wear shirts that expose my dragon, and everybody always asks me about it, wherever I go. It's made it easier for people to notice me. "Let me see your dragon!" I'll show it to them. Everybody looks then. "This guy's got an awesome dragon!" It's an easy pick-up type thing. I didn't expect that, I didn't get it for that purpose. But it's had its advantages.

Z: Do tattoos on other men attract you?

K: Yeah. Well, it depends. If they're in the military and they have tattoos exposed on their arms—when they're in uniform, it looks really trashy.

Z: Some people say the actual experience of getting the tattoo is a kind of sexual feeling.

K: I didn't think that! It was more like getting scratched by a cat. And the one on my chest—I paid for it very much. In pain. But I'm happy with it.

But getting back to some of these fantasies. Dealing with troops, and not only Marine Corps troops—I also helped train [Navy hospital] corpsmen. Corpsmen and Marines have a special relationship. They take care of us, and we take care of them.

There's a Marine Corps-type boot camp for corpsmen. They go through all the stuff the Marines go through, just about. They learn infantry tactics; they learn how to do Marine Corps drill with rifles, just like the Marines. And I got selected to be an instructor. We could do damn near anything we wanted to, except hit 'em. It was great. And that was a big turn-on for me. Some of the men that I come into contact with, especially in the Navy. It's a big sexual fantasy of mine.

Z: What is?

K: Having a group of guys and me the drill instructor.

Z: Ordering them to . . . do stuff for you?

K: Exactly.

Z: Do you have an attraction to sailors in uniform?

K: Yeah. Dungarees are kind of unsat, but the white uniform, it looks really cool, depending on the person. If they have the right haircut. And a big thing is, because I'm a Marine I can pick somebody apart, the way they maintain their uniform, the way they keep themselves squared away. If they take pride in their uniform—that's another big turn-on. Somebody who looks like they slept in their uniform: get out of my face. I don't want to associate with you.

One thing I've always had a problem with is, I stare. I still do that to this day. I just stare—especially a Marine out of uniform with a leather jacket on. 'Cause it seems like all Marines have a black leather jacket. It's almost like a prerequisite when you get out of boot camp.

When I first met Jim, he was really interested in the Marine Corps. He was on the SWAT team and stuff like that. One of my hobbies is collecting guns and swords [and Nazi paraphernalia], and he liked that. I gave him a pair of boots and two or three uniforms. He said, "I'd like you to do dirty things to me while you're in uniform." I wanted to do stuff like that, too. Me as a drill instructor. "*Come here, you!*" He'd play the part of the PFC. He'd explain what the situation was: he had a problem that he wanted me to take care of. It was cool!

Z: How strong is the sense of brotherhood you feel with other Marines?

K: Very strong. We can hate each other, but if another Marine is in any type of danger, I'd be there for him. The trust, the relationships you have with these people—Yeah, everybody's different, but when it comes right down to it I would back them up one hundred percent. That closeness really ties in. It's just like a big family. And that's how I look at my gay friends, too. That camaraderie, esprit de corps.

Z: You mentioned you were disappointed you missed the Gulf War. You were in Saudi Arabia, you said, but left before it started.

K: That goes back to brotherhood. All those guys, I'd been working with them for so long. We were very close. It was very emotional because I couldn't be there with them.

Z: Was it more important to you, the idea of being with them, than being in combat?

K: Right. Well, that, too. Ever since I joined the Corps, I felt that one day I would be in a war. The attraction—I just liked the ribbons. No one likes the war. But just the aura of, "Yeah, I've been in combat," people really get off on that.

Z: What does masculine mean to you?

K: Masculine means being able to act like a man.

Z: How should a man act?

K: Not like a woman. I don't want to be a woman, and I don't want to be with a woman. I want to be with a real man.

I'm still looking for somebody. I just . . . want to find somebody. I just want somebody to love me. You know? I want that relationship again. And to me—a simple touch. It doesn't have to be a sexual touch. A hug means a lot to me. It means a lot. It feels like I know that person cares.

Part Two: One and a Half Years Later

It has been suggested that a "gay soldier letting out his gayness may begin to see its theatricalities as incompatible with the monolithic theatricality of military masculinity." Adopting a gay identity led Keith to explore new and different ways of voicing and advertising his Marine masculinity. He found himself at home in the leather scene, and even appeared in the pages of *Drummer* magazine. But this is not the ironic departure from being a "real" Marine it might at first glance seem. Keith continued to view both his Marine-ness and his gayness with utmost seriousness—so much so that he undertook to have a custom tattoo designed featuring the Marine Corps anchor, globe, and eagle logo superimposed over a gay rainbow flag, and had it tattooed over his heart.[3]

Z: How has your life changed since the last time we talked on tape?
K: I'm a lot more comfortable than I was then. I know a lot more people. I'm still looking for the perfect relationship. Which I thought I had, with Pete.
Z: How long were you and Pete together?
K: Six months. I'll chalk that up as a record! At least since I've been in San Diego. I've had some other freelance relationships . . . A year ago I was going out quite a bit. And it's basically old hat now. You see the same people. But every now and then I'll beat the bushes and see if I can't find me a quail. [Laughs.]
Z: How have things changed for you with the Marine Corps?
K: Well, one thing that happened was—there was a misunderstanding with somebody at the barracks. As you know, I now have this really elaborate tattoo on my chest. There had been talk in the barracks that—just 'cause they hadn't seen me with a girl, that I was gay. And I basically confronted everybody: "If you have proof that I am, let's see it." They just shut up about it. Well, one afternoon I had my T-shirt off and I was walking around the barracks. And the first sergeant just happened to be strolling through the barracks to see how we were doing. She says, "I like your tattoo." "Thank you." She says, "Later on I want to come by your room and we'll talk about it." "Excuse me?" "Just wait."

She comes in the room. She says, "What does that [tattoo] mean to you?" I said, "The rainbow flag means different things to different people. It means pride. And it means a new beginning." And I said that's what the Marines stand for. We go somewhere, we try to help people out. Like in

Somalia for instance. We gave them a new beginning. She says, "Is that all it means to you?" "Yeah." "You sure?" "Yeah." And she's like, "Well, I've got some questions I wanted to ask you. And please, don't get agitated. Are you gay?" "Do you have substantial evidence that I am?" She says, "No, but I've seen the rainbow flag. I know what it means. That's a gay pride flag on your chest." I'm like, okay, I'm busted. But then she says, "Don't worry about it. I'm a lesbian." I'm like, shit, this is great! She said, "I think it takes a lot of courage to put that on you. You really are proud to be a gay Marine, aren't you?" "Yes I am." "I'm sure a lot of people will see that and share that pride." And they do. I get complimented on it every time I have my shirt off. They always ask me what it means. And like I said, basically I tell them it means pride and freedom.

Z: Have other Marines picked up on the gay association?

K: Not too many. Unless they're family. If they know what it means, they've got some affiliation with the gay community, or been exposed to it. And they don't have a problem with it.

Z: How is your relationship with the first sergeant now?

K: Oh, it's great! She's a real inspiration to me. She said, "I'll back you up a hundred percent if you ever have any problem of any kind."

Z: Have your feelings about the Marine Corps changed in any way?

K: No. I'm still as gung-ho as I was.

Z: After our first conversations, you spoke to me about a quest you were on. Certain images, including skinheads and leathermen, appealed to you, and you said you didn't understand why. What were you looking for, and what have you since found?

K: I have since associated with the leather community. I find that image attractive. When I go out in leather I scare the shit out of people. As you know, just my presence alone sometimes intimidates people. I've got a military bearing. And I can use that to my advantage.

Z: How?

K: When I go into a place—it's not like I'm taking over this place, but the aura . . . most people, as soon as they see me, they're like, "This is a guy you don't want to fuck with."

Z: What connection is there between the Marine image and the leather image?

K: Well, they just kind of combine into each other. That's how I like to project myself: a Marine in leather. It's a very attractive thing.

Z: What does that combination convey?

K: Masculinity. The hard attitude that a Marine has. Most people find it very erotic to see that military attitude in leather, and they associate that with the very forceful, take-charge type of person that most people are looking for. That's what I've noticed.

Z: You've talked about striving to become more masculine—

K: Yes. And I don't know why. I shouldn't even have to feel that I have to improve on my masculinity 'cause, I mean, I'm reeking with it. In a way it's more a fantasy for other people. I like to project that attitude, and that also helps me to keep away people that are weak-minded. There are a lot of people in the [gay] community that are not strong. If they're put in a corner, they don't know how to take care of themselves.

Z: Would it be fair to say that you're looking for strength and security from these images—

K: Yes. Yes.

Z: —and also enjoying whatever erotic charge you and your partners find in them?

K: Exactly.

Z: In the first part of your interview, you mentioned taking pleasure in being a bottom—

K: I don't like to consider myself a top or a bottom. A good way of putting it is I'm a top who likes to get fucked. There's really no other way of putting it. I mean, most people assume that you play a certain role. When people confront me: "What role do you play?" I usually just look at them and say, "I don't play games. I don't have no reason to." It depends on the person I want to be with—if I play top or bottom.

Z: What kind of person would make you feel like you wanted to be a bottom?

K: Very masculine. I hate to say it, but I think I might be a size queen, too.

Z: It's a big dick you want to be fucked by?

K: Yeah. [Laughs.] It's just—the guy has this big dick, and you're thinking: damn! I wonder how this would feel. I think it's a challenge for myself. Can I take this thing on? I've pretty well given this impression that I'm a hard core motherfucker; I wonder if I can really take it. I guess that's my way of proving I can.

Z: What kind of guy would you like to fuck?

K: A very hard determined person; the kind of person that I like to project myself as being. It's more of a fantasy. You have this really huge, very masculine man; you're thinking: well he's the top, right there—and you turn around and find out he's your bottom! It's just a turn-on. You find out it's the smaller guy who's the top.

Z: But describe the thrill. [Pause.] Is it—

K: Just to say: I fucked him.

Z: Strength?

K: Yeah. Power!

People assume that all Marines like to get fucked. I don't mind getting—I like getting fucked, yeah, I do. But it depends on the person.

Z: Do you believe that the typical Marine likes to get fucked?

K: Maybe so. I guess that it's—I've heard a lot of instances, a lot of straight Marines just want to see what the experience of it is, to see if they like it.

Z: In a lot of cultures a man is only considered a fag if he's effeminate and exclusively on the bottom. Being penetrated is equated with femininity. So why doesn't that idea hold true for Marines? Why does being penetrated not make them feel female? Or does it?

K: I don't think they would want a wimpy person to do it. They would want that strength. That's how I would see it.

Z: Is there any part of you that would ever want to feel female? In any way?

K: Well—[Pause.] I'd like to be better at decorating. I don't consider that really a feminine thing, but most people will.

Z: But how about sexually or physically? Is there an aspect of getting fucked that feels like being a woman?

K: I consider myself always dominant. But if I can find somebody who's an equal, I don't mind stepping down and letting them be in control. I think that's where my femininity would come in. Let them know that I'm hard, but I'm giving as well. Pretty much ever since boot camp I've always been a take-charge type of person. Always leading. And when I find someone who's an equal: "Let's let you lead now. I want to follow you. I want you to tell me what to do for once. I don't want to have to always make the decisions." Also, I find that I want it to be somebody younger than me telling me what to do.

I was up at [the] L.A. [gay] pride [parade] last month, and was talking to a dominatrix. Very interesting woman, very nice person. She said, "Looks to me like you need a little discipline." I was like, "Oh really?" And it's kind of funny, because—I am a very arrogant type. Because I don't want to have to give up what little dominance I have. So it's interesting to me to see how dominant the other person can be, after you've already shown your rebellion. She said, "You look like you need to be whipped." I said, "Thank you ma'am, may I have another?" "Oh is that right? We could have some fun!"

I have never been the kind of person who liked to get whipped for any reason. But I was like, what the heck, let's see what happens. Well, come to find out, it didn't hurt, not at all. And while she was whipping me, the crowd that it drew—I liked being in the limelight. I liked to have people looking at me like: "Oh my God, I can't believe he's actually taking it, and liking it." She was hitting me; I could feel a sting, and it would get very sharp, and then lighten up. I could tell the lady knew what she was doing; it was very erotic. I wouldn't say I was aroused, but I enjoyed the attention that I got from it. The other people was watching me. And they seen me as this hard individual. But I tell you what, it ripped the shit out of my back and I was black and blue for three days afterwards!

There was a man there who said we could have some fun. I said okay. Because I wanted to see what the difference was between a man and a woman doing it. And he did it different—she did it with a nine tails, he did it with a flog. It was basically the same intensity, but it was different. And with him I did get hard because the guy was a very attractive, hard, Marine Corps image type guy who was just beating me. I enjoyed it.

Z: Of course already a year and a half ago your former lover Anthony said in his interview [in *Sailors and Sexual Identity*] that you needed to be spanked—

K: I honestly find it sometimes helps. I like it when somebody grabs me on the balls. It's just an intense feeling. I like to play rough. Most people see me as a bulldog, and I like that. I've always been protective of my friends, and I think that's where that hardness—it's more of a protective type thing. Not trusting everything that goes on around me, not being afraid. That's probably what I mean, the attitude that I have: I don't walk into a situation like, I'm going to kick somebody's ass. It's more that I'm very aware of what's going on around me, and I'm not afraid of it. Whereas most people I see—they're very confused. I go into a situation not knowing anything, but I don't let them know that I don't know what the fuck's going on. And I find that some people find that very attractive. It's like a male peacock holds out his . . . spread, so to speak. That's what I'm doing—having my feathers out, trying to attract, more than anything.

Z: Marines are like peacocks?

K: Exactly.

Z: The Marine Corps dress blue uniform, in particular, makes a theatrical and dramatic presentation. Some Marines display a certain overplayed matador-like hypermasculinity that calls to mind drag queens. Drag queens perform an exaggerated super-femininity. And I remember one time when you were at [a gay bar] and saw one of those "cigarette girls." You stared in rapt fascination. You couldn't believe that it was—

K: A man.

Z: And you finally walked up and said, "Excuse me, I'm naïve. Are you a man or a woman?"

K: She was so good at it, it had me confused. I've also seen a woman trying to look like a man, and I thought, God, she would make a good-looking man! And it was very attracting to me.

Z: Alex mentioned that a large percentage of the prostitutes in Oceanside are transvestites.

K: Right. I have a hard time believing that it exists, but it does, and I'm like, damn, these guys got balls. It's unbelievable, but they are drag queens. Some are really good-looking. I'm surprised that the young Marine will do it. I guess they're so hard up.

Z: So you just think the Marines are just desperate and unable to get anything else?

K: Well, I guess they feel that they have to go out with women. Even though they might want to play—they're bisexual or whatever—they have to be seen with a woman.

Z: This brings me to a story that's maybe a little painful to bring up. You and some other Marines were in Thailand . . .

K: Oh yeah. To tell you the truth, I think I was just trying to cover up for myself. What had happened was, we had a young Marine that was on float with us. We were on the ship. We were making a six-month tour through all of Southeast Asia. We had a kid that had never had sex before. Everybody was bound and determined to get him laid. So we went to the bar and picked out a good-looking girl. Even though I am gay, I still look at women and I can appreciate their beauty. I'm not like some gay guys who are focused on men and nothing more. But, we found this young woman, that I swear to God I thought was a woman. The kid goes upstairs with her, and comes down white as a ghost. We're like, what the fuck? He had broken a bottle and was waving it at us, he was wantin' to try to kill us. He says, "You sons of bitches. I can't believe you fuckin' got me a faggot. I'm not a faggot! That's a fuckin' *dude!*" "Fuck!" So we go up there, and—I was just tagging along with the gang. I was like, oops! I didn't really give a shit if it was a dog, for that matter. But I did feel bad for him. I felt bad that we didn't get him a real woman. I also felt bad for [the transvestite], too. I'm sorry that it happened. And I really—I did not participate in the actual beating. But I happened to be there. And I didn't do nothing about it.

   I'd like to say for the record, if somebody does get offended by this, I was covering my own ass. Because I really didn't know much about myself and the way I am now.

Z: How badly was the transvestite beaten?

K: Not really. [The Marines] were pretty scared. Because [the proprietor] called the cops. We sure the hell didn't want to get busted. So they really didn't—I think they gave him a bloody nose and that was about it. They didn't beat the living shit out of him, I swear. Basically one guy held him, the other guy hit him once or twice, and we all skedaddled.

Z: You don't like queens, you said; that is, you "can respect them," but you "have no sexual attraction to them."

K: That's what I wanna say, for the record. 'Cause I don't wanna piss anybody off.

Z: Don't worry about how people perceive you; it's more important to be honest about your true feelings. What you said about the leather community was "We don't want no queens around."

K: Exactly. That's very offensive to the guys who are hard-core leather: the wanna-bes who put a halter or a leather collar on because they want to be dominated by a man—a real man. You know? "Get the fuck away from me, fag!"

I don't mind associating with [effeminate men], but if I'm out on the street with these people, I'd hope they would respect me by not being so flamboyant. But I try not to associate with people like that because of the fact that it—[Pause.] Shoot. I think I might be stepping out of bounds here. Maybe it's because—I'm not comfortable with myself?

Z: I was just going to ask you: what if somebody suggested that you didn't want to be around queens because you're insecure about your own masculinity? What would you say if they said that?

K: That's a good point. [Pause.]

Z: You'd tell 'em it's a good point?

K: [Laughs.] To tell you the truth, I think I'd be speechless. I'd have to really look at myself again. [Pause.] I really don't know what to say. I hate to say it, but I think that might be—I don't feel insecure about my masculinity. I think it'd be more the fact that I don't want to be outed.

Z: That seems sort of odd, what with your tattoo.

K: Well. Okay, you've got me on the wall! Shit. It's maybe because I don't want people to have the feeling that, okay, that I'm like them [queeny men] too. That's probably it.

Z: Because?

K: Because I'm not that way.

Z: In addition to going out to the clubs in leather, you also went out in a kilt.

K: Yeah! Well see, that is a very masculine thing, too.

Z: In Scotland.

K: It was just one of those wild things I did. And yes, it was more of a mini skirt—

Z: People came up to me in the club and said, "Keith is wearing—well, he says it's a kilt, but it looks more like a Catholic school girl's dress!"

K: [Laughs.] I had a good time with it. I got some really good compliments on it. I've always had very athletic legs. And I don't mind showing them off.

Z: I complimented you on your bravery.

K: I have to admit it was pretty brave. Especially with the monk.

Z: Who?

K: This guy, he used to be a Catholic priest. He looks like a monk. Evidently, that's where his gay side came out. He's a very nice guy. He's very effeminate. I honestly don't see him as a man. At all. It's a really scary thought that this guy is a man. I don't mind associating with him, but it would be the last person I'd take home to mother.

Z: What does he have to do with the kilt?

K: The night I wore it I went home with him. Basically I just wanted to fuck somebody, and he seemed to be easy prey.

Z: Did you keep the kilt on while you did it? I know you weren't wearing underwear.

K: No, no. I had a little jockstrap thing on. I had to wear something, because I have a tendency to—if I freeball I get hard. I didn't want to embarrass myself, have a dress on with a hard-on. Hey guys, how's it going!

K: Just to let you know, since the last time we talked, everybody knows about me in my family now. I feel much more at ease with the entire family. Mom's still—she wants to understand so much, and I want to try and tell her everything, but she—she's really shocked me with some of the questions she's asked. She's been very blunt in wanting to know about my sexual experiences. You know, Mom was in the Navy. And she asked me, "Well, do you like getting fucked?"

Z: Did she say it like that?

K: Yeah! And she said—I had no idea that way back in 1950 there was the "typical Marine." But she said, "Are you the typical Marine?" I'm like, oh God!

Z: Your mom said that?

K: Yeah. Old girl's been around.

Z: What did you answer?

K: I couldn't answer that question. She asked me straight out; she was wanting to know what role I played. She said, "Are you masculine? Or are you more passive?" And I said, "Do you see anything about me that's feminine?"

"Well, no."

"Okay let's go with that." Because it kind of pissed me off when she asked that. And then she wanted to know about, you know, getting fucked. I didn't wanna tell her. I kinda lied to her. I wanted to tell her that I was on top in all situations. "Well, why do you think guys like getting fucked?" I was like, "I don't really know. I can't answer that question."

I'd like to be more descriptive with her, but there's just some things you can't tell your mom.

Lance Corporal Ted:
The Absent-Father Tattoo

Escaping finally from Camp Pendleton on the Sunday of the great flood, Keith and I accompanied Ted to Tiger Jimmy's tattoo parlor on Broadway in downtown San Diego. The shop was filled with Marines newly graduated from recruit training—"boots"—and one took the chair opposite Ted to get a USMC logo tattooed on his left shoulder. As the artist went to work, the boot—who looked no older than 15—began to cry, and he had to be moved behind a partition. Ted bore his pain more stoically, leaning forward with his eyes closed and his hands folded, as if in supplication; occasionally, he threw a glance in my direction to confirm he still held my rapt attention.

He need not have doubted. From the moment I stepped into his barracks room and first saw the small but sinewy 22-year-old—shirtless, playing solitaire, regarding me with eyes beautiful, sad, and crafty—and heard him address me in his soft North Carolina drawl, I was smitten.

To protect his identity I cannot describe Ted's tattoos, but each of them held some special significance for him. One symbolized his hurt at the father who had abandoned him, one his Native American ancestry, another his survival of Marine Corps boot camp. Having lost Keith for an hour, we came to my room for this interview; Ted stripped off his shirt and asked if I would swab antibiotic ointment on his new, difficult to reach absent-father tattoo.

It was a request I took quite seriously.

Ted: Since I've been in the military, I've only met two people I could go and really have fun with. There's only been a guy back in school and Keith. With the others, we'd go out, and I'd end up being a baby-sitter because they'd get so drunk, or try to start fights, or just be boring.

It was kind of weird because at first he was sort of afraid to tell me. He told me he had a gay twin brother. But then after I opened up to him, he realized, yes, there's a friendship here, so he opened up to me and let me know about it. He was kind of shocked that it didn't bother me. He was also kind of shocked the first time he took me to a gay bar and I was sitting there having a good time like everybody else was. He told me to have an open mind before I went in. He ended up being the one who was shocked because I can make myself fit in, and really not cause a commotion or draw attention to myself.

Zeeland: Had you ever been in a gay bar before?

T: No. Everybody there was doing something that's different to me, but it's no big deal. The club itself was one of the nicest I've ever been in. Therefore, I had a good time. Good music. Everyone around was real nice. They even got on Keith last weekend because of the fact that I didn't feel good that night and I ended up going back to base and didn't come along. I think they enjoyed the fact that a straight guy could fit in with them and have a good time with them. It kind of gives me a taste of the other side, and gives them a taste of the other side at the same time.

Keith meets a lot of people because of me. He sometimes acts aggressive, and it's easy to sense. I just kick back; I'm myself. If somebody comes up to me, they come up to me. And through that, he's met a lot of people he can talk to and make friends with.

Z: A number of guys in the bar found you attractive and indicated that to you. How did that make you feel?

T: In a way I got a kick out of it. It was kind of funny. They'd make jokes, "Oh, you're such a tease."

Z: Are you?

T: Well, not really. I just want to go out and have a good time like everybody else. It's just that my friends are not straight and I am. They can't judge me for that, and I can't judge them for their ways.

Z: It must be flattering, though.

T: Yeah, it's always flattering when somebody's attracted to you. But at the same time it feels—me going into a gay bar and knowing these guys are attracted to me—it feels funny, but it feels good. It's a boost to my self-confidence. Both male and female like me. It makes you feel better about yourself.

Z: The Pentagon says that a straight guy needs to be protected from having a gay guy look at him in the shower.

T: I can understand them in a way, kind of wanting to keep them away from each other, but I don't really think it's an actual problem. It could be a safety problem because some people get very offended by it. And sometimes tend to get hostile about it. I've met some people that have said, "If I ever had a gay in my unit, I'd kill him." And I have met some Marines that would. They're that kind of people. They wouldn't hesitate.

Z: But how do you, as a straight man, feel about showering together with a gay man looking at you? Would that be threatening to you?

T: No. Because no straight guy can say that he never darts a glance. Everybody does. That's not really a reason to feel intimidated. It's harmless. The only thing is, for everyone's safety and to keep camaraderie up, not to make advances. You can tell if somebody wants you to come on to them. If you're aggressively coming on to somebody, that could cause a problem. I could understand the Pentagon saying that. But if gays are good enough to go all this time hiding it from other people, I know they can control their hormones.

When gays decide they do want to come out, the reaction will be, "Here's a good Marine, he's been working his butt off, does a good job. He's coming out, oh no, he's gay now. But I already know this person, there's just a little secret about him I never knew before. How can I condemn him for one little thing after all this friendship and camaraderie and how long we've worked together? Especially when he never bothered me before, never even let me know it was a possibility."

Z: What exactly was your reaction when Keith told you? Were you surprised?

T: Actually, I wasn't because I could already see it.

All day he had been wanting to tell me something. We were at work that morning when he first brought it up. Something about the look in his eye, I could tell. When he started to tell me, I said, "Let me guess. You don't have a twin brother." "How'd you know?" "I could see it. I couldn't see it until today, but I can see it now." He said, "I'm sorry I lied to you." I said, "Don't worry about it. I understand." It kind of made me feel good to realize he could see enough friendship between the two of us to come out and let me know. I know I'm the only person in the whole unit that knows.

I try not to judge people. Everybody does, but I try to steer away from it because I was judged so much in my life. By my appearance I was put in one class, but I'm really at the completely opposite end. I used to look like a hoodlum but I was a straight-A student. I had a good job; if I wanted nice clothes I could afford them. But I didn't care, I just liked to bum around in jeans, T-shirt, tennis shoes, and ball cap.

One thing I like about the Marine Corps: To a certain extent it kind of helps you make friends because everybody's wearing the same thing. They're not in their yuppie clothes or their grunge clothes; they don't have outlandish haircuts. And it kind of makes you get to know the person for who the person is. Because when they're at work, everybody's in cammies doing everything the same way. It's somewhat robotic, but still you get to know people for the person. As a civilian, you go by first impression. You look at them: okay, he's got on such and such, he must be in this class. And a lot of times you'll end up turning away a person that could possibly be a very good friend.

The class that Keith would fit into as a civilian, the way he dresses and stuff—people like that I didn't associate with when I was a civilian. He dresses punk: the combat boots, the leather jacket. He said he's probably got just as much hair now, if not more, than what he did before he joined the military. As a civilian I was considered a redneck. I had hair halfway down my back, moustache, a beard. I drive a Camaro. I have tinted windows, I have mags, the front end lowered. But I do show cars, and that's what makes a car look good for shows.

T: I joined the Marine Corps because I was in a dead-end job. I couldn't go back to school because I didn't make enough money. I couldn't get a job to make enough money because I didn't have the education. I had a degree in computer programming, but that wasn't what I wanted to do. I was just going nowhere.

I've always been somewhat of a perfectionist. So I figured, the Marine Corps is considered the most elite fighting force in the world. It's very rigorous, very strict. They have very strong customs and courtesies. I decided I would take that route so that later in life I could look back and say, yeah, I accomplished that.

I knew there would be a lot of games. In a way I was kind of deprived because I didn't go straight out of high school like a lot of the guys did. Since I had already been physically dealing with the outside world, it helped prepare me. It was still very rough. There's a lot of mental pain; there's a lot of physical pain. You have to be able to handle all that pressure and all the stress. I saw three or four guys in my platoon alone that cracked. And one of them is probably still in a rubber room right now. It's pressure that the outside world could not give. The Marine Corps can put you through so much that you feel like everything is on top of your shoulders, and you don't see the light at the end of the tunnel. It's very rough emotionally because it's getting used to being away from everything. And not just your family, your friends, your home: on the day before we graduated, they gave us liberty to spend the day with our families; I was sitting in a Burger King, and I was so fascinated by just the colors. Because I had been deprived of all that; all I ever saw, all day long, was green, brown, and black. People would never realize how lucky they are to have color until they have it taken away. . . . We weren't allowed to wear watches. So you never knew what time it was. Sometimes, you would forget what day it was. Because it would be so monotonous, the same thing over and over. For the most part you would stay in one square block. In that block you would have your chow hall, your barracks, and your parade deck where you would practice drill.

That was one thing they were very big on: drill, because it increases personal discipline. Being able to stand in formation with a bug biting at you and wanting to scratch it so bad but having the discipline to stand there and just let it go until either you forget about it or the pain subsides. I never thought I could see the day where I could do that. . . .

I learned to go from laughing to an immediate, almost kill-someone stare. Just in a second, because of the way they train you. They train you to kill people and you don't even realize it. I got in a fight right after I got out of boot camp and had to pay attention to what I was doing because if I had finished what I was doing, I would have killed the guy. In a way, it's kind of bad because they somewhat implant into your mind that killing is fun. Whenever they were like, "Do you want to learn a new line move on how to kill somebody?" "Yeah, let's see it! That sounds cool!"

It almost seems like the military has got a stereotype that they have to live up to. Because the military is considered very rigid, almost cold-hearted.

Z: How much are Marines really like that stereotype?

T: When it comes down to it, they are the stereotype. The other branches seem to be more relaxed than the Marine Corps.

Z: Does the Marine Corps attract a certain kind of person?

T: It seems like it's usually the same situation as me. You hear and see that the Marine Corps is considered the hardest, so you join to reassure yourself: "Yes, I can do anything I want to."

For the most part, I almost regret ever doing it, but at the same time I'm glad I did it. I regret being a Marine, but I'm proud of having the courage to become one.

Some of the things I've seen being a Marine—my personal values kick in and I don't believe in. For instance, looking at somebody and saying, "You've been in the Marine Corps for this long and you don't know how to do this? What are you, some shithead?" Things like that. They talk about morale and camaraderie and taking care of each other, but when it comes down to it, they don't. In a battle situation, yes. But person to person, for the most part, no.

Z: You were talking about the elimination of superficial differences that might stand in the way of civilians getting to know each other, but you also said you've made only two real friends in the time you've been in.

T: [Pause.] For some reason, in the Marine Corps it's kind of hard for you to let down your guard and open up to people. In the military, it's like everything's hush-hush. A lot of times it gets into your personal life. And that can hurt you because you can get to the point where you don't know who you are or what you are. All you know is, yes, I'm a Marine, I wear cammies all day. And from there you can't go really much further. You can say, I'm male, and all this, but sometimes you tend to forget your own values.

I've seen a lot of Marines turn their backs on other Marines. They say that the Marine Corps takes care of its own. I tore my knee up almost a year ago, and I'm just now getting to see a doctor for it. They have yet to really do anything for it. In the military, whether you got a headache, the sniffles, or a broken leg, they always say the same thing: "Here, take Motrin [an analgesic]."

The military does not care about anything but the military. You tell them, "I have problems with my family back home." "No, you don't *have* family back home. This is your family now." And that's real hard. Because of my father being an alcoholic, and always in and out, my whole life I've dealt with a lot of emotional trauma. That's a big problem for me. Emotionally, I've been wanting reassurance from him saying, "Yes, you can do it," or "Congratulations, you've done a good job, I'm proud of you." Since I've been in the Marine Corps, I've lost even more contact with him. When I tried to talk to even a chaplain and other people senior to me—when I let them know, they didn't care. They said I'm just imagining things, it's nothing.

Z: You haven't found the sense of brotherhood other Marines talk about?

T: It's not there. I keep learning more and more about the military. How hypocritical it is. How discriminatory it is. Women are not supposed to be in the infantry and carry a rifle into battle. If a woman wants to do that, let her do it. If she can carry her own just like everybody else, she earns it.

Z: Do you regret your Semper Fi tattoo?

T: No. That is one thing I don't regret, along with the title of Marine, the few and the proud. I am proud to say that I went through the roughest training that you could probably ever do, and that I had the strength and the courage to earn that title.

Z: So you look at the tattoo with a sense of . . .

T: It's reassurance that I can do whatever I want to do, and that I can accomplish my goal. Because I'll admit that there were plenty of times when I thought I wasn't going to make it.

Z: What is your idea of what is masculine?
T: [Pause.] There's really no definition for masculinity. I've seen women that could be more of a man than I could probably ever dream of.

[Pause.] One thing I would consider masculine would be somebody able to take charge and handle things. Be very sound and rock solid about it. Supposedly, a Marine never retreats. Forward or to the side, but never backwards. That is considered masculine. But at the same time, you gotta know when to back down. Because if not, you get yourself in too deep and it's a lost cause.
Z: Do you consider yourself masculine?
T: In some senses yes, in some senses no. As far as my appearance, I do. I mean, I hold myself for the most part with confidence. I have a good, solid, firm build. If somebody comes forward and tries to invade my space in a fight or something, I'm usually able to stand my ground and not back down. But a part that's not very masculine about me is my deep emotions. I'm still unsure how to control them sometimes. And I let them get the best of me. And that right there—I don't know if you could say it's nonmasculine, or if it's feminine, or what. I think there's kind of a void between masculinity and femininity. Nobody can really determine where the line is.

With gay guys, they would consider some of the things I do feminine, but in a straight person's mind it's masculine. But at the same time they might consider something they do to be a feminine thing, but I might consider it masculine. [Pause.] I guess I would say masculine is walking somewhat rigid and not really just kind of there. And talking boldly, and not real soft. I don't understand why people talk soft in a situation where it wouldn't really matter. Some gay people tend to—the way they talk, they talk like they're trying to talk like a girl.
Z: Some men you've heard at the gay bars?
T: Uh-huh. And I can't understand why they're doing that because I know deep down inside they still have masculinity, but it's like they're afraid to show it. It's not that they can't.
Z: Growing up, was being masculine something you had to work at?
T: I always had to struggle with that. I was a lot shorter than everybody else my age. Everybody would pick on me. So to prove to them, "I might be short but I can back up my own," I used to beat the shit out of everybody. I went through many a principal, many a paddle, many a being

sent home and suspended from school. People wouldn't accept me because of my height.

Maybe that can be considered the same thing as people being gay. If
people can grow to accept me because I'm shorter than they are, why can't
they accept people because they're gay? Just because they have a different
taste—gay men, they prefer to be with men instead of women. Well, that's
like saying, he prefers to drink milk instead of water. If you're going to
condemn him for liking a guy instead of a girl, why don't you condemn
him because he drinks milk and not water?

Z: Do you think sexuality is like that? Do you think it's just a question of
preferring milk over water?

T: I would believe it is. I can honestly say, until now I never really thought
about it that way. But when I look at it, I would believe that's how it is.

Z: How do you think people come to have such a preference?

T: [Pause.] Some say you're born that way, some say you grow that way. I
don't know which it is. I'll leave that for the doctors to decide!

Z: How important is sex to you?

T: I'm not sure how gay guys are towards it, but I know a lot of the straight
guys are like, "I gotta have it all the time" or "I gotta go somewhere and
find it." I'm the kind of person, if it's there, sometimes I'll take it, sometimes I won't. If it's not there, it doesn't bother me. I don't mind waiting.
At the same time I've had situations where it was spontaneous. Either
one's fine with me.

Z: How old were you when you first had sex?

T: Fifteen. It was awkward. It's like anything you do for the first time,
you're constantly wondering if you're doing things the right way, at the
right time, if things are moving too fast or too slow, if you're being too
aggressive or not aggressive enough. I guess the first time was almost a
negative experience because it made me feel awkward, but at the same
time I enjoyed it, but I wasn't even sure what I had just done. And since
then I've learned different things about it, different ways to make it more
enjoyable for both people. Things to make it last longer, to make it more
interesting.

Z: How old were you when you first started having sexual fantasies?

T: Probably about ten. And the thing that was weird then was, at ten years
old there's no girls the same age as you that are developed. It's women that
are in your fantasies. But at the same time, it's like, girls you know in
school—it's their face on the body. But I can't even really—I can remember having the fantasies, but I can't really remember what would go on in
them. It's a scenario where you're having a dream, it feels like one of the

best dreams you've ever had, and your alarm clock goes off or somebody wakes you up.

Most of my fantasies are in dreams. I've never been the kind of person to sit around and fantasize about doing this or that.

Z: Some men who consider themselves straight also sometimes fantasize about men in their private thoughts. Have had you those kinds of fantasies?

T: I've had the fantasies, but I've never really done anything, or attempted to try. As far as I know, everybody, male or female, whether they're gay or straight, they always have fantasies the opposite of whatever their preference is. And even though they feel they know what they want, there's always still a little bit of something inside making them wonder what the other side is like. And sometimes people decide they want to try that life, and drop the style that they're in. And sometimes they find they prefer their original preferences. Then there's people like me that feel content with the way I'm going now and don't really feel the need to investigate or experiment with the other side. I feel content with what I have. I'm not saying that other people do that because they aren't content—

Z: Let's just talk about you.

T: Um, I'm just content with what I have.

Z: You've spoken about the things you had to give up in boot camp. Last night you mentioned that you did find time by yourself to relieve your sexual frustrations.

T: There comes a time when you have to masturbate. Some people are afraid to admit it and I don't know why. It's a natural thing. Everybody is kind of secretive about it until either they hear somebody else say something about it, or they get caught. After that it's no big deal.

Z: It must have been hard to accomplish it in boot camp where you had so little privacy.

T: You could still go in the head. That's where most people went. That's where I went. There were no doors, but after a while it got to the point where nobody cared.

Z: You would see other guys doing it?

T: Yeah, they'd be in there. It wouldn't bother you. You couldn't really say anything because, one, if you were doing it, it would be hypocritical to say, "You were beating off in the head last night; I condemn you." And if you weren't doing it, it would almost be like you didn't have the courage to push yourself to relieve it.[1]

Z: How does it feel when you get these tattoos?

T: It stings a little bit, and it will kind of hurt—it's a sensation that's kind of hard to describe. It just ends up going numb. And after it's done and over with, for a few days to a week it just feels like a sunburn. It's basically all in your mind, how much pain you can endure. There's pain there, but it's whether or not you have courage.

A lot of people, they get tattoos because they like them. Me, I get them because they all have particular meanings behind them. Like with my Marine Corps tattoo; a lot of people get vicious ones, but I didn't because I'm not a vicious person. My tattoo is a [deleted]. But still there's the sense that, if it comes down to it, the person can be vicious. That's the way I consider myself. I don't want to come across that way, but if the need arises I can be that way.

A lot of people like to get these big, ugly, horrid tattoos with skulls and crossbones. I don't understand that. With all mine, I have somewhat of a sentimental reason. In a way it's like, my problems inside—I can get them out. They're still there, and I know they're still there. But they don't seem to bother me as much because it's like I can get them out in the open.

Z: So you express them through symbols; by making them physical you can better master them.

T: Yeah. It helps me see my problems more. It helps to keep them from sneaking up on me.

Z: And for your new tattoo expressing your sadness at the estrangement from your father, you told me you're leaving room for a solution; when you get the problem solved, there's an addition to the tattoo you have planned. . . . But getting back to the sensation: some people describe the experience of getting a tattoo as a sexual turn-on.

T: I've never talked to anybody who enjoyed it that much.

Z: It doesn't give you a hard-on?

T: No. It gives you a weird sensation from the pain, sitting there knowing I'm putting myself through all this torture to decorate my body. In a way you enjoy it, but it wouldn't arouse me.

Z: It was a lot of fun to watch your face. I know you saw me staring at you.

T: Yeah. I could understand because I used to be the same way, just sit there and watch people get tattoos. I'd watch and I'd watch and I'd watch. You kind of get a kick out of it, but at the same time you're kind of puzzled because you're not sure what they're going through.

In a way that can almost go back to sexual preferences. Because of the fact that you wonder what the other side's like. You wonder what they feel, what they go through.

Z: When you have fantasized about having sex with other males, what do picture?

T: [Pause.] It's almost kind of like curiosity. Because I'm not really sure what it would be like. It's almost like you're trying to figure out in a dream what it's like, instead of me just sitting down and thinking about it. In a dream it's like you're actually acting it out.

Z: But in these fantasies, or dreams, do you picture having oral or anal sex, and is there some emotional feeling accompanying that?

T: [Pause.] I'm trying to think.

Z: There's no right or wrong answer.

T: I know. I guess some of it deals with, in a certain sense, having another male as a form of reassurance. In a way that some men can't do. Actually having a man there that can hug you and kiss you and say, it's okay, I'll help you through this, you'll be fine. And I guess—well, I know that stems back to my father, and I can understand why. But I don't ever really remember fantasizing about actual sex. I remember—it's like you fantasize being with another man, but not actually having sex. You're not really doing anything sexually, but you're there.

It's basically something that's very vague. I guess because of the fact that I don't know what it would be like anyway.

[Keith returns, and waits outside my room.]

T: I hope this interview helps gay people understand that yes, there are some straight Marines out there like me that don't care. We're not going to get mad. Just don't try anything with us and we're fine. That's when it becomes a problem. Some of the people I have seen will try and be very aggressive and don't care. My sexual preference is for females.

That night, Ted, Keith, and I went out to a gay dance club down the street from my Hillcrest apartment. Ted played pool and was the target of stares so incendiary that I wondered if I would be tasked with swabbing Bacitracin on holes so inflicted—and secretly feared the job might go to someone else. Ted's naïve notion that gay men were friendly to him because they appreciated his tolerance and understanding was undermined by loud comments such as, "Straight? Not if he's in this bar!" and "He can be had!" as well as an actual wager over who would succeed in getting first crack. Ted handled this stockyard treatment with convincing aplomb. Keith was out on the dance floor, and he reappeared only to ask if he could spend the night with sailor Anthony on my living room floor. Ted left the bar with me, one of his pursuers yapping at our heels almost to my door.

We sat in my room for a few minutes talking until I became uncomfortably aware that I was in my "interviewer" chair and both of us were occupying the same positions we had been in when the tape was running.

Ted did not voice any concern about sharing my bed, but after undressing, he was quick to jump under the covers, where he lay on his back, arms folded over his stomach. I asked him if he was comfortable. He said yes. We talked for a while longer. Finally I said goodnight. Ted did not answer, and I was left with a nagging uncertainty: Was there something we had left unspoken?

A rare and powerful thunderstorm rocked San Diego that night, blackening the arm of the angel Moroni atop the newly christened Mormon temple in La Jolla. I lay anxiously awake, studying Ted's profile in intermittent lightning flashes as devil dog yells and rutting bear moans periodically rose and fell from my living room floor.

Oh, sweet torture; never in my life have I been more aroused by a man than I was by this young Marine in bed close beside me. What would Ted do were I to slide my hand down his USMC shorts? Would he push me away, angry and hurt? Or would he feign continued sleep and savor my attentions, in time-honored Marine fashion, making no reference at breakfast to what had transpired the night before? His interview statements indicated I was not to touch him— but he had also confided that he dreamt about being with men, and voiced no concern or fear about climbing into bed with a man he knew was attracted to him. Perhaps he was expecting, even hoping for an overture?

But I did not feel Ted's troubled emotional state would be improved by my handling him in the night. Let my friends pronounce me a fool (they did), but I had let Ted know he could trust me, and so with considerable self-discipline I kept my hands at my sides[2] and even managed to get an hour or two of sleep.[3]

But I still woke up well before Ted, who was turned now toward me. I studied the small black hairs of his outgrown high and tight until his eyes opened.

I mentioned the storm. He said he must have slept right through it.

"You know, I'm pretty proud of myself for behaving as well as I did."

With a small smile he said, "Yeah, you did good."

I asked him if it would be okay if I put my arm around him and he said yes.

I considered. "You know, I can't help but wonder if you weren't secretly hoping that I would try something."

Silence.

"I guess I'll always wonder."

"You know I'm happy with my sexual preference the way it is."

"But I wouldn't want to *change* your sexual preference—"

"I know, I know." Precisely: Had we not already so carefully drawn the boundary between our sexual identities our night together could perhaps have been spent differently.

I told Ted: "Well anyway, it was just nice sleeping with you like this."

I rubbed the bristles on the back and sides of his head. He seemed to like this. At length he yawned and said, "We should probably get up." Just as we were about to, rain pummeled the windows with renewed violence.

As the deluge persisted and I lay there holding Ted in my arms, I remembered what he had told of his dreams. And I considered that, maybe for one night, I was that man he wanted to hold him and tell him that everything would be all right.

Corporal Alex:
Marine Biology

"And Alex? What kind of an animal would *he* be?"

Seaman Anthony and I were enjoying a cocktail in celebration of my completion of the manuscript for *Sailors and Sexual Identity*, a book in which he would feature as the first interviewee. Possibly we had already had several drinks when I commented that, in the bar that night, there seemed to be an inordinate number of faces belonging to humans but extremely resembling other kinds of animals. There was a beautiful horse-faced woman who looked like that actress in Almodóvar movies and a Navy SEAL who, due to some imagined slight of mine, hurled me a resentful gibbon sneer. Anthony volunteered that, growing up, he had sometimes been likened to a turtle. I confessed to an awareness of my avian qualities.

And Alex? Anthony smiled wickedly. "Alex looks like a baby seal—*just about to be clubbed.*"

The sobriquet stuck. When *Spy* magazine ran a photo of a weepy Brigitte Bardot embracing a seal pup on an ice floe, I reenacted the shot for my Christmas cards, Bardot-ing Alex atop a snowy eastern San Diego County mountain. Probably, Anthony saw Alex more as a cowbird, I thought—any of various blackbirds who lay their eggs in the nests of other birds: Alex's own animal metaphor for his recent usurpation of Anthony's role in my life. Although I had palled around with Anthony for a year, with Alex it was different.

I have previously described the circumstances of our first meeting, occasioned by Anthony, who discovered the newly gay 21-year-old Wisconsonian of trailer park origins in a (he said) "convenience store." Sick with jealousy, I begged Anthony to tell me that Alex had a small penis. "I'm sorry," he answered, laughing, "I can't tell you that." Alex responded to my inevitable overture by making clear that his taste was for large, muscular men, but offered that he was attracted to me "intellectually." Offended, I explained that, after a year of playing solicitous avuncular confessor to young sailors, I had no such vacancy. Alex continued to call me, and, finding him not only cute, but also quirky, intelligent, and amusing, I condescended to provide him with guidance and encouragement, and one night he surprised me by climbing into my bed.

Anthony left for an overseas assignment. Alex became my special companion.

Ours was, and still is, an unusual alliance. We discontinued having (sort of) sex after a bizarre misunderstanding in an L.A. sex club involving a bottled water dispenser filled with hydrogen peroxide and a living, two-headed rabbit toted by some creepy Venice Beach type. Instead, we honed an uncanny telepathic understanding. Alarmingly, we started speaking in synch. Often our simultaneous pronouncements were predictable enough—the kind of thing that typically happens when people spend lots of time together. But sometimes they were more surprising. Once, on a drive in the country, commenting on some reposing bovines, I said "Big cows." Alex said "Little cows." Turning our faces together, in Bergmanesque fashion, we droned: *"All the cows"*—and shuddered together: "Where did that come from?"

Alex: The first picture I ever had of Marines . . . It was a misconception of mine. When I was little I wanted to be a marine biologist. And—I was an intelligent little boy, but I obviously misunderstood. I told my grandmother, "I could go into the Marines and get training for marine biology." She laughed and said, "Oh, you don't want to go in the Marines. They don't teach you anything about marine biology, they just teach you how to kill people." And I thought, "Oh, I guess I don't want to do that." Then later came the pictures that you get from history classes and TV shows . . . I was never a big war movie buff. I never watched—it's kind of even still a sacrilege; people look down on me at my unit because I never watched *The Dirty Dozen, Bridge Over the River Kwai,* or any of the old John Wayne war movies. I continually garble all the Marine facts. The history part didn't really interest me that much.

So the conception that I had was that Marines go out and kill people. But there was also . . . that mystique. There was honor and tradition. That was inherent in people's recognition of Marines. When you think Marine, what do you think? You think, pride. They're the modern day Knights of the Round Table. Well, [laughs] that was my conception of them before I joined.

Zeeland: Were there TV commercials you saw like that?

A: Oh yeah. There was also a very well-produced video. And I was all ready to go after that. It looked like it was very hard work, and they advertised travel, which was one of my top priorities because I wanted to leave Wisconsin. And then they showed you scenes from boot camp. They didn't really glamorize it although they left some significant parts out.

Z: How was the reality of boot camp different from the video?

A: Um, actually, I look back now, and the time that I did in boot camp and my basic schooling was my favorite time in the Marine Corps. . . .

You had no personal freedom, you had practically everything stripped from you; they told you where to go, what to do, how much to eat. But it wasn't that hard for me. There was only one time that I cried. It was about a week into training, and it was at night, and—I was eighteen. This was the first time I had been away from everybody I knew for a long period of time. And I had gotten a letter from my mom. They had me go up in front of class and open it. And it had, like, comics and all that in there—I guess stuff to cheer me up or something. And they took it. They let me have the letter, but they took all the comics and threw 'em in the trash. At the time it was kind of devastating, but I look back on it now and it was actually kind of liberating, because—It might sound kind of cheesy, but it was a time when I guess I felt I was taking a step from a boy to a man. That night I cried, but when I woke up the next morning I was like, "I'm not gonna let this place get to me."

And it wasn't really all that hard. It was pretty much just a mind game. I'd been through enough already in my life where they would have to do a whole shitload more to break me than that. There's a lot of other people that took it a lot harder; we had a few unbalanced characters there, and it was obviously taking a strain on their sanity. People were begging to get out and it was a horrible experience for them, and those are the ones who ultimately gave all of themselves away, let the drill instructors strip their entire identity straight down to the bone and rebuild them. I allowed the drill instructors to break down my individuality *only to a certain point*. I may have given them the illusion that I was broken down further, but deep inside I kept a kernel of my original self. I learned techniques, like being able to go inside my head. [Laughs.] I have many safe havens established in my head.

Z: What was the point of making you open up the letter from your mom and destroying the comics?

A: Well, they said that they were looking for contraband. But I doubt that, because it was just a letter. And if my mom was gonna smuggle me pot—I wouldn't put it past my mom—but they piss test you and all that. When you go into boot camp, you have no remnants of your former life. You go there with clothes and they take those away and put 'em in a box, and basically the only thing that you have is the stuff that they give you. So I think, that early in training, they didn't want you to have any kind of symbols that you could latch onto that identified you with your family or your former life.

Z: You're not a big guy. Did you have any problems making it through boot camp physically?

A: [Laughs.] When we had our first initial physical fitness test, I couldn't do pull-ups. I failed my PFT because of that. Not because of lack of physical strength—well, that was pretty much it. I didn't have the upper body strength. Running and sit-ups I had no problem with, just the pull-ups. Later on, my drill instructor showed me that physical strength isn't always required to do certain things. This was kind of a big revelation because it broke down misconceptions I had, growing up, that if you're not physically strong you're somehow inferior. He taught me what they call "kipping." It's a technique of getting your body in motion so that you can easily just use the momentum to get yourself up over the bar. I got the technique down really well, and the more we trained, the better and better I got, and I haven't had any physical problems since.

Z: What was your build compared to the other recruits?

A: We had almost eighty other recruits. I was pretty much in the middle. Most everybody had a bigger chest and bigger arms than me, but not too many people had bigger legs than me.

Z: You went to boot camp here in San Diego at MCRD, which I told you I overheard some sailors in the head at NTC [Naval Training Center] refer to as the cradle of "Hollywood Marines." They were saying that "real" Marines go to Parris Island.

A: Well, sailors can't really talk, can they? It's all a farce. The whole boot camp thing is just another Marine Corps melodrama to make a situation out to be something more than it is. It doesn't matter which boot camp you went to. Each one has its own difficulties. If you went to Parris Island you had sand fleas. If you went to San Diego you had . . . well, good weather. But you also have mountains here that they don't have in Parris Island. And when you're doing a hike, and you climb hundreds of feet and the slope is so steep that you can practically reach forward an arm's length and touch the ground in front of you, standing straight up, with a full load on your back—it's difficult. And sometimes I probably would have traded the mountains for sand fleas.

Z: Was there some image of yourself you thought you could fulfill by enlisting in the Marine Corps?

A: At the time I joined I was hanging around my aunt a lot, and she was, and still is, on this New Age spirituality kick. I was following her self-improvement techniques. That's what actually kind of motivated me to go in because I realized that I lacked physical strength, and I lacked discipline.

Z: How masculine did you consider yourself at the time?

A: [Pause.] I didn't think of myself as feminine. I was just . . . a kid. I wasn't thinking about masculinity or femininity.

Z: Did you play any sports?

A: No. I was into the mental kick. I was in the science club. The science olympiad was the closest thing I ever did to a sport.

Z: And you played the cello.

A: Yeah. And the bass.

Z: The other guys never gave you a hard time?

A: About playing the cello? The only reason why they gave me grief was because of the size comparison. They'd ridicule me because they'd see me walking home—I must've been five-four, with this bass that towered over me. And I'd have it on my back.

Z: Okay. So you didn't join the Marine Corps out of any sense of deficient masculinity.

A: I won't say that I didn't, but that was mostly just a supporting reason. It was in the back of my mind . . . I guess at that time I considered it part of the self-improvement.

Z: You have told me how, between the ages of eight and sixteen, you were sexually abused by a cousin six years older, who, with physical force and threats, would force you to let him brutally penetrate you, weekly, for eight years.

A: [Nods.] It caused a lot of problems in my life. During the abuse, and after the abuse stopped, I was very moody, increasingly spastic. Which I still show remnants of today, in my indecisiveness.

Z: Why would being sexually abused cause you to be indecisive?

A: Because the very nature of abuse is that you never know when it's gonna happen. I guess you could never really . . . you can't very well make decisions. I guess. . . . It's so intertangled and confusing.

Z: If we were to paint a picture of what you looked like emotionally after your abuse, what would be on the canvas?

A: [Laughs.] [Pause.] A truck accident.

Z: How would you describe your sexuality at age fifteen, after the abuse stopped?

A: My sexuality at that time was very withdrawn. My family is notorious for being late bloomers, physically. The first time I had consenting sex was when I was nineteen. And then the first time I had sex with another male was when I was twenty-one. [Laughs.] My sexuality awakened pretty late. There were sexual desires, but that was always limited just to dreams, or very brief daydreams or fantasies.

Z: What were they like?

A: [Pause.] Earlier, it was—it was just me having sex with a hole. Just a hole. A human hole, but . . . it didn't have any gender. [Pause.] I guess you could characterize it as not being human. It would be natural, organic, living, but not human. [Pause.] Not like animals, either.

Z: I can't picture.

A: Yeah, it's really hard to picture. I mean, I really didn't have any sexual feelings that I can remember before the abuse started—with one exception.

My mom was between marriages. Me and my cousins were all over at my Aunt Sharon's house. They had a pool. This guy that my Aunt Sharon was dating, he was big, masculine, and very handsome. I remember that we were playing hide-and-go-seek in the house. He was out swimming, with a few of the other cousins that weren't playing hide-and-go-seek. So I went and I hid underneath my Aunt Sharon's bed, and they couldn't find me. He came into the bedroom and began changing. And I remember peeking out from under the bed. He never saw me. . . . I felt so ashamed, but I desperately—I wanted him to . . . I guess just to hold me.

Z: How old were you?

A: Four or five. I remember the details exactly. It's etched in my brain. And I guess that's carrying over to my sexuality today because I'm attracted to somewhat older, big, very, very masculine men.

Z: Your abuser was six years older. Was he—

A: Yeah, he was a lot bigger. I was always the runt of the litter, I suppose. And my cousins would beat me up all the time. But I had a wit and intelligence to me that endeared me to the grown-ups, and I usually found myself associating with the grown-ups. Playing cards with them during family get togethers. . . .

Z: You told me about another experience that you left out today. You crawled into the bed of another man—

A: [Laughs.] Well. Yeah, I was eleven or twelve. He was the same type. Masculine, big. He was our next door neighbor. [Pause.] I mean, what do you want . . .

Z: Tell me what you did.

A: This was—I think my mom was married to my—second father? Third father? So I got an invitation to stay over at [the neighbor's] house. He was a young adult, probably about my age now. His wife was gone. And I snuck into the bedroom, and [laughs] fellated him. He didn't stir.

Z: You think he pretended to be asleep?

A: Yeah.

Z: Was this something you knew how to do because your cousin had forced you to do it?

A: Mmm-hmm.

Z: But doesn't that contradict what you just said, how you were a "late-bloomer" and didn't have sexual desires for other people?

A: I didn't really—I wasn't intending on getting any sexual gratification out of it. I suppose I was trying to use it as a ploy to maybe endear myself, and maybe he would . . . want to—I'm starting to sound really pathetic.

Z: No, there's nothing pathetic about it.

A: That he would just—want me.

A: I had sexual feelings for females; it's just that I was so awkward. I didn't know what to—especially after having been used sexually by a male—I didn't know what to do with a female. It was like getting a complex game with no instructions. It wasn't very fun. Especially poking my prom date in the breast with the corsage, right in front of her father. It was horrible. I guess that's why later on I hung around more and more with females—just to try and get some sort of inkling and perspective on how they operated.

Z: How did these early fantasies of the genderless, faceless hole develop to sexual desires for humans of whatever gender?

A: The fantasies became distinctly male-oriented when I went to boot camp.

Z: Before then they were . . . amorphous?

A: Yeah. They were just sex. No intimacy. There was coming and that was it. And then later on in boot camp I started feeling—

In boot camp I had four very well-built, very masculine drill instructors. All four of them were exactly the type of men that I had sought after in my early life. And I guess by having sex with them, I thought maybe . . . I guess this is all kind of boiling down to a father issue, isn't it? [Pause.] What is the exact question that you want me to answer?

Z: Tell me what you fantasized doing with these men.

A: One thing, early on in boot camp, that I kind of wished would happen— They showed us a first aid thing about hypothermia. The best thing to do if a person falls in a river is to dredge 'em out, strip 'em naked, and put 'em in a sleeping bag. Then, another person strips down and gets naked and gets put in a sleeping bag, too. I would love to do that with any of my drill instructors. Because then I would . . . I mean, I don't know if that's really sex, being naked and close to each other, but that was the core of the fantasies. That and also wrestling. I had lots of wrestling fantasies in boot camp and later on in my military career. Not that much anal sex. That never really came into most of my fantasies. I think maybe only once or twice. And that was with my DIs topping me.

Z: Did you ever fantasize about the other recruits? Were you attracted to them?

A: Only one, and that was because he was basically the same body type as the drill instructors. He was a guy from Texas. Big and burly and masculine. Stupid, too.

Z: At boot camp, did the drill instructors ever hit you?

A: On the record, no, I wasn't hit. Off the record, yes, I was hit a few times.

Z: Why don't you want that to be on the record?

A: Just because. If they start making a big deal about it, they'll stop hitting recruits and the training won't be as good.

Z: They're not going to make a big deal out of it on the basis of this book.

A: Okay. [Alex later granted me permission to include this information.] Well, yeah, they did hit us, but that was good. It's not like they left permanent damage.

Z: Did that figure into your erotic understanding of them?

A: Oh yeah.

Z: You liked being hit?

A: Well, I suppose I liked getting punished when I did something bad. [Laughs.]

Z: But do you associate that with sex? You told me that your abuser used to hit you.

A: Sometimes. But I mean, with [the drill instructors], I did something wrong, so I should get punished. And the severity, them hitting me, I felt like it was deserved. It wasn't like the abuse, when I felt that I was being punished, and I didn't know what for.

Z: You've said that you equate playing the bottom with the humiliations you experienced in boot camp [see Introduction, pp. 6-7]. But you've also explained your sexuality in terms of the abuse you suffered growing up. Do you stand by the fact that it's the Marine Corps that gave you . . .

A: The submissiveness? It was a combination.

Z: In joining the Marine Corps, did you feel any connection between your past trauma—

A: And what I was getting myself into? No, actually I thought it was going to be the opposite. I thought the Marine Corps was going to be—which it turned out to be afterwards—a structured environment where they make men out of you. That's pretty much their advertisement. I thought that it would fill some void in my life.

A: After boot camp I went to MCT, which is our Marine Combat Training. It's kind of like the Marine infantry training for non-infantry people.
Z: What is your job in the Marine Corps?
A: Supply. Administrative. Not a grunt. And then from there—well, it was definitely the scariest time that I had in the Marine Corps because at that precise time, Desert Storm was going on. We were out in the field when they announced that the allies had started bombing Baghdad.
Z: A mutual ex-Marine acquaintance of ours insists that the real reason men join the Marines is to kill. Was that something that you had given any thought to in joining?
A: That came as a shock later on in my training. At MCT they were saying, "You're gonna be going over there. They're going to have a mortality rate of ninety-five percent. Everybody's gonna be waxed." And I was like, "Well, I don't remember this killing part being in my contract. And I definitely don't remember the *being* killed part."
Z: You have confided to me that you have frequent recurring homicidal dreams.
A: Homicidal dreams?
Z: You told me that you kill people in your dreams all the time. Including me.
A: Well, that was a special circumstance.
Z: Did you have these dreams before you joined the Marine Corps?
A: No. No, I really didn't. I don't think I was capable. I was pretty spineless before I joined the Marine Corps.
Z: They teach you how to kill people—
A: With your bare hands.
Z: What kind of impression did that make on you?
A: It made me more confident. I can walk around smiling, thinking to myself, "I don't have to use this force, but if the situation arises, I'll gladly kill somebody."
Z: Did you tell me before that you fantasized about killing your drill instructors?
A: I think that at some point everybody who goes through boot camp wants to kill at least one of their drill instructors.

Z: You were stationed in Japan for a year. What kind of friendships did you have there with other Marines?

A: I had a bunch of acquaintances, but I never really had one friend that I would pal around with. As soon as I got there—I was already promoted to lance corporal after getting out of school, so I was already ahead of the ball game. And I wanted to make a good impression at the first place that I worked at. So I just dove into work. This is what I commonly do: I replace people with work. I was working all the time, so I didn't really have any time to get any really good friendships.

[Pause.] I guess I did have one good friend over there, though. And that was a WM, a woman Marine. She was pretty much the only one that I would confide in. She was very intelligent.

Z: A lot of your important friendships have been with females.

A: Yeah. As a teenager, and then later on, too.

I was overseas when I had my first consenting sexual experience.

I was on Okinawa. I was TAD [temporary additional duty] there with a staff sergeant of mine. The running joke in our office was that I hadn't ever had sex. I admitted that. I thought it was true. I mean, I don't think abuse should be considered sex because it wasn't consensual. [Pause.] So that staff sergeant, he went there TAD with me with the intention of having me have my first sexual experience. He took me to a little red-light district where they have these houses right outside Kadena, the Air Force base. It's called Whisper Alley, because the mama-sans whisper: "Hey GI, come here. We got good deal, our girls are all clean. All have certificates."

He popped for it. I thought it was really funny. He goes, "How much for a blowjob?" The mama-san goes, "Oh no! We no do blowjob here!" She got all upset. He goes, "Well, how about twenty dollars?" She goes, "Okay. We do blowjob just this one time." So then I went inside, and to this back room. She was blowing me. I was laying down. She was completely naked. I wasn't touching her. And she became exasperated because she couldn't get me off. It just wasn't doing it for me. I mean, I had it up; I just couldn't come. Finally she was going, "My mouth sore. I no do blowjob anymore. Mama-san give you money back if you not wanna go fuckie." So I said okay. I was fucking her, I was fucking her hard, too. And she was yelling 'cause I was bumping her head against the headboard. I didn't even realize it. And then finally when I did come—

Z: She was dead.

A: [Laughs.] No. She was just yelling. But it took quite a while. My staff sergeant, after I came out, he was kind of dubious. "That was your first time? You were going at it for quite a while. Did you just come once?" I lied and said, "No, I came two or three times." "You didn't have to pay any extra?" I said, "No, I guess she just wanted it too bad, or something." Which was a lie, but he believed it, so.[1]

Z: How did you look at the experience the next day?

A: I felt a little guilty. I mean, I grew up Catholic. . . .

Z: But what I mean is, how did that impact on your desires and your sense of sexuality?

A: [The experience did have] kind of an impact, because I thought, if that's what sex with females is like, then I don't know if I want to keep having it because it was bad sex. Having sex with other men was the only other option. But I was still in the mode of saying, "Obviously I'm sick." So I drove myself harder and harder, tried to be more masculine. More Marine-like.

Z: At work, you mean?

A: Yeah, being all motivated, thinking that this was the way that I could do it. And not realizing that the dreams that I'd have at night about having sex with other men probably were a result of my becoming more masculine and people identifying with me and hanging around me. The people that were very masculine. 'Oo-rah, motivated, chest-beating types.

Z: You never had sex with any chest-beating men in Japan?

A: No. There was an aborted sexual opportunity. That was with the Cajun corporal from Louisiana. Very, very masculine. He was my type. Very big, not very bright, and when he drank he got exponentially stupider with each drink, to the point where you'd make fun of him, right in front of him, and he just wouldn't get it. I guess I must have felt an attraction to him as a friend because I would protect him when he started getting drunk. And I felt that maybe he would reciprocate and protect me physically.

We were on duty one night, and we were talking. We were the only ones in the building; nobody else could get in. So it was really private. I told him, "You know, out of all the guys in the unit—don't take this the wrong way—but you're the best-looking. You always get all the girls that you want. Physically, I wish I could be like you." He got into that, and we got talking about the subtle beauty of the machine that is man. Then he got on the subject of homosexuals. And at that time I didn't consider myself homosexual, even though I had the desires. I said I thought that was maybe an illness or something. He was like, "Who are you to pass judgment?" Because I was pretty much an open-minded person with the exception of being homophobic. "If you want to be so open-minded, you have to accept gays just as much as you do everybody else." I was very uncomfortable with the subject, and he kind of let up a little bit.

It was getting late, and I went to go watch TV in another room. He said, "Well, I'm probably gonna go to sleep, so." I came back to go to bed, and there he was, stripped down to boxers, laying on the bottom bunk, and the fly on his boxers was open, and—

I didn't take action on it even though I should have. It seemed like an obvious invitation, especially since the room was really cold. I woke up during the night and he had gotten dressed, so.

That was the closest thing I suppose I had to sex before I had sex in San Diego.

The first few months at Camp Pendleton I started coming to grips with my sexuality. I took [the Cajun corporal's] words to heart. "Well, I suppose it is just a different lifestyle." It was pretty hard for me since I didn't have anybody to talk to. Especially being trapped on Pendleton so far from any semblance of civilization.

That's when I met Brian. He was in my platoon. There was a small group of us that would hang out together. Physically, he was very different from me. We became friends; he respected my intelligence, and I respected his . . . bigness, I suppose. His physicalness. We went everywhere together. He had a car, which made things easier. Of course, it was a '65 Mustang which didn't work all the time. But then later on when I got my car, I chauffeured him around. In December 1992 Brian left for Somalia. Then he came back, and he was gone on and off until he left in November of '93.

Z: How would you describe your friendship? When you first told me about him, it sounded to me like a buddy relationship, but then later you seemed to suggest that you considered it something more.

A: Well, I mean, it was a buddy relationship. I knew that I would have laid down my life for him. I was pretty sure that he would have done the same for me. We'd confide in each other. And when he went to Somalia, part of me—it was the closest thing I've ever felt to somebody like a lover, or mate, leaving. I was pretty tore up, because he was going off somewhere and there were people already getting killed. I volunteered, but my gunny [gunnery sergeant] said that I couldn't go because I was too important to be sent away.

Z: Did you have any further sexual experiences with women?

A: During that time? Yeah.

Z: Well, tell me about those.

A: There's only one word to describe them—bad. There were three or four instances, and each one was just as bad as the first time I had it. I don't know; women are just really bad sexual partners. They're very temperamental. They're like Brian's Mustang: They work when they want to and then all of a sudden they'll just give out and sit there lethargically. I realize that it's hard to do everything right all the time, but it's especially hard when they don't give you hints or tell you which button to push. . . .

I do still sleep with women, sometimes. And I've refined that now, to where it's on a personal basis. I sleep with women if they're nice. And it's actually nice to sleep with women too because they're a lot more feminine. I wouldn't sleep with an effeminate guy, because I think that's unnatural.

I slept with a woman Marine this spring. She was actually pretty good in bed. We kissed, and stuff like that. No cunnilinguistics. I didn't let her fellate me. She was very, very active. She'd move and jiggle and all that.

Z: Would she lay on top of you?

A: Noooo. . . .

Z: Are you sure?

A: And she was in really good shape. Soft and feminine. Like a little bunny or something. But it still doesn't compare to sex with other men.

A: I came out in May of '93. I was in an adult bookstore [in] downtown [San Diego]. I had never been in one before. They had all these girlie magazines, and I was looking through them. And then I noticed a gay magazine. I picked it up, and went around to the other side, where you could see everybody that was coming in. There weren't that many people in the store. I started reading it, and my blood started rushing to my head. I started getting very sexually aroused. I had never felt such a rush of anything before. I bought a magazine that was wrapped in plastic; on the cover it had a big naked guy with boots, on a forklift. I also grabbed a copy of [a local gay newspaper], too.

On the way back I was starting to think of what I actually did, that I had got a gay magazine, and I started punishing myself or whatever. How could I ever expect to be normal if I was to read things like this? I saw it sitting next to me, and it was inciting me to think even worse thoughts about me. And then something inside of me kind of stood up, and I started saying to myself: *"This is me!"* Soon this voice in me became overpowering, and I just started feeling happy about myself, happy to just be me. I was laughing, and yelling in the car, "I'm gay! I'm gay! I'm gay!" I was euphoric. I suppose people going by—well, people do weirder things in cars, but I didn't care what other people thought.

That was my gay . . . release. I knew that I was gay and I was going to be happy that I was gay because I had desired to have sex with males more than with females. I would say that that was the happiest moment in my life.

When I got to the base, the sentry looked at me kind of strange because I had this almost unnatural smile on my face.

Z: Where did you put the gay magazines?

A: We had false ceilings, so I just put them up there.

Z: You didn't tell Brian about this.

A: No. I never told Brian.

I was very happy for the next few weeks after coming out. I was almost giddy. People at work were wondering if I had met some girl, but it was actually just the first time in my entire life that I felt—not at peace with myself—but I felt such a release.

I hear a lot of people talk about the first time they went to a gay club, that they had a hard time going in, especially if they were just coming out. And me, as is pretty characteristic in my life, once I make a decision I'm pretty solid with it. I had no problem. I just parked and went in. Used my military ID at the door. Later I thought that was stupid, especially after getting inside the club and the first thing people ask you is, "Are you a Marine?" I'd get really flustered and say, "I have to go," and just walk to the other side of the club.

Z: You also started going to the bathhouses. That's where you eventually met Anthony, which led to your acquaintance with me. Tell me about your first time out at the bathhouse.

A: [Laughs.] The kid-in-a-candy-store scenario. I mean, I had lots of sex. Six people. It was really enjoyable too. Mainly just—what do they call it? Frottage. That was pretty much it.

Z: That's not what you told me before.

A: Well, I did have anal sex. But I didn't have anal sex with all of them. And I definitely didn't play the bottom.

Z: What was it like to fuck another guy for the first time?

A: It was much, much better than fucking women. Whenever I have sex with women I'm always afraid I'll break 'em. But with men it's different. That's what makes the sex so good, because it is so rough. Women are nice, but like I compared the one WM to being like a bunny—I don't get the urge to fuck bunnies too often. It's nice to be sensitive and all that with them, but I definitely prefer the rough sex.

Z: What was the first time in these new experiences with men when you played the bottom?

A: [Pause.] That was through a guy that I met through the classifieds. He lived out by [Naval Air Station] Miramar. It was okay because he didn't have a very big penis, so it didn't really hurt that much.

Z: It didn't give you flashbacks of the abuse?

A: No. I was on my back, and all my abuse happened when I was on my stomach. I'd rather be on my back if I'm going to play bottom. It's just more comfortable. When you're facing down, you're like a turtle flipped on its back. You have to crane your neck around to see what's going on.

A: I can't understand gay men going after anything other than masculine men. There are effeminate men out there, but my idea of being gay is being attracted to men. If they're drag queens, they're in a different category. But if they're men and they act like women, that's totally unattractive. Or if they're small. I don't understand that—men who like young boys or whatever.

Z: You're rather boyish yourself. Or do you think of yourself as big and macho?

A: I don't really consider myself big and macho. But I don't consider myself boy-like.

Z: How do you think of yourself?

A: A cross. I mean, I'm still developing, but I consider myself to be somewhat a man.

Z: "Somewhat a man?" Is that what I'm supposed to type up?

A: I consider myself a man, but—I'm still young! [Pause.] What?

Z: Tell me more about what is masculine.

A: I have a pretty conventional view of masculinity, I guess. Strong, not betraying any emotion, strong of will, big, and muscular—that's how I view masculinity.

Z: And that's what excites you sexually about other men?

A: Yeah.

Z: To include not being emotional?

A: Yeah. I've never been accused of being too passionate during my love-making.

Z: I found you pretty passionate.

A: Well, passionate is the wrong word, I guess. I mean . . . tender.

Z: You tell me that you are looking for a romantic relationship, but how can you ever hope to have one if one of the characteristics you insist on in your men is lack of emotion?

A: Well, at first. I mean. That kind of stoic—I suppose I look for it probably to counteract—Even though I might seem stoic at times, I'm a whirlwind of emotions. I think I seek stability from people who seem emotionless. Masculinity I consider to be . . . a rock in a swirling river, right before the falls. It's there, the water can try to wash it away, but it'll always be there.

Z: So you don't want them to yield to you at all? Or do you?

A: It becomes more exciting if they don't yield: it becomes something of a fight, and then they'll be even more emotionless, and that excites me even more. If they give in a little bit, then it's like they're letting down a section of the wall to allow me in.

Z: Do you think there's any special connection between Marines and drag queens?

A: Well, I told you I went up to Scandals, that [now defunct] skanky gay bar up in Oceanside, and there was one other Marine who walked in there, after this really bad drag queen walked in. And they left ten minutes later with each other. I didn't get the impression that they knew each other before that. And every time I tried to rent *The Crying Game* at the base video, all the copies were always checked out. I think Marines are attracted to drag queens because, for myself, there's such a rigid standard of masculinity imposed on you every single waking moment of your life as a Marine. I mean, it's hard to be masculine. And I think drag queens offer, where you can still be essentially male because you have a penis, but . . . For, like Marines, you're always expected to be rah rah rah.

My first impression of drag queens came when I was in Marine Combat Training. We were getting a liberty brief before we were going out to Oceanside. And of course one of the briefs was: "Stay away from the prostitutes. Most of them aren't actually women." I didn't see any, even though I was kind of wanting to see one or two.

Later on when I went overseas, they have the boy-women of Bangkok. There was a big scandal; one of the Marines who came back in a group right after us had picked up a [transvestite] prostitute. The other guys had pictures of her sitting on his lap; of course they'd bring 'em out to taunt him, and make Xerox copies and put them on his desk every day. Their version of the story was that he was totally trashed and that it took a while for him to figure it out. So he must have been kissing on her for a while, which I found funny.

I saw a really bad drag queen when I was first waiting for the bus to go back to Pendleton. Very drunk, too. Or drugged. I felt kind of sorry for her, but. Then there were drag queens getting attacked in Oceanside by Marines, and you hear stories about Marines picking up drag queens, and even more recently a drag queen stabbed a Marine. I guess the Marine actually knew the drag queen.

I was at [a gay dance club] one night, when the candy drag queen was going around. I know her, and I'll buy gum, and she'll give me a kiss. But there's this evil queen that was there who said he wanted to glue her heels to the floor. I told him that was a really stupid thing to say. And then there were other friends who said similar things; rip her panty hose or something like that. It's kind of sad to see gay men, who want to be accepted into society, ridiculing somebody because they're different. I mean, I see drag queens as breaking down conventional stereotypes people have to fill, and I think that's exciting. They're warriors in a sense.

I'm not really attracted to—well, [laughs] there is a slight sexual attraction to some drag queens. But it's not really for men; it's for women. They put on a show like they're women. Like I said, I still sleep with women sometimes.

Z: What do you picture doing sexually with the drag queens?

A: I've never actually fantasized sex with a drag queen. I mean, I've gotten aroused, but it's like . . . in a fog or something.

Z: You told me before that the drill instructors are "nurturing."

A: Not in the same way women are nurturing. Like a father nurtures . . . his son. You can be nurturing and not overly emotional. That's what I meant before. Women are generally overemotional. They are run by emotions. Men are run by logic.

Z: [Laughs.] Is that true?

A: I believe it is. Pretty much. [Pause.] What?

Z: You want to divide people up into "masculine" and "feminine," but I see a lot of both in me, and I see a lot of both in you.

A: Well, that's why I'm gay, I suppose.

Z: What can you tell me about women in the Marine Corps?

A: Most women in the Marine Corps are just like women on the civilian side. They whine, they bitch, they fuss about their hair. But there are exceptions. They're the women Marines that forget they're women. And they try to prove themselves to men, or try to outdo men.

When I was stationed in Japan there was this WM named Lance Corporal S. She was just about as boon-dyke as they come. She was six-foot-six, weighed over two hundred pounds—just an Amazonian woman. And she'd go around and tell the Captain and the [master gunnery sergeant] what to do. One time, the Master Guns wanted S in his office. She was his receptionist. And she didn't want to put down what she was doing. She told him to hang on. He called her a second time, and she said "Didn't you hear me? I said hang on." When he called her the third time, she slammed down her note book and swaggered over to his office and said, *"What?"* And the Master Guns—even though he was six foot, he only weighed probably a hundred and seventy pounds, and he was very intimidated by her. She got transferred out of the unit not too long afterwards.

Lance Corporal R, he was from Indiana. Big farmboy type. He was over six foot two. He was the only one in the platoon that was close to S's height. So when the Marine Corps ball came around, and S remembered that she didn't have a date, she flat out told R in front of the whole platoon that he was going to be her date. And he said, "No, Lance Corporal S, I'm not gonna be your date." She said, "I don't think you heard me. You are going to the Marine Corps ball with me." And he wound up going with her.

Lance Corporal S was infamous for her "foot massages." She'd come to a barracks room, and she'd always make sure that the guy's roommate was gone. She'd start with the foot, go up his leg, and work her way up.

Z: Did you ever get a foot massage from her?

A: Nope. She always told me, "Lance Corporal [Alex's last name], I want to give you a foot massage." And I'd say, "No, no, Lance Corporal S, I've got ingrown toenails. I don't like foot massages." But there were plenty of other guys that were interested in foot massages, so I was spared.

Z: Was she thought of as a Marine, or a woman Marine?

A: I think she was thought of as a Marine. There was one forced march when the Master Guns wound up falling out of the hump, and she had to take his pack. I was two people behind her, and she bitched bitterly the whole way about how much of a goddamn wuss he was. The captain overheard it and he just laughed, because he didn't like the Master Guns either.

Z: What would it take for women Marines to be fully accepted as Marines?

A: This is something that I feel strongly about. First off, they'd have to revise the physical standards. Women would have to do the same exact things as men. Secondly, they'd have to redo the grooming standards, so the women would have to get the same haircuts as men. And wear the same clothes as men. If they made them essentially equal, not different, then people wouldn't think of them as different. That's what I don't like about most WMs; they think it should be separate but equal. You can't have that in the Marine Corps. Everything has to be *together* and equal.

Z: You said that most women Marines, like most women, bitch all the time. But aren't all enlisted Marines famous for bitching all the time?

A: They bitch, but. [Pause.] Take that out about the women Marines bitching.

Z: You have expressed regret that you weren't a "real Marine." What would you have gained had you relinquished your individuality?

A: I probably would have stayed in the Marine Corps. There would have been that camaraderie and esprit de corps that I didn't feel by staying an individual. I guess Marines can smell it like bloodhounds. Individuality: they can sniff it out on a person.

Z: Is that why other Marines don't like you?

A: Yeah, I think that's why.

Z: You read part one of Keith's interview. What was your reaction?

A: I have two words for that. Chee-sy. It was hokey.

You asked me to attest to the authenticity [of Keith's stories]. They are authentic. But the malarkey about brotherhood in the Marine Corps is—it's not even—in the Marine Corps, I've found that there's a false sense of brotherhood. There's all these guys who go around thinking that their buddy would help them out if they got into a jam. But I found that people in the Marine Corps are self-serving and vindictive. That's probably one of the biggest ruses of the Marine Corps. I mean, you can *feel* a sense of brotherhood. That's different from there actually *being* a brotherhood. They create that illusion and give you a security and give you some sense that if I fall, my brother will be there to pick me up. And it's all a facade.

Z: When I told you that Ted called the brotherhood a hoax, you reacted angrily.

A: I was probably in a Marine mode or something.

Z: So maybe you're just saying these things now because you're getting out of the Marine Corps?

A: No, no, no, no. I mean—it might have been that I wasn't at the right units. I am only a support Marine. I wasn't with the grunts, where you actually lay your life in other people's hands. I believe that there might be some genuine brotherhood there.

Z: It's too bad you weren't with the grunts that Keith talked about. You would have won the over-the-line contest.

A: I probably would have.

A: One time we were just being naughty in the field. We were drinking Wild Turkey and playing spades in an abandoned [tear] gas [training] chamber, not far from where we were bivouacked at. Sergeant Ski, he was the psycho one. I told you about him; he was the one with an eagle tattooed on his penis.

Z: Where exactly?

A: On the head.

Z: Would he display this fairly often?

A: Oh yeah. Whenever anybody wanted to see. He was our Motor T [transport] NCO [noncommissioned officer]; he'd go back into his little room, undo his cammie trousers, and pull it out. It was uncut.

The other two Marines got drunk, so they left. It was just Sergeant Ski and me. He was asking me if I've ever done anything evil. He was rubbing me on the chest. I was totally smashed, and I didn't want to risk anything because this guy was former Force Recon. I thought he was capable of extremely psychotic deeds, and I didn't want to press it. But he was rubbing my back and stuff like that, asking me if I'd ever done anything evil.

Z: What did you answer?

A: No, no, I'm good! I'm entirely good! I don't have an evil bone in my body! He was like, "Sometimes I just get the urge to be *evil.*"

Another time, me, Sergeant Ski, and Sergeant B were all in the instructors' tent, my tent. We were talking, and we were starting to fall asleep. Sergeant Ski asked me what position I liked my women to be in. I didn't know, so I just said missionary style. He said, "That's old." Sergeant B, he gets on his hands and knees and sticks his butt up in the air, and says, "This is the position I like." Sergeant B got kicked out of the class later on for wanting to have a three-way with one of the other students and his wife. Actually, with Sergeant Ski and his wife. He was re-assigned to a different unit.

Z: You told me about some remarks you heard the other Marines in this class make.

A: They got in a discussion about whether their wives or girlfriends would give them head. There were some Marines whose wives wouldn't give them head at all. Not to be stereotypical, but half the Marines were married to Filipino women that they met over in the Philippines, and they would always give them head, and the Marines always bragged about how good it was. They would jokingly invite all the other guys over. Only one guy made any protest. He was ultra-religious, and he never had a girlfriend. He said it was gross and he couldn't imagine it. Everybody just ignored him. Then they got on the topic of if they could suck their own dicks. The married ones said that if they could do that, they would never have gotten married. The single ones said that they would never even have girlfriends.

Z: Did you tell me that they agreed that it wouldn't be queer to get a blowjob from another guy?

A: Yeah, as long as they beat the guy up after they'd come. That was the only restriction. The other thing I overheard, most of 'em said that the only problem they would have with fucking another man would be the hairy ass.

A: I have a friend who was in my unit overseas. He came to California, and he brought his wife over from Texas. She was flying home to visit her family. Shane asked me if I would drive them to the airport in San Diego.

After we dropped her off, Shane asked if there was someplace I wanted to go down here. I said, "Well, there's a few gay bars." So he agreed. We went to [a gay dance club]. He sat there and he was drinking. He got pretty drunk, since I was driving. We were going down University [Avenue], and he started talking about his ass, and about his wife's vibrator, and how he sometimes liked to turn it on and stick it around his ass, and how good it felt. When I dropped him off at his house, he wanted me to go inside. I said, "No, I have to get up in the morning." "Well, you can't drive on base because you've been drinking." "I only had one beer." He was pressuring me to stay the night. It was unnerving.

Z: Why?

A: Because I slept and showered and dressed in front of this guy, and here he could have been secretly fantasizing about me. It was kind of frightening.

Z: [Laughs.] Isn't that sort of reverse homophobia?

A: It's not homophobia at all! He was doing it secretly, without my permission. It's like—it just wasn't right.

Z: You never lusted after him?

A: He was totally not my type. He was small, redheaded, plus he had a belly. Plus, he was married.

Z: Do you think he would want somebody like me to fuck him?

A: No. He was a pretty private individual, normally. I couldn't see him asking that of somebody he didn't really know.

A: I met [another enlisted Marine] at [a gay dance club]. Obviously, he was in a gay bar, so I started hitting on him. He was pretty rough-looking. Not scruffy, just rough. Sloping forehead, slightly neanderthral-looking. He said that his friends dropped him off and he didn't have a ride back. He was going to take a taxi. I offered him a ride. We drove by a canyon. We stopped there and we were talking. He was obviously really liquored up. I was kind of tense because I hadn't been out for that long. I was quite ineffectual at coming on to people. I'm still not very good at it. But he said, "Do you, like, do stuff?" "What stuff?" "You know. Stuff." So finally, I'm not sure if I laid my hand on his thigh, or he laid his hand on my thigh, but. There were cars coming. And plus there were lights on in the house we were parked by. So we went down into the canyon.

He gave me a really bad blowjob, then he was like "I wanna get fucked by you." So I said, "What a minute. Stay here." I went up and got the condom and lube I keep in my glove box. He was definitely a better bottom than he was at giving head.

Afterwards, he was really quiet. I just dropped him off at the place he was staying.

Another time I was driving around up in Oceanside. I picked up a Marine who was waiting at a bus stop after all the buses had stopped running. He was from Texas. About nineteen, average build. Nice butt. He'd been drinking a lot. We were driving up to Pendleton. I was trying to open him up a little bit, asking him what was his favorite part about being in the Marine Corps. He said, "The physical part." Which I thought could be an invitation, but I didn't want to be too open. Then he said, "I gotta piss." So we pulled off onto this tank trail. He got out and he was pissing. I was pissing too. He was standing there for the longest time. I looked over and he was jacking off. So once again—I think it must be that if they drink they don't give good blowjobs, because he was raking his teeth across it. And once again he wanted to be penetrated. So of course I went to my glove box again and we did it. But there wasn't—when you go to bed with an out gay man, there's open kissing. With [this Marine] there was a little bit of kissing on the neck, but that was about it. Oh, and in the ears. Yeah, so. I dropped him off. He was kind of apathetic afterwards. But I felt okay.

Z: You told me that the experience was disappointing for you.

A: It was disappointing, because there was no . . . exchange.

I don't really like having sex with [enlisted] Marines anymore. I still am attracted to officers. It's more of a status thing, I think; people in power positions excite me. And officers, most of 'em have that typically masculine look, too.

Z: Are they different sexually from the enlisted Marines?

A: They're usually better bottoms. They just know what to do, and they get more into it; they move their butts up if you start to pull out a little bit. They're more active than the enlisted bottoms. I guess I can't speculate why, besides practice I suppose.

There was one officer, I don't remember his name. I think he was a major. He was very cute. We went to his house. He was fantastic in bed. And then the next morning he starts playing religious music, hymns or something. It was pretty much understood that I would just leave.

There was the one I saw again last week at the Camp Pendleton commissary and he didn't acknowledge me. Probably because his wife was there.

Then there was that other guy. I met him at [a gay dance club], and I drove up to Oceanside, where he lived. He was a talker. He was like, "Fuck that officer butt." I don't usually like that. Besides being kind of embarrassing, ultimately it sounds hokey. But that was another thing: most of the officers were more open about their sexuality, in general. They would actually kiss on the mouth.

Z: You liked him. You wanted to see him again.

A: Yeah.

Z: But generally, you told me that you only wanted to sleep with a man one time, and that afterwards you lost all respect for him.

A: [Sighs.] It's true, but I guess it's not entirely true anymore. This last Marine I met, I slept with him three times. He was one of the first nice Marines that I met. Nice, as in comfortable with his sexuality, I suppose. Even though he doesn't openly talk about it. And nice in the sense of not psycho. Or married. Or to not want to talk or be affectionate afterwards.

Z: How much were you like that though, with these guys? The stereotype of the cold, emotionless, just-want-to-get-out-of-there-afterwards Marine?

A: I was like that to a point. But that's what's expected. They want you to be a Marine.

Z: Why do you have a penis tattooed on your arm?

A: I don't have a penis tattooed on my arm! I have a cobra.

Z: Could you have possibly chosen a more phallic tattoo?

A: A penis, I suppose. [Pause.] I thought it kind of described my personality. I didn't think of it as a phallic symbol!

Z: You thought of yourself as a cobra?

A: Well, yeah.

Z: Um, how are you cobra-like?

A: [Laughs.] Well, I mean, like the cobra, you put on a big show keeping people away. And you're ready to lash out and bite people. [Pause.] What?

Z: That's how you picture yourself?

A: Well, I did when I got that tattoo. I got it in Japan. It was . . . I felt like . . . like I needed it.

Z: What was the physical sensation?

A: Like getting the open end of a jar of mosquitoes put on your arm. The place we went to was really horrible. It had this old, ancient machine. It was like a foot pedal thing. It probably hurt more than it would in one of the tattoo parlors here.

Z: Was there any aspect of the experience you found erotic?

A: No. It was pretty painful.

Z: What about looking at it on yourself afterwards?

A: That I liked. You know, 'cause it's actually under the skin. It's part of me now. It's like an extra bedroom added on to a house.

Z: Last question. As I'm debating, and you so patiently listen to my exhibition of the quality you most hate in yourself, indecision, about what I'm doing with this potential book—you and Anthony both discouraged me from doing it. Actually, you were more ambivalent. In the beginning you said, "Don't feel you need to write it just for me."

A: [Laughs.] I don't remember saying that.

Z: What words of advice would you have for me on doing this book?

A: You could do an interview book just like your previous two. Not that much interpretation, because you'd have to do a very in-depth case study of each Marine for it to be a thorough, analytical, scientific piece of material. Marines are very complex. The reasons they join aren't so simple, usually. Like I said before, you'd have to co-author it with a psychologist. Marines are psycho. [Laughs.] You probably know that more than I do! No, I know that more than you do.

Part Two: One Year Later

Alex got out of the Marine Corps and enrolled in college, majoring in marine biology. The two of us rented an apartment together, adopted abandoned Siamese cats, went hiking on weekends in the back country of east San Diego County, and in general pursued a quiet and satisfying "lesbian" lifestyle. I avoided gay bars and balanced out my needs with healthy doses of wordless public sex while Alex explored various alternative venues. After one especially liberating experiment, he received a phone call from our friend ex-Naval Lieutenant Tim, who mentioned that some friends of his had described an incredible scene that had occurred the night before at a San Diego leather bar. A hooded young man, nude but for his briefs, boots, and socks had been shackled to a fence for half the night, and anyone who wanted to could have their turn twisting his tit clamps, fondling and pouring beer on his genitals, whipping him (with leather accessories available on-site for purchase), and so forth. Tim said he heard that when the hood was finally removed, the guy was revealed to be really cute. He said that now even he was considering going to the leather bar. Alex deliberated for a dramatic moment and took a deep breath. He confessed that it was he who had been shackled to the fence.

Z: When I read you the Leo Bersani quote about gay Marines from *Homos* [see Introduction], you scoffed, and said that military masculinity "hardens and melts" all the time anyway. You said that Bersani was looking from the outside, without any understanding of what "real" Marines are really like.

A: Right. Once you're a Marine, you've already proven yourself. So you can get even borderline "feminine," and it's okay, because you've already established that you're a man. Brian wore nail polish and nylons! And he wasn't the only one. The Marine Corps is only concerned about the image you portray to the outside world.

Z: Why did Brian wear nail polish and nylons?

A: He said that nail polish strengthened his nails. Usually he used the clear stuff, but he did have some stuff that was a little bit red. And the nylons he wore out in the field to help keep him warm.

Z: But don't you think the average young Marine still buys into the idea that men should be hard and act tough and always be in control?

A: You couldn't tell it from the Marines I knew. But it depends. There's two types of Marines. Some of them act it out without knowing it, and then there are some that are aware of it being an act. Like my gunny, he even said: "The Marine Corps is all an act." He believed you have a Corps identity, and that you're just doing what they say, to conform to what they need you for. Even in boot camp, if you get depressed to the point that a drill instructor sees you as a possible suicide candidate, it's not like the old Marine Corps where they kept pushing you until you shot yourself. They tell you that it's just a mind game, that it's just an act. But I don't think most Marines are conscious that they're performing an act.

Z: Well, I think that's Bersani's point. If they became self-conscious, they might not take it seriously anymore. Do you think there's any more likelihood that you would have stayed in the Marine Corps had you not come out?

A: [Pause.] It did influence my decision. I suppose, to be totally truthful, I went into the Marine Corps, I guess, to masculinize me, and I guess with me coming out, I proved that the Marine Corps couldn't masculinize me. Since I'm gay. It failed. So why spend any more time with something that's a failure?

Z: So you still think you can't be gay and masculine.

A: It's something I'm still working on. It's like a section of a building that's not fully constructed.

Z: On one of our recent visits to that E-club at one of the outer camps at Pendleton, you expressed regret that you had traded the sense of belonging and intimacy you felt with other young Marines for the fast pleasures of being an out gay. But in your previous interview, you said that sense of belonging was just an illusion.

A: Well, I did say that. But I didn't realize that I needed that illusion until I lost it. The purpose of that illusion is to make you feel like you belong, to feel like there's a group of many people that are like you, that care about you. Marines really do take care of Marines, at least nominally. And there's something to be said for sitting around in the barracks not really doing anything, just drinking beer with your buddies.

Z: Does being tied up to the fence in the leather bar have anything to do with being a Marine?

A: No, not really.

Z: I know that it doesn't, but if it did, what would it have to do with your being a Marine?

A: I would have done things like that if I was in the Marine Corps and other Marines were doing things like that. 'Cause it's like an exercise. Not of physical ability, or even mental ability, but it would be an emotional exercise. You would have to trust your fellow Marines to take care of you and not be mean to you. If I was in the Marine Corps, and they did things like that, I would wholeheartedly agree to it.

Z: How come out of all my friends, the only ones who have done things like this are you and Keith, and none of the sailors?

A: Because sailors are wusses.

First Lieutenant Frank:
Parris Island Is Burning

"With our relationship," Scott tells me, "Frank and I have broken three major taboos": the taboo against two Marines being lovers, the taboo against fraternization (Scott is a corporal, Frank an officer), and the taboo against interracial love (Scott told me that he had never recognized racial prejudice until he experienced how people always mistakenly assume that of the two he, the Caucasian blond, must be the officer, and not black Frank).

Scott comes from Lincoln, Nebraska. At nineteen he received a phone call from a Marine Corps recruiter. "It was like a hand coming down from heaven. 'Let me help you. Let me do something for you.' . . . It didn't really have anything to do with the macho image because I've always been fairly secure with myself." Scott did however mention that he grew up a "puny, skinny momma's boy."

In boot camp, Scott had "raw sex" fantasies, "big-time, about all these totally hot guys. I just couldn't understand how a guy could be eighteen or nineteen years old and have a body like that. Built, musclebound oafs. In my platoon there were husky wrestler and football player types." He also fantasized about his DIs. "I had three drill instructors. One was really skinny. One of 'em was white, two of 'em were black. One of the black guys was really buff. To be totally honest, I had sexual fantasies about all three of them. Because for three months, they were our mother, our father, our wives, our girlfriends, boyfriends, whatever. They were our leaders, our mentors—our life. And I think a lot of people in boot camp thought about having sexual relations with them. Because—just because of the situation."

But Scott still had never had sex with another male, and six months after enlisting he got married.

After he had been in the Corps for several years, Scott and his wife divorced. He celebrated his adoption of gay identity on National Coming Out day, and that same night entered—and won—a wet jockey shorts contest at a local gay bar. Not too long afterward he met Frank. The two have maintained a "closed relationship" for more than three years—surviving even Frank's absence during two six-month Western Pacific cruises.

I asked Scott, now 26, to describe his attraction to Frank, 30. "Size really turns me on. I'm not big by any means, yet I have always been attracted to bodybuilder types. Frank is really big: broad shoulders, big chest, big arms." What does size means to him? "Safety. Power. I would never be with a queen. Just the fact that if anything were to ever happen, he would be there to protect me. He's a really great guy, and I know he could do whatever needed to be done. He's just . . . big!"

Part One

Zeeland: You're an officer in the Navy now, but you were an enlisted man in the Marine Corps for—how long?

Frank: A little over six years. I used to be a sergeant. I joined back in 1983, and I picked the Marine Corps—I grew up pretty poor, and it was just a way to get out of poverty. To at least put a few dollars in my pocket, keep a roof over my head, and think about what I wanted to do later on.

Z: But why, out of the four service branches, did you pick the Marine Corps?

F: There was just something about the Marine Corps that I wanted to be a part of. Actually, to be honest, one night I was sitting around the house and I saw a commercial: it was like Excalibur, a guy comes up and pulls the sword out of the stone. And I thought, "You know, I could do that." I went down to the recruiter's office. They showed a motivational film that was called *Take Up the Challenge*. And whoever made that thing did a pretty good job because after you saw it you wanted to go. Just the whole aura of it. It was a real macho kind of thing. And I guess at the time, now that I reflect back on it—it's been almost ten years—it was one of those things where you're—I was struggling over whether I was gay or not, and at the back of my mind was, "If I could do this. . . ." It's obviously not that effeminate stereotype.

Z: Did you join the Marines to be a man?

F: Yeah. Very much so.

I was seventeen when I signed up. And away I went to Parris Island.

Z: Was it like the movie?

F: There is no truth in advertising. It was not like that goddamned film! And hell started from day one down there. I often wondered if I had done the right thing. There were a couple of times when I thought, "God, I'm in the wrong place. What am I doing?" But then I thought, "What have I got to go back to?" And then I thought also, "If I can't hack this, maybe I am gay." So I just knuckled down and did what everybody else did, and got through fourteen weeks of hell. That was just about the hardest thing I've ever done in my life. Getting through that mess. But I guess a lot of it was the masculinity part.

Z: How old were you when these doubts about your sexuality began?

F: Probably fourteen, fifteen. When other guys, my friends, started to date girls. And I just wanted to hang around with them. It wasn't necessarily sexual arousal. I just thought it was . . . buds, companionship. When I started getting seventeen, eighteen, I started—when some guys see a good-looking woman they turn their head. If I saw a guy I thought was attractive, I about broke my neck. And I would do it without even thinking. And as I got older, especially in the Marine Corps, that got to be real difficult for me. I thought the Marine Corps would take all that away, I really did. I thought that was the panacea. But it just got worse.

I had a good friend in the Marine Corps. I had been in a year. He came from the same town I did. And that's kind of how we got to know each other. I didn't know him in the town, but I knew him when I got in the Marine Corps. Went through boot camp, went through school together, and then we got stationed right at the same place together. We did everything together. And I really started developing a liking for him. I mean, more than just friends. He started dating one of the girls that worked there and I got extremely jealous. I was just—I was livid. Without even realizing it. And that's when it got worse, because that's when I began to realize. . . . My interests, everything I thought or did always revolved around him. I didn't want to do anything without him. I didn't want to be without him.

He got married, and I was best man at his wedding. I remember standing up there, and they're going through all this ritual, and they said, "Is there anybody who has any . . ." And I just stood there and I wanted so badly just to cough, or tap my foot, or just nudge somebody. But I think the worst of it came—

His wife went home on leave for three weeks. And I stayed at his place, and we went out and stuff. One night we stayed up late and got drunk together. And I just decided, screw it. I'm going to try something and see what happens. I did, and he responded, and we ended up having sex together that night. But the next day I felt really bad because I knew his wife real well. In fact, I introduced them because she had a big crush on me. I just did it as a friendly thing, I never thought anything would come of it. But that's why I said it got worse, because that was—I couldn't believe I had done that.

Well, then we talked about it. I started telling him that I had feelings for him. He was . . . surprised. "I don't feel that way about you." He thought we were just friends. And I said, "What happened between us?" "Well, that was just a one night thing." But then every time his wife would go somewhere else, he would call me up and ask me over. We got together a couple more times, and then I just said, "I can't do this anymore. This is a thing of convenience for you."

Z: Do you think that he wanted to continue having sex with you, but that he just didn't want to view it in the same way?

F: Right. He wanted to view it as a purely physical thing.

Z: Do you think he loved you as a buddy?

F: Um . . . Yeah. I think he somewhat still does today. And maybe even more. But he just had a real hard time accepting that part of it.

Z: What kind of sex did you have with him?

F: The first couple times it was just oral sex. Both he and me. Then it progressed to anal sex. He was the bottom, I was the top.

Z: Did you get a feeling that he had done this before or was at all experienced?

F: No. And I asked him about that. I guess the last time I saw him was about a year ago. And he had no reason to lie to me. He told me I was the first man . . .

But, that's when it got worse. And you know, I was even to the point—I felt so bad at what I had done, and I felt something was wrong with me, I got super depressed, and I actually . . . I thought about it. I said: I can't live like this. I really thought about doing myself in. I honest to God did. [Pause.] And he talked me out of it.

Z: He did?

F: He was the one, yeah. Because I told him I was just going to go away and not come back. He was very astute; he honed in on what that meant. I don't think I'd ever felt that bad in my life. Not only what I had done, but then his sort of rejection of me afterwards. That was the hardest thing. And after that I kept to myself. I didn't—feelings I had for anybody else—I led a very closeted life, and kept those feelings to myself for the next three or four years. I started to date just women after that. There were a lot of female Marines where I was at who always wanted to date me. And I'm not a bad-looking guy. When so many of them try to ask you out, and you say no, no, no all the time, and nobody ever sees you with a woman—rumors started floating around about me. I got wind of it, and I just said, well fine, I can fix this problem real quick. They start asking, I'll just say yes. Then the frustration . . . you go out, they want to go back to your place and have sex. It's just—you just get fucking frustrated.

Z: Did you go through with it sometimes?

F: No, I never did.

Z: But you did get married.

F: Yeah, I did. [Laughs.] My wife—she pursued me. I met her coming out of the gym, on campus one day, going down the stairs. I had no shirt on. She just went, "Oh!" I was going through ROTC to get commissioned. I don't remember which ball it was, but I had to bring a date. I bumped into her again, we talked a little bit, and I just happened to ask her to the ball. It was more of a convenience thing. After that she kept coming over to my apartment and we'd just talk. She kept coming over at night, and after a while I felt—I think I responded sexually to her under pressure. I guess it's a lousy thing to say, that I just went through with it, but that's my honest opinion.

Z: How did you feel while you were doing it?

F: Almost every time I thought of a man. Or just tried to remove myself mentally from there, put myself someplace else. . . . It was a very hostile relationship. Finally, she decided on her own that the marriage just wasn't going the way she wanted it to, and that was the biggest relief of my life. It was like a ton of bricks had been lifted off my head. But I still carry around a great deal of remorse over the fact that I hurt somebody so bad. And I just couldn't tell her what I was feeling. She has no idea.

Z: To this day?

F: Yeah.

Z: I assume you think of yourself as gay now.

F: Right.

Z: So you were straight when you were in the Marine Corps, but you're gay now that you're in the Navy.

F: I don't think I was straight. I was just closeted. And, I mean, I fit the picture of the model Marine. I modelled for a number of advertisements, I'm in a number of brochures. I'll even tell you—what the hell!—even for the Navy, I've done several. So I don't know, but whatever this poster image is they want, I guess I got it. [Laughs.]

Z: Why did you have to leave the Marines?

F: While I was in the Marines and going to OCS [officer candidate school], I got hurt. And they said "You can't come back to us anymore because you're not physically qualified." It was pretty depressing, because I really had set my sights on that. I thought about it. "What am I going to do? Do I want to be a civilian? No. I put all this time in; I have a technical degree; the Navy says they'll take me." So that's what I did. But they're just two different worlds. The Marine Corps is a much more macho kind of thing. That's what drew me into it at first. And I guess it was—it's an easier way to hide any sort of sexuality. It's just really butch. The Navy isn't that way. And I guess that's one problem I'm having to adjust to because I conditioned myself to be this way for so long. And part of that help fit the great screen. If you do all these things as a Marine, nobody's going to think you're gay.

Z: But why is that a problem and not an advantage?

F: Now, you mean? I guess I'm just so used to everybody else around me having been that way too. And it's not that case.

Z: The Navy isn't as butch?

F: Oh, no, no, no. In fact, there are several sailors who I've met since I've been commissioned who I just immediately looked at and thought: "You're gay." And sure enough, you'd see them out at the club. They didn't really give a crap about hiding it. So I came from a really strict, regimented, masculine-type environment over to something that isn't as much. It's an adjustment!

F: When I was in the Marine Corps I thought I was the only one. And I remember reading about a Marine Corps major who was court-martialled because he was gay. And—I think that kind of eased things for me, because it was in the papers, and this guy, in his picture, he was like, six foot one, two hundred and twenty pounds, and he was just . . . [Pause.]

Z: Not wearing a dress.

F: Yeah! Because I had those kinds of images in my head. I certainly don't wear a dress. I don't think I could find one that fits anyway. But that's not necessarily true in the Navy. You see some guys you can just peg!

Z: Navy hospital corpsmen, some of whom work closely with Marines, are often stereotyped as likely to be gay. Was there any talk among the Marines about corpsmen, or the Navy in general, being gay?

F: That was always kind of the joke, Navy fags. I didn't actually meet a gay corpsman until I was in the Navy. But there is all the innuendo and stuff.

Z: I hear that in the Marines there's a lot of joking, horseplay, and sometimes even more than that.

F: There were always a bunch of guys in the barracks who would wrestle, just grab each other and start rolling around on the ground, and just be a pain in the ass when you're in the TV room. You'd tell them to shut up and they'd grab you and pull you down to the floor. And you're getting grabbed in your crotch, or your ass, or somebody's hand is going down your pants—all in the name of just fun and games. I didn't really think anything of it at the time, but when I look back on it now, it's like, you've got to fight pretty hard to constantly keep your hand in somebody's crotch. So, that was the only thing that was really commonplace where I was at. And, depending on who was wrestling, I didn't mind.

Z: How did you meet your lover?

F: [Laughs.] I was out by myself at a club one night. I saw him dancing with another guy. These two guys were obviously Marines. That's what caught my attention. And so I watched him. He had a close "high and tight" haircut and this USMC sweatshirt. I went up to him and said, "You know, you should be just a little more discreet." He just looked at me. "Oh yeah? Really?" And I just kind of walked off. That was Saturday. I went out again Monday to [another bar]; I saw him there with a couple lesbians who I found out were his roommates. There was a drag show going on. And he went up there with a dollar bill in his teeth. I was like, "Sonofabitch! That's how much he heeds my advice about discretion!" I didn't even talk to him that night, I was just so pissed off. But I went out again Wednesday, and saw him again, and I started talking to him. We exchanged numbers and agreed to go out to dinner. Met again a couple more times. I started really taking a liking to him, and vice versa. One thing led to another, and it's been a year now.

Z: Is this your first major relationship?

F: Yes.

Z: What attracted you to Scott?

F: Um. At first, and I'm not going to lie, when I saw him it was—I'm not trying to justify this, but when you see somebody, the first thing that attracts you is the physical. You're like, wow! I wonder what this person's like. And then I got to know him. And he's a genuine person. I had some reservations because he's enlisted and I'm not anymore. But then I said, "Well, there's a lot of things I'm doing right now I probably shouldn't be fucking doing. Screw it; I'm not going to look back twenty years from now and do a "What if?" So I started developing a liking for him, and eventually . . . I can honestly say I love him.

Z: Is it just a coincidence that he's a Marine?

F: No. That is one of the things I guess attracted me to him. Having been a Marine, I knew he was. When I saw him walk off the floor, just by the way he was dressed—his shirt was bloused, and tucked very neatly—ding ding! So I guess that was a lot of it.

Z: Why is that attractive to you?

F: [Pause.] The whole macho aspect of it.

Z: So more because of the image than a commonality of interests?

F: I think that draws a commonality of interests because I've been doing this now for ten years. We already have that bond. But there's also that . . . just the fact that . . . I don't know. The guy's gonna read the book and say, "I'm a Marine! That's the only reason you love me!" [Laughs.] And it's not.

Z: Well, is it part of his attraction to you?

F: Yeah, because—well, he didn't know if I was or wasn't a Marine. Normally my hair is pretty short, so most people just automatically assume that I'm still in the Marine Corps.

Z: What is masculine?

F: The opposite of feminine! No. To me, what is masculine? I don't know. [Pause.] And I've worked so hard at being it. I'll be honest about that.

Z: Were you masculine as a boy?

F: No. In fact, when I was born, my mom was so pissed off—because I was the sixth boy and she wanted a daughter—that she didn't cut my hair until I was six years old. I had this damn ponytail hanging halfway down my back.

Z: And all your brothers made fun of you?

F: Oh, fuck! And I hated it. They called me "Geraldine." I just loathed it. I hated it I hated it I hated it I hated it I hated it I hated it I hated it. I think that's part of [what has] driven me to be the way I am today. I was always a kind of a skinny kid with a wee voice and . . . I don't know. What is masculine?

I had a lot of trouble with this. To me, I guess physical presence has a lot to do with it. Strength. And especially the way a man speaks. I just—I hate queens. Okay? I do. [Laughs.] But when I think about it now, it really causes me to question my way of thinking because I don't think that anybody can naturally be that [queeny], and yet I've worked so hard to—artificially, I think, at times—be the way I am. That's how I got into all the weight lifting and all that stuff. That was the macho, masculine, butch sort of thing to be doing. I often look on that as a big aspect of it. . . .

Hmm. To be masculine: how well somebody handles under stress.

Z: That's the first thing you've mentioned that isn't just image.

F: Yeah, but a lot of it is image.

Z: And how others respond to the image?

F: As well, yeah. I work so hard at having an intimidating presence just for that reason. It's to the point—and I still have some trouble dealing with this now, as to who I am, because I've doctored up all these images and everything masculine I could ever associate with it, including my speech pattern, sometimes I get lost and don't know who I am. [Pause.] This is something I haven't even told my lover about yet; he'll probably flip if he ever sees this: I got to the point where—to me, the bigger you were, the more masculine you were. And in my early days of weightlifting I dabbled around with steroids. Thinking it was masculine. . . . And all those things. How you talked. How you dressed—just your overall presence. I carefully thought about everything I ever said, and how I said it and how it could be construed. To never give an inkling of a feminine characteristic. That's how bad I used to be. I do it now; it's just second nature, so I don't know if it's really me, or—who am I? I'm kinda lost in that. I'm still sorting that out.

Part Two: Two Years Later

Frank told me that he had observed very different attitudes between Navy and Marine Corps men toward the male body.

F: In the Marine Corps, physical fitness and your appearance—both in uniform and in civilian attire—are things you don't take for granted. You present a good appearance, and that is the norm. In the Navy, even for me, as an officer, if you are that way you stand out. You're looked at a great deal. I know I have been looked at a great deal. People have assumed the right things about me for all the wrong reasons! [Laughs.]

Z: You're telling me that Navy men interpret the care you put into your appearance as a gay thing, when really it's a Marine thing?

F: Exactly. Those are things that I grew up with in the Marine Corps and carried over into the Navy with me. Most sailors, whether they're enlisted or officers, aren't overly concerned with their physical appearance, or even physical well-being. I think most of them look at the military as a job, as opposed to a way of life.

A couple months back I was leaving work to go to the gym, and a senior [Navy] enlisted guy I work with made the comment that he had read in the *Advocate* that "a gym bag is a gay man's purse." I told him I hadn't had a chance to read that edition of the *Advocate* yet, but that I would be sure and pick it up. And the next day I mentioned that if he ever said anything like that to me again I would carry *him* out in my gym bag! He went on this spiel about how it was just a joke . . . but it's because you just don't see it that often. In the Navy, you have guys who are more into power lifting, but they're the obese kind. So when you see a guy like me who's that much different—it's an anomaly, whereas, it isn't an anomaly in the Marine Corps.

Z: The Marine Corps trains physically every day. In the Navy it's once every six months?

F: Yeah. Folks say they're in the Three Mile a Year Club because you have to run a mile and a half every six months. And that's all they run. It's a different world.

One thing I've noticed though: I've done two Western Pacific deployments since I've been commissioned and what's ironic about the Navy is—the only time that men seem to care about their body is when they are stowed away at sea for six months. And when they come back to their wives, they don't really care how they look; they let themselves go to the point of obesity and being unkempt. But out at sea, it seems men care more about their physical appearance, and the only people around them are other men!

Z: Of course, one reason for that might be that they don't have much else to do. But you think that they were conscious of other men looking at them?

F: Certainly. Particularly in the gym. Yeah, maybe some of it was just an admiration and looking towards a goal—

Z: And rivalry and competition.

F: That's part of it too, but I thought that there was—Being gay and being out, you know how other people look at you; there's sort of that sense you pick up on in other people. And this was more than just the manly camaraderie.

Z: These sailors wanted to look desirable.

F: Definitely. And the only people around to desire them were other men.

Z: You said that whenever it's mentioned or realized that you were in the Marines, that Navy men treat you a certain way.

F: For one, just when folks meet me, because of my size, there is a lot of intimidation. And I guess because they're not acutely familiar with the Marine Corps, there's a lot of fear. So, if you tell somebody to do something, or you want something done a certain way—it's just amazing how things are interpreted. "He jumped all over me!" A lot of it is the fear of the unknown. A lot of these people have an image of what the Marine Corps is, and then they take a look at an officer who used to be a former enlisted Marine; he's bigger than anybody they've ever seen, for the most part, and he still looks like a Marine, only in a Navy uniform—a lot of people have a problem with that.

Z: You're smiling. Do you enjoy causing fear and intimidation?

F: I do now. But at first it really bothered me, and I became really conscious of how I spoke to everybody, once people started complaining about how they were intimidated by me. Then I got to the point where I said: "To hell with it." I'm not gonna change what I do because there's nothing malicious in it. I'm not berating anybody; it's their inability to just simply do what they're told and perform their daily functions without being intimidated. I haven't raised a hand; I don't raise my voice. But there is that image that you're gonna come running in there and just do all kinds of bad things. Because I look different. Hell, I'll go ahead and say it: the other thing is, I'm not white. And that bothers a lot of people. It does. I'm the only black officer in the whole command. There aren't many black officers in the Navy—less than one percent. So a lot of folks haven't worked with them.

Z: How does the Navy compare with the other service branches in that regard?

F: The Marine Corps is the worst. The Army is the best, with ten percent of the officers being minority, followed by the Navy, then the Air Force, with the Marine Corps last. The Army is more representative demographically; they have been able to do that because they start commissioning folks with associate degrees, and allow them to work towards their bachelors. So they play with the numbers a bit.

Z: Have you noticed any differences in attitudes toward homosexuality between black and white guys in the military?

F: Yeah. [Laughs.] From what I've seen, the gay aspect is not spoken of that much amongst black Marines and sailors. You don't talk about it. Nobody is gay; even the guys you think are, aren't. The talk that you hear on ships when you're underway for a period of time—most of that is amongst the white sailors. Black sailors: "No man, I don't play that shit! I don't even wanna talk about it. Don't even bring it up." It's just something taboo.

Z: You said that the intimidating effect you have on people has to do in part with an unfamiliarity with the Marine Corps. I wonder if that isn't a big part of the Marine Corps' appeal. What can you tell me about that mystique?

F: I think it's an individual thing. You could ask any one person, and it could mean any different thing to them. But by and large, one thing folks have in common, at least on the enlisted side of the Marine Corps, is that they come in with a similar image, then develop themselves into what they think it is. The mystique grows out of what you learn in boot camp. I think

I'm one of those people that have carried that over—for the last twelve years. Most of my mannerisms and characteristics were developed there.

Z: What exactly have you retained?

F: Even to this day, an extreme sense of discipline. I'm very regimented. I plan everything, even my weekends; I make a schedule of events. That's a little overboard, and my other half lets me know that. My appearance, not just physically, but the types of clothes that I wear—it's gotta be the neatest thing. Even though I'm a Navy officer now, I get a haircut once a week. Having a certain sense of values that you don't deviate from. Those are the kinds of things that I developed there and identified as me. And that's what's allowed me to be successful—and to be ahead of my peers, and to become commissioned. Because very few folks, especially in the Marine Corps, rise up to get commissioned. So [Marine Corps training] can be a very positive thing. Then there are folks that take it and turn it around and make it the most negative thing in the world.

Z: Lee Harvey Oswald. Oliver North. [Laughs.]

F: Those are good examples! In the Marine Corps, I was a legal services specialist. Working in that field, I saw Marines involved in all sorts of crime—taking that discipline and diligently applying it to their criminal efforts.

Z: I remember you telling me that there does come a point, though, where being a Marine becomes just a job; you said that you then realize that you are still the same person underneath. [Pause.] Do you remember what you were telling me?

F: I think there gets to be a point after so many years gone by, if you continue service, when you begin to develop more as a person, and you start to look outside of that image. And realize—in my own case, that what has changed in me is what I have allowed to change. That I'm still the same guy, with the same feelings, only that I've structured my life a little differently now. No matter what you do, no matter how regimented you make your life, how clean your uniform is every day, even if you're the number one Marine, you can't take away the other part of you.

Z: So you just meant your gay desire?

F: Right.

Z: Do you think that coming out might incline gay Marines to see the whole Marine Corps masculine image as just a theatrical performance, and to not be able to take it seriously anymore?

F: I think, from my own experience, that there's an awakening, maybe at the end; you just stop one day and ask: "What have I been doing all this time?" [Pause.] At least in my own experience, it was more a question of, could I actually do all this stuff? And if I can do it, can I do it better than anybody else? Again, I think largely because it's stuff that some gay effeminate man shouldn't be able to do, and by God, not be able to do it better than somebody straight. So maybe when you are doing it better, it ceases to be a challenge anymore.

Z: Sometimes there's a certain joy in the pain of self-discipline; I'm reading Nietzsche, and he talks about "the ascetic ideal employed to produce orgies of feeling." Some people say that the humiliations and pain of boot camp instill in men a certain element of masochism.

F: I've never personally felt that way although I could see where it is quite possible. When you graduate from boot camp, you got guys crying. Because you're leaving this group of people that you've bonded with. But a lot of that is missing those experiences that you shared with these people. And what were most of those experiences? You were crawling through mud. You were cold. You had bugs biting on you. You were made to do push-ups with a pool of sweat in front of you, just dying in agony. And you're crying because you're missing that experience! So I could understand why some folks would translate that over. I would not discount that.

Z: Were you ever physically struck in boot camp?

F: Once. That was more prevalent back then. I didn't think it was a bad thing. It's something you thought went along with the training. If you screwed up, you got whacked. Or even if you didn't, you got whacked once or twice. If you didn't get hit, you were kind of disappointed!

Z: What about getting blood stripes?

F: Oh yeah. When you make corporal, you get the red stripe down your trousers for the dress blue. You're expected to endure that pain. You're punched or kneed in the leg by half the company, if you're promoted by them, but the ones here are only done by the individuals who actually promote you. They only did one side on me. And they drew blood. It was like, oh my God. Shit. But you're supposed to tolerate this, suck it up, and go on.

Z: You didn't find that fun?

F: No. It was not fun. In fact, my stomach was in knots just thinking about it because you knew it was gonna happen.

Z: You have a USMC tattoo. Anthony [in *Sailors and Sexual Identity*] said that he thought getting a tattoo was masculine because it was "putting yourself through pain to make yourself look good."

F: [Laughs.] I got mine in part for that reason. Not so much for the pain, but for the masculine. That's the reason why I got it where it is clearly visible, and not someplace hidden. I've had opportunities to get it removed, but I just said: "Screw it." I had some concerns about it when I first became an officer, especially being a Navy officer. But in dealing with other officers, it's made life a lot easier for me.

Z: More fear and intimidation?

F: Yeah.

Z: What did you think about the representation of Marines in *Sailors*?

F: [Pause.] I think there's a certain amount of truth as far as gay Marines wanting—the submissive aspect, and still being able to maintain . . . I don't want to say dignity, but your masculinity, because being a bottom is always associated with being feminine. For me, I never viewed it as being not masculine, or passive. Maybe because just looking at me you would never assume that. So maybe it does relate in the sense that you still have, at least physically, the image of everything to the contrary. I think a lot of it is—from what I did, and what I know from my present lover now—you can hide behind that macho image of the Marine. You can go out and be in a so-called submissive bottom role, but you're still macho. I think that's probably a good way of explaining it.

Z: Do you remember what your sexual fantasies were like as a teenager when you first started thinking about having sex with men? You described at fourteen or fifteen just looking at other guys and wanting to be around them, and you said that a couple years after that, it became a pronounced physical attraction. But I'm wondering how your fantasies might have changed after you first began conceptualizing what you wanted to do sexually with other men.

F: The change probably came during Marine boot camp. I remember there were a couple guys in Marine boot camp who I was just completely in awe over. I would lay up at night, and start jerkin' off just thinkin' about 'em. I was like, "Oh fuck! What am I doing here?"

Z: In your rack?

F: Oh yeah. You got the fire watch goin' around, you're not even thinking about it. But there were a couple of 'em; I used to think about 'em all the time.

Z: Other recruits?

F: Yeah. So I started doing that. I would never do that before.

Z: Before then you didn't fantasize while you masturbated?

Z: No, actually I didn't. And this was when I first started. It got to the point where it was killin' me! Thinkin' about 'em, bein' around 'em all the time. Being close, regardless of what you were doing. When you first start boot camp you're just worried about trying to adjust, but as you go through, you get more settled in a routine, and you get accustomed—particularly for me, because I had been through it before. [Before joining the Marine

Corps, Frank served for one year in the Army reserves.] Some of the fantasies were at first to just spend time together, talking. And then they did develop into sexual fantasies. Mostly just oral sex. That was the first time that I thought that. Then I kind of just put it out of my mind when I left boot camp and went off to my school. But those feelings were the most intense I had ever had in my life. And I guess for one, it was the longest I had ever been in an environment like that. And you certainly get much closer to people in Marine boot camp than you do in Army boot camp. I've been through both of them; not many people can say that. And I think some of that excitement came from [other recruits'] admiration of me. I've always been very athletic. I graduated number one out of Marine boot camp. There was nobody that could outrun me; nobody could do more pull-ups than me, do more sit-ups than me, or shoot better than me. And the guys I liked the most seemed to be the ones who would come and ask me for advice, who wanted to be around me for me to help 'em out. And yeah, it was a friendship bond, but for me it was more than that. Because I started thinking: this is what I want. Through that I always thought something sexual could develop, but just jerkin' off was as far as that would go. I remember laying in my rack feeling tremendously guilty: "Oh my God, what have I done! I could get kicked out." And then I thought: "You stupid idiot, nobody knows what you're thinking except you!"

Z: So before you went to Marine Corps boot camp, when you masturbated, there wasn't something that you would picture?

F: It wasn't so much the act of sex, it was just certain guys. When I was in high school, there were certain guys that I had a major attraction to. So I would just think about them. Try and picture their face, and being close to them. Maybe the sexual thoughts were there, but I certainly did a good job of suppressing them. But in boot camp, being around a bunch of other men, you're half-naked all the time, in the morning everybody's jumpin' up to get on line, half the guys got hard-ons, and you're just like, oh man!

Z: Did you ever have fantasies involving your drill instructors?

F: Not about my drill instructors, but one from our sister platoon. I'll never forget his name, Sergeant A. He was just—God—the biggest, most handsome guy I ever saw. We would always go and do different training evolutions with them. And it's kind of an unwritten rule, the drill instructors don't really bother recruits from other platoons; they'll come over and screw with them for a bit only if they're doing something blatantly heinous. So I would just do something that I knew he would see and come over and yell at me for. Just to get his attention. I'd put my head down on my legs like I was sleeping or something. Then you'd hear his mouth from way over. It was kind of a rush for me. Actually, he was the first one that I fantasized about just, you know, having sex with him where I was a bottom. 'Cause for the most part, there aren't many guys that are bigger than me, especially not now, but then . . . that was something that I just fantasized with him. I don't know why. I used to think about him all the time. And that kind of bothered me for a while.

Z: Why did that bother you? What did you associate that with?

F: Well, because at the same time—I had this stupid idea in my head: "You can't think of people senior to you like this." I thought that was a big crime. So I told myself: "Maybe you're just thinking that because you want to be like him." I toyed with that a lot. I remember watching all of his mannerisms and how he did things, and how he wore his uniform, so I just started doing things like him. That was close enough for me. I became satisfied with that. Because you get this thing about discipline, and rank structure, and I thought just thinking that was a cardinal sin.

Z: Your own drill instructors didn't inspire those kinds of feelings?

F: Oh no. They were tired guys. [Laughs.]

Z: Do you ever think about how your sexuality might have developed differently had you not joined the Marine Corps?

F: I wonder about it. I probably would have stayed in the same town I grew up in. I don't know. It was the best thing that could have happened to me!

Z: You told me that, more than the Navy, the Marine Corps is "a man's job." How do you feel about women in the military?

F: I worked with women in the Marine Corps. In fact, I worked *for* women. I've worked side by side with women in the Navy. I have no bias. I think it's a great thing. In the Navy, more than the Marine Corps, women can easily perform most of the jobs, with the exception of the boatswain's mates, hauling in lines, that sort of stuff. But I don't think there should be any limitation. I've never—and maybe for me, just being raised by my mother only—where my mother was mom and dad, did everything a man did as well as a man—I don't look any differently on that. A lot of guys have problems with that.

Z: You appeared in recruiting posters for both the Marine Corps and the Navy, and now you are doing some modeling work again on another project. How do you feel about being a sex object?

F: [Pause.] That's a question I never expected to be asked. As a Navy officer I don't appreciate the attention I get from enlisted people, particularly the women. It makes life difficult. But ironically enough, most of the comments are from men. In uniform.

Several months ago I gave a presentation to a three-star admiral. He came in and sat down. I'm ready to talk to him all about the wonderful things we do. I dim the lights. He says, "Hey, turn the lights back on. I just gotta ask you: how did you get a *body* like that?" And he proceeded to sit there and talk for fifteen minutes about what I did to train! Questions about my waist, and size, and measurements. I have never been more embarrassed in my entire life. Then he looks over at my department head and says, "You need to stop eating all those donuts and look like this guy." Here's a man who's perhaps third in line of succession to lead the entire Navy, and he wants to know all about my body.

Z: Do you think he had some hope of attaining a body like yours for himself?

F: At his advanced age, probably not! I think he was interested in fitness. But it was embarrassing. Especially comparing me to my boss.

The comments at work now—I just kind of slough 'em off. Some of the senior enlisted will be like, "Your waist is smaller than my wife's." That's a routine comment! When the analogy is one of femininity, it goes overboard. Now I just say back, "I get a little concerned when a man is more interested in my appearance than his wife's." Then nobody says anything else to me.

Z: During the gays-in-the-military debate, it was widely theorized that straight men were afraid of the idea of having gay men looking at them in the shower. But I wonder if that's completely true. I think that, even before the last ten years or so, as we've started to see more and more homoerotic images of men in advertising, Marky Mark and all—Marines have a long tradition of building themselves up to resemble young gods; the Marine Corps is practically a cult of the hard male body. And it's directed at an audience of men. I've been looking at videotapes of hundreds of Marines who performed sexually for some guy's camcorder in Oceanside. And I wonder if there's not something about becoming a Marine that makes men more inclined to want to show off what they've built up.

F: I think there is. That's true about me. In fact, Scott and I were just talking about it, and I admitted it as candidly as I will here. I think a large part of it is that you're just proud to be a Marine. In and out of uniform, you want to be identified with that. The greater you enhance that identity, the better it is. That I've grown up this much over the years—I never envisioned myself getting to look like this. But there is a certain sense of . . . you want to be admired for who you are and what you've accomplished. I won't say I live for it, but I do enjoy it. It's an uplifting thing. Off-duty, that is. In the workplace it's a problem for me. In the Marine Corps, people would look, but it wouldn't be commented on the way it is in the Navy, where I'm treated almost like a freak. "Look at the rest of us running around here, fat, dumb, and happy! What's wrong with *you*?"

Z: In our first conversation two years ago, you said that you had worked so hard at incorporating a masculine image, that sometimes you felt a little bit lost; that you couldn't tell how much was just a performance, and how much was really you. You said that you were still sorting that out.

F: [Pause.] I am still sorting it out. I guess I just wonder how much of it is learned behavior. Putting on a uniform was my first exposure to anything outside the life I had growing up. So maybe I wanted so closely to identify with that, to be a man, that everything about that I simply took on and made it my own. Everything I've ever done has been focused on that . . . It's hard to explain.

[Pause.] In order to get through boot camp and to do a lot of tasks means that you have to be indifferent to a lot of things. Sometimes that's emotional stuff. And sometimes I find myself being indifferent, and I wonder what is the cause. I look back and ask whether that is a trait of mine or a characteristic that I have taken on.

Z: What kinds of things?

F: [Pause.] Most of it's emotional feeling. Like nothing bothers you. And particularly in my relationship, there's sometimes—if I hurt my other half, and I see him visibly hurt, it doesn't bother me like I would want it to. It doesn't mean that I'm doing it intentionally. I want to feel something there, and I don't know . . . what to feel, or how to feel. Or if I am feeling it, how to interpret it, what meaning to attach to it. Because I got so used to being indifferent.

Z: You built up an armor.

F: Yeah. Because that's the way I always thought I was supposed to be. It can be done so easily; you walk the walk, you talk the talk, nothin' bothers you. And if you think that long enough, then nothin' really does. And I know a lot of it stems from takin' on all those characteristics back at Parris Island. Wantin' to be that way. The drill instructors comin' out there—they belittle you and they hound you, and sometimes they look like they're *enjoying* it! And I guess to that person who is looking to mold themselves into something—I've seen that in a lot of Marines. You take on those traits, and it's not really reality. I'm this way because that's how I desired to express myself—I don't think it's a natural thing; I think it's a learned thing, but it's done so subconsciously that it seems innate. I think maybe I've gone a little too overboard with it. I want to try to figure out what some of that stuff is.

FIGURE 1. Dance floor, San Onofre Enlisted Club, Camp Pendleton: 1990s Marines dance and sing along to the Village People's "Y.M.C.A." (Zeeland)

FIGURE 2. 2nd Marine Division, Saipan, 1944.
(Peter Stackpole, *Life* Magazine, ©Time, Inc.)

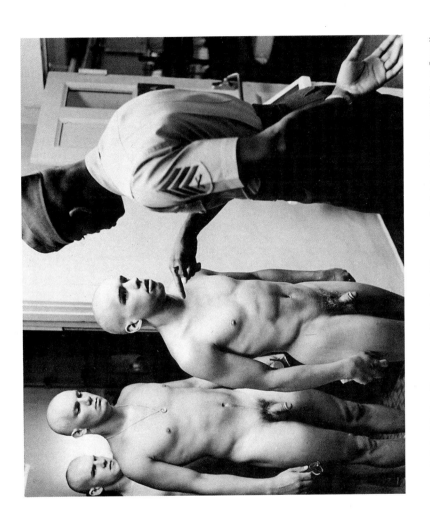

FIGURE 3. Marine Corps recruit training strips away individual identity. (©Volker Corell, reproduced by kind permission from the cover of his 1982 book *Goodbye America*)

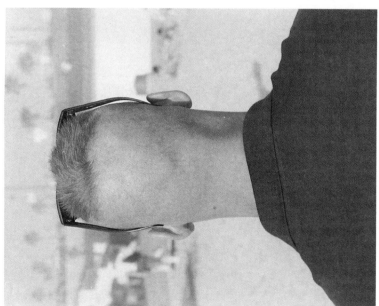

FIGURES 4 and 5. "High-and-tight" and "regulation" Marine Corps haircuts. (Jon-Paul Baumer)

FIGURE 6. Oceanside. (Jon-Paul Baumer)

FIGURES 7 and 8. Marine in drag—as a woman, and as a Marine. (Zeeland)

FIGURE 9. Tattooed Marine. (Zeeland)

FIGURES 10 and 11. "Straight" Marines . . .

. . . posing for "gay" porn magazines. (David Lloyd)

FIGURE 12. Cartoon representation of Oceanside Marines circa 1983.
(© The estate of Jerry Mills)

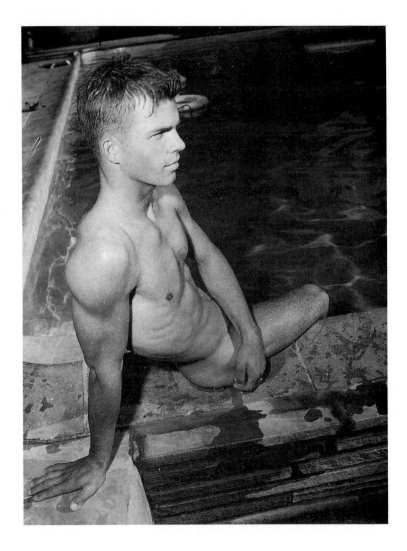

FIGURE 13. In 1993, the story of as many as 800 Camp Pendleton Marines performing in "gay" porn videos made national headlines. But Marines have long been offering their nude bodies for the delectation of other men. Pictured above, and on the following three pages, are five of the more than 1,000 active-duty Marines who bared all for the cameras of the Athletic Model Guild in the half-century between 1945 and 1992. (Photo courtesy of the Athletic Model Guild)

FIGURE 14. "Marines like to be looked at." (Photo courtesy of the Athletic Model Guild)

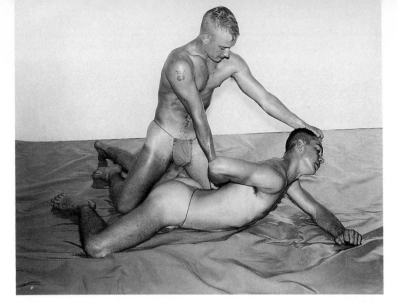

FIGURES 15 and 16. Marines wrestling. (Photos courtesy of the Athletic Model Guild.)

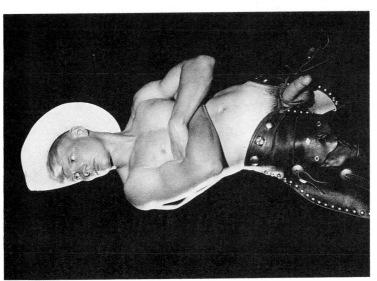

FIGURES 17 and 18. Two macho icons in one: 1970s Marine as cowboy. (Photos courtesy of the Athletic Model Guild)

FIGURE 19. Camp Pendleton. (Zeeland)

Captain Eric:
Marines Like To Be Looked At

A muscular blond Marine, wearing a tank top and jeans open at the fly, lies propped up on pillows on a double bed with a mirrored headboard. In his right hand he holds a can of Budweiser. It looks as though he's had a few. With his left hand he masturbates. An off-camera television blares high-pitched moaning. He says, "Hey, Bobby, come here."

"Bobby," an older civilian man with dark skin and hair, wearing only an oversized T-shirt, enters and walks past the camera. He kneels by the side of the bed, snorts an unknown substance from a small flask, then leans over and sucks the Marine's penis. After a minute or two, he instructs the Marine to remove his pants. The Marine has thick, meaty legs and wears argyle socks. He copulates with Bobby's face. When Bobby interrupts to snort some more chemicals, the Marine tries to stroke himself. Bobby slaps his hand away.

He directs the Marine to put on a condom. Bobby kneels and bends down low before the camera, his genitals hidden by the big T-shirt. The Marine mounts him. The bed creaks noisily. In between gasps, Bobby inquires of the Marine, solicitously, in heavily accented English: "You okay?"

"Mmm-hmm."

"Nice and tight, I told you— *Oh!*"

After a few minutes, the Marine grunts. He slaps Bobby's buttocks. (Pause.) "I'm still comin'."

"I know!"

Bobby extricates himself, pulls the condom off the Marine and marches past the camera carrying it like a trophy. The Marine reclines, holding his penis; he looks dazed. Sound of flushing toilet.

Bobby: "It was *full*, man! You okay?" He gives the Marine another can of Bud.

The Marine wipes sweat off his face, yells "Oh shit!" as the beer spills on the bed.

Bobby: "Don't worry about it."

The Marine hands him back the can: "Here. I can't drink no more. I can't be sick today."

The Marine reaches off-camera for a big two-liter bottle of Mountain Dew and drinks directly from it. He says, in a pleading tone: "Can you call your girlfriend now?"

We hear Bobby making a phone call.

The Marine sits on the edge of the bed, adjusts his socks. He looks down contemplatively. "Damn. First nut in almost three months. Well, not exactly. I did jerk off five times."

Bobby: "A day?"

Marine: "In the past three months."

Bobby: "I used to jack off—"

Marine: "*Eight* times! About ten nuts a day! I still do it, but now I come even more, I noticed. I fuckin' shoot farther." The Marine gets up, walks past the camera holding his still fully erect penis.

Fade to black.

From a gay porn video distributor's advertising flyer:

> RIGHT NEXT DOOR TO CAMP PENDLETON IS OCEAN-SIDE, CALIFORNIA. BOBBY LIVES THERE SMACK IN THE MIDDLE OF 44 THOUSAND MARINES. AN EXPLOSIVE SITUATION. . . . OUR BOBBY INTERVIEWS AND VIDEO TAPES WHAT SEEMS LIKE THE ENTIRE MARINE CORPS. . . . SOMETIMES OUR BOBBY PUTS TWO OR THREE MEN TOGETHER FOR A "CIRCLE JERK": SOMETIMES, IF HE FEELS THEY'RE UP TO IT, HE SIMPLY MOVES IN FOR THE KILL! EVERY SCENE HAS A PAYOFF THAT WILL LEAVE YOU WONDERING, "HOW DID HE GET THEM TO DO IT?"

In the summer of 1993 the story of as many as 800 Camp Pendleton Marines posing nude for "gay" videos made national headlines,[1] catapulting an amateur pornographer, Luciano Ceballos, alias Luciano Vazquez, alias Bobby, eagerly into the spotlight. Police had obtained, from the unhappy wife of one of Bobby's Marines, a mail-order advertising brochure and a photo album containing Polaroid shots of 311 men. The scandal ended with Bobby's arrest and imprisonment for parole violation charges stemming from a conviction for check forgery. After three months, a probe by the Naval Criminal Investigation Service concluded that only nine Marine Corps men and one woman were guilty of improper conduct, and "none engaged in homosexual acts." A review of scenes such as the one described above included on the 56 commercially available Bobby videotapes[2] belies this assertion, a motive for which is baldly evident in the statement of a Marine Corps spokesperson: "We are still the few and the proud, and I hope something that was alleged but not proven does not tarnish the great reputation we have."[3]

In fact, this was at least the third scandal involving Camp Pendleton Marines performing in porn videos—two previous police and military investigations occurred in 1976 and 1988[4]—and Marines have been offering their nude bodies for the delectation of other men at least since World War II.[5] Other video producers in the San Diego area regularly make use of active-duty Marines. Some porn industry insiders have even claimed that, in some years, Marines and sailors outnumbered civilian actors.[6] Certainly, the many pseudo-Marines to be seen donning cammies in slicker porn videos with military themes could not have convincingly acted out the parts of the guileless middle-American boys who passed through Bobby's door.

So how *did* he get them to do it? Why *would* hundreds of young, virile Marines agree to be videotaped having sex with, or having "solo sex" for, the erotic entertainment of a 42-year-old Mexican ex-con?

We know what Bobby sees in Marines. Their youth, gullibility, small paychecks, and large numbers in the Camp Pendleton area make Marines easy enough targets to those who would exploit them. Bobby promised his Marines money and sex with girls, and, as the videos document, did not shrink from using deceit and intimidation to get what he wanted. Some of his videos were taped with a hidden camera.

But the videos also document how *Bobby's ruses may have been recognized and yet eagerly swallowed by young men who welcomed a suspension of disbelief that would permit them to act on, while at the same time disavowing, forbidden secret desires.*

REMEMBER—THESE ARE NOT ACTORS. THIS IS
NOT STAGED.

Well, sort of not.

Certainly, there is a sometimes almost painful humanness to these young men, most of whom are patently only-too-real Marines. Overexposed in Bobby's floodlights, they display a touching abashment, a cocksure bravado, unexpected grace, a blond-trash coarseness, and the desperate horniness of rutting beasts (more deer-in-headlights than devil dog: galvanizing, this fear in the eyes of men trained to kill with their bare hands. There are moments when the viewer may register these as potential snuff films—though probably that Bobby has not himself been snuffed is the most incredible fact of all)—sometimes all in the same sequence.

But there is a definite script to these videos, which reveal much less about Marines than they do about Bobby's interest in reducing Marines to meat-mannequin representations of his straight-stud ideal.[7]

In Bobby's world, all Marines are tops. He leaves little doubt as to how *he* conceptualizes the bottom role. In a sequence taped with a camera hidden in a bedroom closet, an olive-skinned, smooth-bodied young Marine anally penetrates Bobby (without a condom) in a variety of positions, some assumed so as to better allow him to watch the straight porn video Bobby is copying for him, apparently as payment. Bobby, clad in jockstrap and sweater, asks the Marine to *talk to him as though he were a female Thai prostitute.* The Marine obliges.

Bobby (imitating the voice of a young girl): "What am I good for?"

Marine (with relish): "You're good for a *good fuck.*"

"What I am [sic]?"

"You're a *whore.*"

"Do you like my beautiful Thai pussy?"

The Marine (having misheard). "Your pussy ain't gonna *be* so tight."

"Oh! You destroy my pussy! No Marine fuck me the way you do! I'm a good trash [sic]?"

"Yeah."

"Fuck me like a Marine . . . Call me names. When straight guys fuck me, I want to be called trash names. My pussy get tighter."

"Bitch."

"Oh no! Help! I have to save my pussy! More guys comin' to fuck me. [*Pause.* Then, plaintively:] You don't caaaare. You only care to be feeling good. You abuse my pussy?"

"Yeah, if you want me to."

"Abuse my pussy good!" (Perhaps the Marine Corps was not altogether incorrect in determining that, in this video at least, no homosexual act was committed.)

A few of Bobby's Marines are adamant that they would never have sex with a man. One man (perhaps significantly, one of the few apparent non-Marines in the tapes; he has longer hair and wears a San Diego State University T-shirt), staring at a monitor, says: "I want a girl like that. If you can get me one of those, we'll be good to go." Before he ejaculates, he asks for and receives assurances he will be paid. Afterwards, he says "I can't believe I did that, to tell you the truth. It's not as bad as I thought, though. I don't mind doing it, as long as it's, you know, totally straight. If anyone ever put the wrong move on me, I would *kill*." (Bobby does not seem uncomfortable with this threat. When another, more adventurous Marine reaches for Bobby's penis, the videographer rewards him with a punitive slap.[8]) However, all of Bobby's Marines display a certain submissiveness, to include being lubricated, measured against a ruler, handcuffed, fitted with cock rings, impaled on plastic vaginas, and otherwise handled by Bobby. All *take orders* from him.

One recalcitrant Marine, wearing a stars and stripes "Proud to Be An American" T-shirt, dares to push back Bobby's grabbing hand, protesting "I want to wait for the girls."

"Let me play with your cock!" Bobby commands.

The Marine submits. Meekly he requests, and is granted permission to come.

A cuter, buff Marine meets a similar fate. Slathered with great quantities of baby oil (Bobby: "I buy that shit by the fucking case! I got coupons. Two for one!"), Brad lays nude, belly up on a kitchen table, shielding his face with his forearms, accepting a massage from the hands—and mouths—of Bobby and a second, half-nude Marine. As Bobby "moves in for the kill," Brad asks, "Aren't the girls coming over?" Bobby's only audible reply is "*Give it to me, honey.*" After Bobby, with mechanical efficiency, brings him off, Brad gesticulates . . . disgustedly? Helplessly?

But most of the Marines betray no emotion after coming, or even grin. It is hard to guess to what extent any of these Marines *mind* being objectified and used.

Bobby asks the shy, embarrassed Brad: "When was the last time you came?"

"Yesterday."

"By yourself?"

Brad mutters, "Wife."

"*Oh!* So you're—married?" But in another, solo segment, Brad reveals that before joining the Marines he performed as a male stripper in Concord, California, and placed second in three swimsuit contests. Brad, too, likes an audience.

Perhaps the most instructive of Bobby's productions is *The Bi-Wars*, in which a select few Marines are singled out for the ultimate reward: money for sex with a woman on camera.

BOBBY USED THE PROMISE OF THE MARINES MEET-ING A GIRL AS "BAIT" TO GET THEM TO COME BACK AND "AUDITION" FOR HIM—OVER AND OVER. ONCE IN A WHILE, HE WOULD DELIVER WHAT HE PROMISED.

Inadvertently, Bobby does an excellent job of sabotaging heterosexual identity.

As the video opens, a beautiful young black woman with large breasts and a Marine Corps tattoo is sweating profusely, positioned between two male Marines: fellating one, being penetrated (vaginally?) by the other. A third man stands a few feet off, masturbating. Anyone familiar with contemporary commercially available gang bang videos would probably be shocked to hear the woman Marine, identified as Samantha, gruffly assert herself: "*Damn* Bobby. You got a fan?"

Bobby: "Yeah, I go get one right now."

Samantha: "*Damn.* Sore, man."

Bobby: "I know why. It's too tight."

Samantha: "No. It's *fuckin' big!*"

Bobby (dubiously): "It's not that big."

Samantha: "Oh *bull!* Jesus! You wouldn't know a big dick if it was in your *face.*"

Crudely, the editor cuts to a shot of Bobby fellating the penis in question.

[*Fast-forward to a new tableau.*] Samantha is sucking a baby-faced Marine of adolescent build. Quietly, he signals his impending orgasm.

Samantha: "What. Huh? *Puh!*" (Baby-faced Marine ejaculates in her mouth.) "I said *say something.* Don't do that shit. *Man.*"

Bobby enters the room. "He's getting hard? Oh—Oh my God."

Baby-faced Marine: "Sorry, Bobby."

Bobby: "What happened? He came?"

Samantha: "Yeah."

Bobby: "Squeeze his fuckin' dick, Samantha! No mercy on this young man."

Baby-faced Marine looks chagrinned.

Samantha, considering the semen, shakes her head. "I can't do that. Hand me a towel, man."

Baby-faced Marine (trying to save face): "C'mon, Bob. First time in front of the camera. Nervous, couldn't get hard—" The camcorder pans down over his slender white body.

Bobby: "How long before you can give me another come shot?"

Samantha (pained): "Don't even *attempt* it."

Baby-faced Marine: "I'm young. Five minutes. Give me a cigarette and I'm ready to go."

Samantha (as if to herself): "I *cannot* do it."

[*Fast-forward.*] Samantha kneels before a huge, handsome, muscular Marine. She is sucking on his penis and giggling.

Bobby (jealously): "Nice, huh?"

Samantha: "Not really."

[*Fast-forward again.*] Samantha masturbates a cute Texas Marine to climax. As he comes, she mocks, laughing: "Dude, muscle spasms and shit."

Two Marines I spoke with told me of an Oceanside encounter with a woman fitting Samantha's description who claimed to have been the only person discharged from the Marine Corps as a result of the Bobby investigation—victimized by the Marine Corps' interest in heterosexualizing the "gay" scandal. She was wearing rainbow lesbian/gay freedom rings. *The Bi-Wars*, it seems, shows her becoming a lesbian before our very eyes.

In the same spirit, though Bobby wants his Marines to be "totally straight," in getting them to perform sexually for his pleasure he cannot help but make them "situationally homosexual."

After his uncomfortable interlude with Samantha, we see the Baby-faced Marine, who looks about 16, sitting on a bed next to a non-Marine who sports long sideburns and a pierced lip. He says, "I'm still soft, Bobby."

Bobby: "Don't worry about it."

"Okay." Baby-faced Marine pours baby oil on his penis, then hands the bottle to Sideburns, to whom he suggests, grinning: "Rub it all over your chest."

Bobby (off-camera): "I like a lot of Thrifty baby oil!"

Sideburns: "This won't sting my dick, will it?"

Baby-faced Marine: "Naw, it feels good."

[*Fast-forward.*] The two men lay close together, watching straight porn, smoking cigarettes and masturbating. Bobby: "Beautiful, guys. You guys have what it takes. Just watch the movie. . . . Remember, the more straight you guys are, the more I like it."

Sideburns: "What?"

Bobby repeats the remark, and adds. "The only thing you guys have to do is listen to me." To Baby-faced Marine: "I'm not very pleased about you coming. You come when I *tell* you to."

[*Fast-forward.*] Sideburns turns his head to look at Baby-faced Marine's penis. Baby-faced Marine grins, indicating Sideburns's erection: "Look at that!" He makes a partially audible comment apparently about how cool it is to get paid for doing this; laughing, he says something about "pussy." The two men appear to be enjoying themselves. Sideburns is the first to finish. Baby-faced Marine masturbates frantically, straining to come; with his free hand he fondles his collar bone. Sideburns cruelly mimics him, making a floppy imitative motion with his penis, and winks at the camera. Baby-faced Marine ejaculates, shooting high up into the air.

Sideburns (surprised): "Look at that one!"

Bobby reappears. Baby-faced Marine, beaming winsomely, says: "Wait 'til you see that one on film, Bobby. *You're gonna like that one.*"

The advertising flyer asserts:

THEY ARE EAGER AND DETERMINED TO DISPLAY THEIR NEWFOUND MANHOOD FOR THE PORN PRO-DUCER.

Might Marine Corps training incline young male Marines to want to show off what they have worked so hard to build up? Does the imagined armor of hypermasculine Marineness insulate young men from the fear of being reduced to a "feminine" sex object that has been widely assumed to underlie military objections to lifting the gay ban?

Far from being the isolated, embarrassing transgressions of a few "bad Marines," the Bobby videos may showcase some predictable results of Marine Corps training. In the following interview, Eric, a 28-year-old Marine Corps officer from the South, asserts that "Marines like to be looked at."

This, at least, was true of Eric. The dashingly handsome captain of German, Irish, and Cherokee ancestry—an aspiring author—contacted me after reading *Barrack Buddies and Soldier Lovers*, offering himself as material for this book.

Eric: My first picture of the Marine Corps? I was in between the eighth and the ninth grade and I had a summer job working in the cafeteria at a nearby college. They allowed fourteen-year-olds to work as long as you didn't work past seven p.m. The head of the dishwash crew—oh man, he was a stud. He was a Marine. He had just gotten off active duty, but he still had a flattop. He was the epitome of the perfect Marine gentleman. And I thought: If this is what the Marine Corps is made of, this is something I want to be a part of.

Zeeland: He exhibited qualities that you wanted for yourself?

E: Very much so. That was a very traumatic time of my life. I reached puberty a little bit before the other guys. As a result, my voice started to change. Instead of going right away from a little boy's voice to the deep, manly voice it is now [laughs], I went through a period where I'd answer the phone, and the person on the other end would say, "Oh, hello Mrs. [Eric's last name]." I'd just totally freak out. So I was kind of in that phase, and here was a guy that was just a total man. Don't get me wrong— my dad was definitely a perfect gentleman, a perfect man, but my dad was pretty laid-back, easygoing. This was a young attractive man who had qualities I definitely wanted to emulate.

Z: Were you conventionally masculine as a boy, or not?

E: No. Well, it's kind of hard to say. I was small, I was nerdy, and I don't know if I was—I was never called a sissy until these two guys that were a year ahead of me used to call me that. David L. and Ernie L. They would call me a fairy, and if I saw them walking down the sidewalk, I would just duck behind the building. It's something I would go home and cry about, but—[Pause.] Some guys, the queens that you see out, they probably went through that same thing, and it just made them more bold and defiant in their effeminacy. I said, "Well, I must have a problem here if these guys are calling me a sissy." So I started concentrating on the way that I spoke and the way that I walked, to try and not be a fairy. I was not an athlete; I could run a little bit, but that was about it. I could ski, but I couldn't play ball. I played the piano. So by some standards I was not the most masculine of boys. And I know what you're leading to with this! [Laughs.]

Z: What am I leading to?

E: No, I did not join the Marine Corps to try and fulfill my sense of manhood.

Z: A lot of men do join for that reason, don't they?

E: Yeah, they do. And you can see it. [Pause.] There's definitely a Marine stereotype, but I don't think most Marines live up to the stereotype.

Z: How would you describe this stereotype to someone who didn't know about Marines?

E: Six-foot-six, barrel-chested, looks like a bulldog, and he's got the IQ of a bulldog. He parties hard, and works hard, and lives like a pig. Then there's the more realistic stereotype—it's a little bit more modern, probably—of the Marine as precise, punctual, thorough, militaristic. But I think that old stereotype of the rabble-rouser is what a lot of guys are trying to live up to.

Z: Those two stereotypes would seem to contradict each other.

E: That's what I'm saying: even in the stereotypes, there's duplicity built in.

I knew we were going to have this interview, so I thought about some things I wanted to bring up. When I was a little kid, driving down the road, my mom would always take her tea with her. And if she spilled the tea on her blouse, we turned the car around and went home and she changed. If it happened to my dad, his attitude was, "Oh well, I guess I got a spot on my trousers," and we kept going. So right off the bat I have this image of the man [as someone] who doesn't really care that much about his appearance, or not as much as the woman. Now, there's no way on earth that a Marine would ever show up to work, in even his cammies, with a stain on his clothes. This week I'm having to wear the service uniform; the short sleeve khaki shirt and the green trousers. And I had a little spot on my shirt. I had to drive all the way back up to Oceanside and get another shirt. No Marine—I don't care what type of person he is—is going to show up for work with any type of flaw in his appearance. Marines are so masculine and butch—the stereotype—and yet that is kind of a feminine thing, I think. Well, I don't know if it's really feminine, but it's definitely associated with that.

Z: So you didn't join the Marine Corps to be a man. Why *did* you join?

E: When people ask me this, I usually say, "I had a hundred reasons for joining and, one by one, I've forgotten all of them." But about a year ago I finally admitted to myself the biggest reason: I love being in an all-male environment. I think I had a hard time admitting that to myself because I couldn't separate the sexual aspect from the—any type of other aspect. But now I realize, it's not that I want to have sex with all of these men. I don't. I just like the way they look, the way they are; I mesh with their personalities a lot better. When I'm around women for a long period of time, I start to really get annoyed. And—I just love being around men. That's part of the reason. And I work well in a structured environment. It sounds trite, but it's true. I work well with rules and regulations. When I joined, I couldn't foresee where I would be now, but I can't imagine any place on earth I'd rather be.

Of course what always follows is, "I didn't ask you why you joined the military, I asked you why you joined the Marines." To me, there was no other choice. Joining the other services never really crossed my mind. I wanted to go to the Naval Academy, but even when I was sixteen and seventeen I knew that I would go the Marine track. It never occurred to me to go anywhere else. And I don't know if it's just the eliteness, the tightness, or—I can't tell you why I chose the Marines instead of the Navy or the Army. I don't know. It's like, why do I choose men over women? [Laughs.]

I didn't get into the Naval Academy so I joined the reserves. I went to boot camp and to my training school, and once I was done with that, I went back to college. I went through Officer Candidate School during the summers. When I graduated from college, I was commissioned and sent on active duty. I did five years in the reserves; now I've done almost that much time active duty.

Z: You went through the same boot camp that every enlisted Marine goes through?

E: Right. We went through a winter company so it was smaller; there were sixty of us in my boot camp platoon. And thirteen of us were in the reserves.

[Recruit training] was an eye-opener for me. I grew up in a very sheltered, fundamentalist Christian environment. I went to a private Christian high school. I had a lot of acquaintances, but very few close friends, and they were very sheltered themselves. And there were a lot of things I didn't know about. I hadn't really learned a lot about sex. Of course, I was still a virgin. I had never even jacked off at this point. I remember the first night (and I don't want to give away too much of my own book here, but), standing on the yellow footprints outside of the building, and they filed us inside this rickety old building from World War II. It was midnight, and I hadn't slept in the longest time. And the recruit next to me, said—there were male drill instructors yelling and screaming at us, but there was this female Marine that was in charge of getting the paperwork done. And she was a very attractive Hispanic woman. She had a little bit of a moustache. The recruit sitting next to me said, "Damn, I bet she's got a bush! Wouldn't you like to eat out that pussy?" I had never heard of eating pussy until that moment. And I thought: that is the grossest thing I've ever heard of! And through the course of boot camp—of course, I learned all about the Marine Corps, and how to be a Marine, but I also learned a lot about life. The phrase "cocksucker"—that was something I'd never even pictured, taking another man's genitalia into my mouth. But I learned that at boot camp. "Blowjob," "jack off," "buttfuck"—my first exposure to things like that was at Parris Island.

Z: Who did you learn these words from?

E: The other recruits, mostly; even though there was very little opportunity for recruits to converse with each other. I had a very professional senior drill instructor, but the junior drill instructors would resort to [using language like] that when they didn't think anybody else was around. . . .

They shaved our hair off, then we went next door to this building. We're standing there, and the drill instructor goes, "Ready! Strip!" Everybody strips naked, you throw all of your stuff into this bag, you put your name on it, and tape it up. We walked into the shower room, and it was similar to how you might picture the Final Solution, where they went in with the Zyklon B. All the showers come down from the ceiling, and there's just a handle there beside each shower head, and whoever was running the showers yells, "Ready! Pull!" You had to reach up and pull this ring and the water would hit you. The guy that was doing it, some Marine who worked at the uniform issue, was playing with the temperature, and he would make it scalding hot, then cold, then back to hot. But you were just thankful because you were finally getting a shower. At least *I* was. They gave us a towel, you dried off and put the towel on, then you went in and got fitted for your uniforms. And from that day on, you stood on line, the drill instructor would come out and say, "Ready. Strip!" And the first couple times I would start getting a hard-on. But it would instantly stop, just 'cause of the stress of the situation.

Z: Did any other men get hard-ons that you noticed?

E: Yeah, a little bit that I noticed, but of course you couldn't even look. But a lot of the things that we did—One of our drill instructor's favorite games to play was, "Everybody get at the front hatch!" The whole platoon would run to the front hatch. "Strip off your blouse!" (I think that's funny, too. Marines wear "blouses." And to me that sounds perfectly normal sitting here ten years later. But at that point in time I thought, "*Women* wear blouses." I remember one time this one recruit referred to his trousers as slacks. And the drill instructor went off, "Women wear slacks!" And I'm thinking, "Well goddammit, women wear blouses, too!" But anyway.) We would get to the front hatch, and we'd strip off our blouses. "Get to the rear hatch!" We'd get to the rear hatch. "Take off your right boot! No, you're not fast enough!" We'd have to put it back on. . . . It would take an hour to go through this little game. Meanwhile, we'd gone all the way around the room, all of us putting each article of clothing in a big pile. By then we're totally naked. "Okay, get in the showers!" There's sixty of us crammed in this shower. And guys were—[Laughs.] One time I did feel the guy behind me getting a hard-on. I was like, "Whoa, I don't know what this is." I mean, at that point I didn't know if I liked it or not. But he'd make us turn the showers on, turn 'em off, turn 'em back on, hot water now, cold water now. Then we'd have to run out, and we'd have five minutes to get dressed. You're grabbing somebody else's skivvies, with their stains, throwin' 'em on your body. . . . It was an experience. I remember some guys going, "God, I can't believe these fuckin' faggot games we play." I'm like, "Yeah, well, this is the Marine Corps."

Z: Would you say you enjoyed boot camp?

E: No. I counted down the days. Nobody likes boot camp. Anybody that says they liked boot camp is lying to you.

Z: Did you ever become really depressed or despondent about it?

E: Oh yeah. I was depressed a lot, simply because I missed . . . just the normal stuff. But as soon as you get done with boot camp, you miss . . .

I went back to college. I was dating this girl. Every once in a while you would see a Marine that had just graduated from boot camp. Whenever I saw a Marine in charlies, I would go up and talk to him. Just because of that bond that was there. My girlfriend's like, "What do you guys do this for? How come every time you see a Marine you gotta go up and talk to him?" And I thought that was the stupidest question. How do you explain that to somebody? You can't. Here's a Marine; this kid's just graduated from boot camp, and he's overwhelmed by the world. I wanted to go up and talk to him, and tell him, "Hey, there's lots of Marines out here; we're all here for each other." That we can count on each other. But at boot camp, when you're going through the process, there's nothing enjoyable about it. The only things you look forward to are taps and chow.

Z: Were you ever physically struck in boot camp?

E: No, I wasn't. We were in second battalion, [which] had a reputation for being more . . . politically correct, simply because we were the closest to the headquarters building; if there were ever any visitors on the base, they would bring them over to us. Third battalion was way out in the boonies; they'll tell you that they were hit and all this stuff. Because there was nobody there to witness it.

E: All throughout high school, I always had the best-looking guy in class as my best friend. That's the way I wanted it. I wanted a best friend just like David and Jonathan in the Bible. I remember praying, when I was a young kid, asking the Lord to give me that. . . . In periods of mental weakness I would allow myself to picture lying naked side by side with him. As soon as I realized what I was doing, I would just totally—[Makes sound of despair.] The guilt—I can't even describe. And I wanted to go to the dean and confess what I was thinking and see if I could get some help. In fact, at one point I was walking over to his office and somehow got sidetracked. Thank God I did. So, I put it out of my mind and kept thinking: once I meet the right girl. . . . And going to boot camp and being in the reserves didn't have much of an effect on it at first. I dated a lot of girls. I was never really serious with any, but I had a lot of female friends; a lot of short-term relationships and long-term friendships.

The first time I had sex was very much an accident. The timing—I don't know if it was coincidental, but it was the day after I got commissioned. I graduated from college; it was three weeks before I reported to active duty. I had a party. Everyone was really drunk. Most of the people left. We were just really horny, this guy and me, and we had sex.

Z: What kind of sex?

E: Everything. Hot and heavy. It was twenty-three years of pent-up frustration. We had anal sex, we did everything short of bondage. We would probably have done that if we had handcuffs and leather.

Z: Did you kiss?

E: No, that's—Okay, yeah, we did not kiss.

We did it once. Then about an hour later we did it again. The first time was his initiation; the second time was mine. . . . I wanted to stay there [with him]. But as soon as we were done the second time, he let me know that that was it. He wanted me to get away.

The next day—I never felt so guilty in my life. I wanted to talk to somebody about it. When I got a chance to talk to this guy about a week later, he said, "Don't ever bring it up again." And then I was off to see the world in the Marine Corps.

I went to Quantico, and suddenly I'm starting to notice things I hadn't noticed before. I realized, God, if I had done this, there's no telling who out here has done what. I started noticing one lieutenant in particular. But nothing ever happened. . . .

About a year later I was at an Army base. I was in the gym, there was this guy in the jacuzzi with me, and suddenly he started touching me. I thought, oh great; I know what this means. But I didn't move my leg. And he started giving me a handjob there in the jacuzzi. He was an Army E-4. He's like, "You want to come over to my house?" I went over to his house about three times. Until my guilt finally got the best of me again.

Once I went to the gay bar in my hometown. I just went in there to see what was there. Kind of like how I joined the Marines; I went in the reserves to see what it was like, and I liked it, so I went full-time. I went in this bar to see what it was like and totally hated it; I left thinking, "Good. Now I know I'm not gay 'cause I hated this gay bar." That solved it in my mind for a while.

I went to Okinawa. I got a chance to go to the Philippines before [the U.S. bases] closed. I said: "I'm gonna have sex with a woman and prove to myself that I'm straight." It didn't work. I thought: "I'm not even gonna think about this. I'm not gonna deal with it." And on Okinawa you really don't have to. It's not constantly in your face; you've always got the out of, "Well, there's only Asian women here; there's all these men and no women; therefore, I don't have to deal with my thoughts." And I just concentrated on my job and started drinking a lot. Put on weight. Then right before I came back to the States—it was the '92 election, gays in the military was a big issue, and I started thinking about it a lot. That was when I was at my most homophobic. I said, "Gays don't belong in the military. They have no place in the military."

Z: You said that to other military people?

E: Oh yeah. I was homophobic, and yet I was offended by other people's homophobia. And eventually all of this coming together, and knowing I was coming back to the States—I thought, "I'm twenty-five years old. I'm gonna have to settle down; people back home, by now they're already on their second marriage. What do I want to do?" And the thought of—the whole family thing just made me shudder. It repulsed me. I mean, I love the family, don't get me wrong. But I don't want to be a father or a husband. So I looked in the mirror, and I said, "Eric, you're a faggot. Accept it. You're a homosexual." And the weight of the world instantly came off my shoulders.

I knew when I left Okinawa I could request North Carolina or California, and the thought of requesting California never entered my mind because I figured I [had to] request the East Coast [in order to] be near my family. About six months before I left, the monitor from Washington, DC was on Okinawa, and he said, "Tell me right now if you want to go East Coast or West Coast, and I can guarantee it to you," and I just said: "West Coast." As soon as I said it I thought, "Why the hell did I say California?"

Z: So this for you is the gay coast?

E: Oh yeah. [Laughs.] I remember landing at LAX, thinking: "There's a whole gay world right near this airport, and I want to be a part of it."

I didn't know where to go out here. I went up to the Boom Boom Room in Laguna Beach, but I didn't see any other Marines there. And at this point, I guess I was looking for other gay Marines. That's what I wanted to find. Just because I figured they would be masculine. Most of the guys I met at the bar that night were the stereotypical effeminate gay man, and I was not attracted to that at all.

I went out to [a gay bar in San Diego]. There were quite a few military guys in there that night. And there were these women on stage, and I thought, "Whoa, I thought this was a gay bar. Why is it advertised in the gay magazines?" Well, I spotted this really good-looking blond, blue-eyed young Marine. He was obviously a Marine. He was there with a buddy, and his buddy was actually pretty good-looking, too. I went up and started talking to him. I asked him, "Well, what are the other bars in this area like?" "Oh, they're gay too! Why do you ask?" "Oh. So this is a gay bar?" "Yeah, what were you thinking?" I said, "Why are there all these men watching these women on the stage?" And they just started laughing. "Look again." I realized what was going on, and it was hilarious. From then on I had a good time. Through those guys I started meeting other guys.

Z: And you know quite a few gay Marines now.

E: Yeah. I've had this group of friends now for about a year and a half.

Z: You told me you underwent a physical transformation upon coming out. You lost weight; you did other things to change your appearance. You were talking about the stereotypical modern Marine's concern with his appearance. Why weren't you that way already?

E: I was only half a person. Your ability to form relationships, not just serious relationships but friendships, is based in large part on your sexuality. And that was completely missing from my life. And I didn't know it; I couldn't recognize what the problem was. And so it was a very frustrating time. It was boiling to a head when I was on Okinawa. Even before that, I just wasn't as disciplined when it came to physical fitness, simply because I didn't have a goal or a purpose. Being a Marine should have been goal or purpose enough, but—I just didn't take it seriously enough.

The first six, seven months I went to gay bars, I never hooked up, I never went home with anybody. It used to really frustrate me, but I realized, hey, I'm not good-looking enough. And it's hard here in Southern California. It's a buyer's market! So I started running five, six, seven miles a day. I got contacts 'cause I was wearing these thick glasses. I hadn't put any time or effort or money into clothes. I did that. I just started paying more attention to my appearance.

Z: Well, you look great now.

E: Thanks. [Laughs.] I work hard enough at it! You know, but it's ironic because everything I did to make myself more competitive in the gay marketplace has also helped me immensely in the Marine Corps. My last PFT score was a two ninety-six; if I hadn't been chain-smoking the weekend before, I would probably have gotten a perfect three hundred.

On the Marine Corps fitness report that your OIC, your commanding officer, writes on you, [two of the items are] military presence and personal appearance. Basically, how good-looking you are. I was noticing this the other day as I was filling out one of these things; that's just another area where the stereotypical gay world crosses over. . . .

I think it's amazing how you can go into any Marine barracks, and what are you going to find there? Stacks of muscle and fitness magazines that are full of photographs of beautiful male bodies. And these guys will sit there and they will pore over these magazines for hours, just staring at these guys. Is there anything sexual in that? I don't know. But there's definitely a sincere appreciation and love for the beauty of the male body. And they know that.

I think the Marine Corps attracts men who appreciate beauty. You asked me why I chose the Marine Corps over the other services. I think that's one of the reasons. The Marine Corps' emphasis on attention to detail and appearance—I mean, just the uniform. Just the poster Marine. It attracts people who are that way.

Z: You told me another reason you had for not joining the Navy.

E: Their uniforms are disgusting.

Z: That's not what you said.

E: [Laughs.] Their uniforms make them look like faggots! That's one of the things I thought at the time, yeah. Their uniforms make them look— gay. They're really tight in the ass, real tight around the crotch—the dungarees. And then the whites, they usually don't fit very well. I don't find that attractive at all.

Z: What does the Marine Corps dress blue uniform symbolize to you?

E: It forces you into an erect posture, forces you to hold your head up. You look proud; you look like you've got it all together. It's a very good-looking uniform. And I think all of that symbolizes this attitude of "I am going to be as precise and perfect and as excellent as I can be." That's why the standards for those uniforms are very strict. We must have gone through a dozen uniform inspections before we got out of Quantico. And the guys in boot camp go through almost as many. And if a Marine starts gaining weight, his platoon sergeant is going to make him have it refitted or buy a new one. And I like that.

Z: Do you find the uniform sexy?

E: No, in fact I find it almost not sexy because it kind of just hangs. The snug belt does kind of emphasize the waist a little bit, but still—I guess here I'd have to explain what I find sexy. To me, the sexiest thing is a lean, muscular man with rippling muscles, but not very big. And most Marines look big in that uniform. When I'm in that uniform, I'm like, damn, sign me up for [Eric's home state football team] or something. So I find it appealing but not sexy.

Z: You invited Alex and me over for dinner one night, and there were five or six other Marines in attendance. One of them pointed to the underside of a cake box that he had brought, and showed you the inscription there that read, "THIS IS THE BOTTOM." He said, "This is for you, Eric."

E: Well, first of all, they're all bottoms. So [that] could have [applied to] any of 'em. [Pause.] I tend to think—I guess I've really accepted myself for who I am, for what I am, for what I like. And most of my gay Marine friends—I'm not gonna judge 'em, because they're great guys, and I love 'em all to death. But I don't think they are as sexually fulfilled as I am, or as they would like to be. I queen out a lot when I'm around them, just because it makes light of the situation. I think I'm a good actor. And it is an act. They play along with it, and it's all in good fun, and whenever I'm around them, I tell them that, yeah, I'm a bottom, I'm proud of it, and any gay guy that's not a bottom is a frustrated heterosexual who is unfulfilled sexually.

Now, let's go back to the truth: I'm not a bottom. I'm not a top. I like to think of myself as a team player. Nothing turns me off more than when I meet someone who says that they are an exclusive top. It is a sign of selfishness. Because the attitude behind it is: "That's all I like. And why should I do something that I don't like?" Well, because maybe that would make *me* feel good. And an exclusive bottom, *that* I don't understand. Because I think I do get more pleasure out of being on top. Just the physical satisfaction; the stimulus is better. But at the same time, I get a certain amount of pleasure out of the other.

Z: What do you mean by "team player"?

E: Marines I think understand this better than [members of] the other services. It means that I'll have duty this weekend, and you can go do whatever you want to do, then next weekend you'll have duty and I can go do whatever I want to do. That way we can all get a certain amount of satisfaction. There's a lot of reasons for the stereotype that "all Marines are bottoms," but for me, and for the guys I know, that's the primary reason. They're not bottoms; they're versatile. Of course, all these homos in Hillcrest—if you've ever bottomed even once you're thought of as a bottom.

That "Marines are used to being so macho that when they get in the bedroom they want to fulfill their feminine side"—I think that reason's a crock of shit. Because—another reason why I think Marines tend to be bottoms is that Marines like to see how much pain they can endure. Marines are taught at boot camp that pain is weakness leaving the body. And I know I've carried that idea to the bedroom. The first couple times when I had sex, and I was a bottom—it was painful, but I was proud of myself for enduring the pain. And that's very much the opposite of a feminine thing. So the idea that bottoms are women or sissies or queens I think is bullshit because I think it takes a lot more masculinity to be a bottom than to be a top.

Z: Do you think straight Marines who end up in bed with other men and want to be fucked by them want that for the same reasons?

E: It's probably because it's generally what's expected. And Marines, more than most people and most other servicemen, want to do what's expected. I know for me, the first couple times I bottomed, it was because I thought I had to. I thought that's what one man did when he had sex with another. So the first guy I had sex with, he fucked me, and I thought, okay, now it's my turn to fuck you, and he said no. I didn't realize that was an option; I was totally stunned. And from that point on, I've really been turned off by that attitude. These guys that are married or straight-identified and want to get fucked, I guess it's because they think that's what they have to do.

Z: You've talked about playing the bottom out of a sense of fairness, and enduring the pain, but of course a lot of people take *physical pleasure* in—

E: Yeah. There's thirty seconds of pain and then it's pleasure. Speaking from my experience.

Z: Alex theorizes that boot camp instills in Marines a "craving to serve" that may carry over sexually.

E: At TBS [the basic school] at Quantico, there was a second lieutenant named Bob. He was very well-respected, because he had been a staff noncommissioned officer. In fact, he had been a drill instructor. He was an open-minded person, and it was surprising to me, because he was kind of a gruff older guy. Not your typical second lieutenant. And he made the comment that, when he was a senior drill instructor, he was so well-loved by the recruits (because it's the junior drill instructors that are the real hard-asses, the ones that they hate) that he could have gone up to any recruit and said, "I want to fuck you up the ass," and they would have let him.

Z: You have a tattoo.

E: I don't know why I got this tattoo. Because all my life I said I would never get a tattoo. And it was, once again, those last two months I was on Okinawa. My life just completely changed. There was another officer, a straight guy that I worked with—I really liked him. I don't know if it was a sexual attraction. But we were drunk, and he was like, "Hey Eric, let's go get tattoos." I thought it'd be really neat to go get a tattoo with this guy. I said, "Oh your wife will never let you get a tattoo," and he said, "I know. She's out of town, so we gotta go right now." So we went and got tattoos. And I have to admit, I got a certain amount of gratification from going with a buddy and getting a tattoo.

Z: Did you tell me that you held each other's hands?

E: Yeah. Well, he would deny this, but—it wasn't really holding each other's hands. He grabbed hold of my wrist. I joked about it the next day, and he denied that he did it. He was in some pain when he was getting his tattoo. Of course, then he denied the pain, too.

Z: Was that one of the closer buddy relationships you've had with other Marines?

E: No, not really. In fact, we were butting heads a lot. No one else really liked this guy. But I did.

Z: So you haven't had any experiences with the Marine Corps bonding spilling over into something sexual between men who don't think of themselves as gay?

E: No. I wish! It's not for lack of trying.

Z: Do you think being an officer has made it less likely that you would experience that?

E: Oh yeah. In fact, I spent six months last year on ship, and reading your book about sailors, all about their experiences—that was totally foreign to me. I knew it would be; being an officer makes it a lot tougher, because you're not down in their berthing areas, and—I'm just too high profile. Everybody knows who you are. That's what I liked about being at the gym there at 32nd Street [Naval Station San Diego]. I was there in gym clothes; they could tell I was a Marine because of my tattoo, but they thought I was a sergeant or something. I don't want anybody to take this to mean that I was hitting on these guys; I wasn't, but it was great to be able to talk to enlisted guys like I was one of them.

Z: Do officers in the Marine Corps bond with each other at all?

E: Not really. When I first got to this battalion, it seemed like there had been some officers that were really close. I don't know if it was because they were in Desert Storm together, or what. Now it's not that way at all. I don't know what's changed. We call ourselves a "band of brothers," and at TBS you might feel like that, but you certainly don't feel it out in the fleet. At least I haven't.

Z: Do you have any other comments for me on the sailor book?

E: I think it's interesting as to how they all had their reasons why all Marines are bottoms, and I think most of their reasons were wrong. "Marines want to fulfil their feminine side." Or that Marines are upset because they're just a branch of the Navy. Bullshit. They are our department of transportation. And they know that full well! Now, I'm being facetious; it's just these guys were so quick to come up with these ideas, when in reality they don't know what they're talking about. That's a quality I despise in anyone. So, to answer your question, I can't say too much because I don't know too many Navy guys. And I don't wanna be guilty of what they're guilty of. But a lot of the Navy guys that I have met are a good deal more effeminate than the gay Marines that I know. I don't know why.

I'm taking a class down [in San Diego] this week. I met this [Navy] chief [petty officer] today. I looked at his row of ribbons; he's got medals like you wouldn't believe. Obviously, he's very good at his job, but he is the biggest *woman!* There are three women there, and they're more butch than this guy ever was or will be. Actually, there's a few Marines I know that are straight but effeminate. But that's not normal. And I see that more in the Navy.

Z: What is there about effeminacy in military men that you find distasteful?

E: I don't condemn them. A lot of my gay Marine friends (and I have a couple gay Navy friends; they're different though; they've always worked with Marines; they actually act more like Marines than Navy)—they despise queens, and when we go out they'll just laugh in their faces. And I don't like that. I'm not gonna condemn these guys, because that's what the Republicans do to us just for being who we are. But I'm not attracted to it, and I don't want it around me. I just think that. . . . What do I find distasteful about it? I like men. I like masculinity. Why do I like it? I don't know.

Z: How masculine do you consider yourself?

E: On a scale of one to ten, about a fifteen! No, just kidding. [Pause.] I can't cook, so that makes me a little more masculine. It's kind of hard to say because I have never met a gay man that did not consider himself masculine. Even the biggest queens, they're practically wearing a dress, but they'll tell you "I don't think I'm feminine."

Z: Well, you know that you think you're more masculine than them, though.

E: Yeah, but I don't want to answer your question—I think I'm pretty masculine. And I've been told that. I've gone up to the door at a couple of gay bars, and the bouncer's like, "Excuse me, this is a gay bar." So, I don't know, maybe that means I'm a little more masculine than the average gay guy.

Z: How do you think you compare to the average straight guy?

E: I'm much more tasteful. [Laughs.] I don't want to be identified as straight any more. Because I find straight people, although somewhat quaint, to be rather tacky and plain, and totally without flair. No, I think I'm about average.

Z: Tell me again what you told me about "We all put on drag every day."

E: I was watching one of the talk shows. This drag queen said, "We're all born naked, and from there on out everything's drag." I think that's an interesting point to remember. And what is a drag queen doing? Well, she's putting on clothes, and fixing herself up to make the world think that she is something that she is not. And I think that in the case of a lot of Marines, especially the ones that have something to prove, they're putting on this tree suit [i.e., camouflage] to make the world think: I'm a Marine.

And a lot of Marines will tell you that. The Marine regards his uniform as sacred as a drag queen regards her—tiara, or whatever.

Z: Do you think Marines realize that there is perhaps a parallel there?

E: No. Marines don't realize a whole lot. And they certainly don't realize that type of concept. [Laughs.]

Z: Not even on some other level, to understand that Marineness is to some degree theater?

E: No. Marines don't realize that.

Z: I kind of wonder though, when I hear about Marines picking up street drag queens in Oceanside knowing that they're not women—and when I think about Keith, seeing a drag queen at [a gay bar], just staring in rapt fascination, moving ever closer, finally getting up his nerve to ask: "Excuse me, I'm naïve; are you a man or a woman?"—I wonder if this couldn't sometimes be an empathic thing, where they recognize that this is somebody else who is pursuing an extreme gender ideal. [Pause.] You think I'm taking this too far.

E: Yeah. You give us so much credit, it's almost flattering! I'm gonna go grab a beer, Steven.

Z: [Reads Leo Bersani's theory in *Homos* that "the gay soldier letting out his gayness may begin to see its theatricalities as incompatible with the monolithic theatricality of military masculinity."]

E: I don't think I'm playing a role. I think the only time I am playing a role is when I'm around my gay Marine friends and I queen out just to amuse them.

Z: You don't play a role in uniform?

E: No, I don't. It's good conversation to talk about how putting on a uniform is like putting on drag, but there's a reason for that uniform, and that's the bottom line. I don't think a Marine who sees a drag queen is gonna notice the similarity between what he does every day and what she's doing. There may be some. But I don't put on the uniform to help me play a role. I put on the uniform to help me do my job.

Z: But doesn't your job require a certain kind of "hard" masculinity that isn't supposed to be bending or soft or "versatile?"

E: There's no question about that; there's no room for anything less than what's masculine. But then we get to the question of what's masculine. Masculinity and femininity cross sometimes—

Z: But do other Marines know that?

E: No.

Z: Does your knowing it make you any less inclined to be the kind of Marine the Marine Corps wants you to be?

E: No. In fact, in my position as an officer, it makes me better; it makes me smarter; it makes me more cognizant of what's happening. The more that I am able to understand, the better leader I am.

Z: But doesn't your sexual identity threaten what the Marine Corps thinks it's supposed to be about?

E: My sexuality now, because I am aware of it and because I have accepted it, does not. My sexuality, before I came out of the closet, was definitely a threat to the good order and discipline of the Marine Corps. Because I thought that I was normal. Here was my thought process: I thought, I feel this way toward other men, but I can't be gay because being gay is awful and terrible, and I am not an awful and terrible person. Therefore, I must be heterosexual, and because I'm heterosexual and everyone else is heterosexual, they must be feeling the same way I am. So I didn't think anything was different about getting possibly too close to the Marines in my platoon. I thought that's what was normal because I was normal. The Marines in my platoon might be having a beach party somewhere and invite me; I didn't think there was anything wrong with me showing up. That may be fraternization, it may not be; it depends on what happens. If I show up and say, "Hey devil dogs, how's it goin'?" maybe drink a beer, and leave, that's not fraternization. But hanging out with 'em, gettin' trashed with 'em, and not seeing anything wrong with that—now that I am aware that I am different, I can take a step back and I can say, "What the fuck were you doing? You're gay; you have the potential to have feelings for these guys. You need to take steps to be sure it does not interfere." So now that I am an out-of-the-closet gay officer, I am a much better leader than I was before, and now I am definitely not any type of threat; in fact, I can look for signs in people who were going through what I was going through, being in the closet, and I know how to deal with them.

Z: I guess what I meant to ask was if they would feel threatened by you in some psychological way. Do you think the Marine Corps would be threatened by the kinds of topics I'm addressing with this book?

E: [Pause.] Yeah, most of them would say that it is. Threatening. . . .

We were on ship last year, and we had to wear these [underwater demolition team] shorts (and I have some stories about UDT shorts that I'll tell you in a minute), the really tight, short khaki shorts; that was our uniform because it was so hot in the [Persian] Gulf. And this one first sergeant—who by the way was a piece of shit first sergeant—kept saying, "I hate having to wear that. Why do we have to wear that? Only faggots wear those shorts. Those are faggot shorts." So, he kept saying this, and I was standing there—I mean, I listen to antigay comments all day long. Actually, not that much, but it's not unusual, once in a while. And so finally, after about the fourth time that he said it, I said, "First sergeant, why are you so fixated on the Marines wearing these UDT shorts?" He goes, "When I used to work at MCRD I used to have to ride my bike through the gay part of San Diego known as Hillcrest, and at five o'clock in the morning they would be out there still looking for their trick of the night; they'd be wearing shorts like that, and I hated to have to look at that shit." Well, there were a couple other lieutenants standing there as I'm talking to this first sergeant. And I said, "Somebody was sticking a gun to your head making you look at these faggots patrolling the streets?" "Well, no, but I made sure I didn't stop at any red lights when I was riding my bike through there! I just went right on through." "So you were . . . *afraid* that one of these faggots might grab you, and you're not enough of a man to fight them off?" "Well, no—that's not—" He was kind of speechless because the other lieutenants were laughing their heads off. So this first sergeant—gays were a threat to him. And I'm just quick to point out: How is homosexuality a threat?

It doesn't make any logical or rational sense. I think a lot of it is because there is a script out there, that somebody has written, and everybody goes by it. The Marine thinks, "Well, everyone else is saying it, therefore I'll say it: I don't want some faggot staring at my ass in the shower." And he thinks that he has to say that. Does he mean it? Probably not. Most Marines like being looked at, that's why they're Marines.

Z: You think they like being looked at?

E: Yeah. I think it goes along with the dress blues, working out, and keeping themselves in shape. They like being looked at.

Z: You said you had some stories about the UDT shorts. . . .

E: These shorts come up to here. Marines don't wear underwear with 'em. They're sitting on ship with one leg propped up here like this—their balls are hanging out of these shorts. But because it's all men—it was just, "Well, we gotta wear these shorts, and it's too hot to wear underwear." I had to go around ship with my hand over my eyes. Marines are famous for not wearing underwear anyway. At least that's what the doc tells me; *I* always wear underwear. He's like, "Eric, what is it with your Marines? None of 'em wear underwear!" I would always come back with an anti-Navy comment, like "I don't know; maybe they ran out, and you guys only let us use the laundry room once every other week."

Z: Since you joined to be in an all-male, balls-hanging-out environment, would you prefer that there not be women in the Marine Corps?

E: No—and there are no women in my job field, but—my opinion on women is that, there needs to be a standard, and everyone has to be held to it. I know that [Commandant of the Marine Corps] General Krulak is going to be reading this, so I want to commend him on his decision this year to raise the standard for women's PFT's, the physical fitness test. But it's still not the same. He brought the women's run up to three miles, which I think is great. But they still don't do the pull-ups. I think we should all be measured by the exact same standard. And if women can meet that standard, by all means let them serve.

Z: But would you prefer not to work with them if you had a choice? You said you didn't like to be around them.

E: Yeah, I guess—Steven, you're kind of asking me a leading question so I'll fall into the trap: yeah, I would prefer not to.

Z: I just want to hear what you really think.

E: [Laughs.] I know, you want me to be honest, and I want to be politically correct. But yeah, the basic, politically incorrect me: I like working with men, and I don't like working around women. But I get that from my mom! She hates working around women too. She says women are whiny and complaining.

Sergeant Wood and Corporal Marie: Gay and Straight Are Identical

One day, falling prey to a suspicion that none of the men I had interviewed so far for this book was a "typical Marine," except perhaps in the sense of that phrase as Keith's mother used it, I jumped on a commuter train and rode up the San Diego County coast to see what kinds of Marines I would randomly encounter in a Friday night stroll through downtown Oceanside, the disreputable beach city that licks/bites at the foot of Camp Pendleton.

At the train and bus station, I espied a Marine in baggy black nylon shorts carrying a 35mm camera with a long zoom lens. As he saw me walking up to him, he ran away. Later, I caught this fellow in the practice of his hobby: photographing street prostitutes (female ones, I think, but I am not sure. Lacking Keith's boldness, I was unable to approach them and ask, "Excuse me, I'm naïve. Are you a man or a woman?").

At the newsstand on Coast Highway, I observed a small Marine with glasses reading war magazines and wearing a Smiths' "Meat is Murder" T-shirt. He walked over to his buddy, a strikingly handsome blond Marine perusing *Casting Call*. The two left the store, cattily commenting that a certain *Details* magazine cover model had *no talent*.

The pier and the adult bookstore were bereft of Marines. I also did not see any at the Hill Street Coffee House, an oasis of urbanity in this still gritty but no longer pleasingly sleazy burg, where, sipping a double café mocha, I stared with tepid interest at three pretty boys decked out in the height of mid-nineties youth culture fashion. One sported a fey International Male rendition of a gas station attendant's uniform while his buddy perspired under paisley pants and a thick woolen cap. The third was expounding to a girl with blue hair and black lips on how much his new nostril-piercing had hurt. Then, with a jolt I realized that these men *were* Marines as I overheard them bitching about their gunnery sergeant.

Obviously there was some sort of lesson here. The archetypical Marine I sought was but a fantasy. But just as I reached this conclusion, standing in line to purchase a train ticket back to San Diego, *I saw him*: His hair was cut high and severely tight; over his broad, sinewy shoulder he carried the freshly laundered uniform of a staff sergeant; his "meaty" mesomorph ass was a marvel of perfectly controlled movement as he strode purposefully toward the train. As I boarded, he met my wide eyes with the requisite Marine scowl. Or was it—dared I even hope—an invitation?

It was. This living embodiment of my Marine ideal turned out to be a gay sailor who liked to look like a Marine.

How I wish I could have interviewed even one of the nameless, seemingly archetypical Marines I enjoyed public sex with, who hastened away immediately after the act, their cold, emotionless faces growing increasingly worried as they observed me tagging close enough behind to confirm the Department of Defense decals on their windshields. But had I cornered one of these men, what could he have said that would convince you that he was not merely a closeted gay?

Though I took a few pictures, I never made any use of my tape recorder at my favorite Camp Pendleton enlisted club. Attempting to engage in dialogue the gung ho School of Infantry boots we saw there, Corporal Alex and I felt as though we had stumbled, sans script, onto the set of a 1950s bad boy movie. Of course we knew how to ad lib our way through, but we never got any of the actors to break character. Had one of them done so, how typical would he have seemed? And what pleasure would it have given, when the performance was so captivating?

In *A Member of the Family*, John Preston wrote of his relationship with his younger brother Marvin, a "blond, blue-eyed Marine Corps jock":

> The idea that a Marine and a gay activist could be as close as Marvin and I became over [the] years always attracted atten-

tion. How could it be, people wanted to know, when you seem to be diametrically opposed in every way. . . . In the end, when someone asked Marvin how we could possibly get along, he came up with the best answer: "Given the way the world's going to hell, being a gay writer and being a Marine are the two best options I know of."[1]

At a San Diego reading, Preston recounted the story of his brother's wedding. Preston was best man. One by one, each of the Marines in attendance approached him, explaining that, while all the other Marines were hopeless rednecks who would never understand that a man could be gay, he was a sympathetic and open-minded guy. If any of the other Marines were to give him the slightest trouble, Preston only had to let him know.

This, I believe, is a lesson: Marines look most typical in *numbers*. It is the sameness of appearance that, reassuringly, allows us to think of people as clones. Alone, even the most uniform of persons can be dangerously different.

I met Sergeant Wood through his "top," a master sergeant who was retiring from a 20-year Marine career (he was gay only during the last five). Wood, 30, came to his interview with his fiancée, Marie, 22. Though we had not met before, I recognized him at once as the brother of a sergeant I had met (and had sought, unsuccessfully, to interview) two years previous. The identical twins, sons of a rust belt steelworker, had joined the Marine Corps together.

Wood: The reason Mark and I joined the Marine Corps was basically to get out from under our parents. We were 20 years old. Ran out of money for school. We both went to boot camp, and then we both went to Okinawa. Both of us were cooks, but he did his own thing; he had his own job. We saw each other, but not 'til the end of the day. He had an easier job, which I hated him for. [Laughs.] I had long hours. He would always be going out and doing stuff. But we would always talk; he would always include me in things. He still had not told me that he was gay. The suspicion can be there, but as long as nobody says anything, you kind of wonder but you just don't know. Finally, we went out one night, and on our way back to the barracks he told me. I was like, "Well, so what?" Everything just felt a lot easier. At least it was in the open. Now, I got to ask all the questions. Like, hey, what's this like? Or, why is this like this? And I asked him also, "Here we are identical. What made you choose this way and me choose my way?" And basically I feel, and he feels the same way, that it's more or less a choice, but also a subconscious choice, from the way we perceived things growing up. It's just your preference, and there's nothing wrong with that at all. And after awhile, through the years, I started realizing that it is no different. That the intimacy is the same between guy and girl, girl and girl, and guy and guy. The only difference is that he has to overcome the stigma—society's label.

Zeeland: Was there a time, especially in the beginning, when it disturbed you to think that you were identical twins and he was gay?

W: [Pause.] Nobody's ever asked me that one before. No. I found it more intriguing. I appreciate differences in people, cultures, stuff like that. I want to know what's up. I find difference appealing. [Pause.] So why did I join the Marine Corps? [Laughs.]

Z: Why did you guys pick the Marine Corps out of the four branches?

W: To see if we could do it. I never really asked Mark about it, but maybe at that point in time it was an identity thing. He didn't want to try and change himself; he went through that already when he was in high school. He was accepting of himself, but maybe he wanted to not be so obvious about it. Both him and I feel the same way on this: Just because you are gay, it doesn't rob you of your masculinity at all. Him and I definitely agree on that. It doesn't change anything. I think the reason he chose the Marine Corps is that it's a good representation of the stereotypical masculinity. I don't think he wanted to give that up. He's not feminine.

Z: You said you'd had suspicions that he might be gay, and I wondered whether that was because there was any difference in the way he . . .

W: Talked or walked? No. He behaves exactly the way I do. You could never tell. He doesn't like the nelly people; he doesn't like the drag queens. He feels that your choice of sexual preference has nothing to do with your conduct, or your proficiency, or your ideas, or the way you stand up for things you believe in. It has nothing to do with it.

Z: I guess when I asked if you were disturbed at first by the idea of your identical twin being gay I wanted to know whether you were at all bothered by the idea that there could be some capacity for that desire in you.

W: In me?

Z: Yeah.

W: No, it didn't bother me. If I was gay, I'm sure I would go through the whole range of emotions that he went through. But I feel that I would turn out like him if I was; I would be accepting of it. But I can't see it now. [Laughs.] [To Marie, taking her hand:] I don't think you'd love me as much.

Z: A lot of gay-identified people resist any challenge to the idea that same-sex desire is an innate "orientation" that they have no control over.
W: I believe it's a choice. And it's kind of an excuse to say, "I don't have to take any responsibility because I was born this way." I don't understand that. Being gay is no different than being a musician, or being an artist, or being whatever you want to be. Most of the time it's a choice on a conscious level, but it can also be on a subconscious level. It's what you feel you're comfortable with. And eventually it becomes a lifestyle.
Z: You brought up the connection between the Marine Corps and masculinity. It's popularly thought that, of the service branches, the Marine Corps is the most . . .
W: Rr-rr.
Z: Was that something that appealed to you in joining?
W: The uniform [appealed to me]. And at that point in my life, I felt I wasn't assertive enough. I wasn't able to get my point across. And I wanted to learn how to. And I wanted to be on my own, do my own things, and take control of what I wanted to do. I think that's one of the major reasons Mark went in, too. Yeah, we chose the Marine Corps because it was a masculine thing. To get rid of that lost little boy thing.

Z: What was boot camp like?
W: I always look back on it and say it wasn't as hard as I thought it would be. But when you're going through it, yeah, it's hard. Mark and I were trying to outdo each other. It was always a competition thing between us. All through life, and even to this day, we're still competitive. Who can get the most this, and who can do better on that.
Z: I think you told me that you guys went everywhere together for eight years?
W: Yeah. Mark and I went everywhere together, until he got out two years ago. Because we had the same job. Same rank, same time in grade, same everything. So him and I got stationed everywhere together. It was like we were married or something. [Laughs.]
Z: Did it help you get through boot camp, that you were there together?
W: Oh yeah. We relied on each other a lot in boot camp to help each other through.
Z: What kind of impression did boot camp leave on you? Some Marines say they were really broken down and fundamentally changed; others say it was no big deal for them.
W: Yeah, I felt broken down. When I was done, I felt a lot more sure of myself. I was a lot more capable of accomplishing things than I had been. Even something simple, like not knowing where something was. Before

I'd be hesitant about going up and asking somebody for directions. Then after boot camp, it was easy. I felt a lot more confident. But I still clung to my individuality. I tried to find that happy medium of trying to conform and still be accepting of other things and other people.

Z: Were you ever physically struck in boot camp?

W: My brother was. My mom died during our first phase of boot camp. We went home for three days and we came back. I guess one of my drill instructors didn't know that my mom died. And Mark was late for getting in line on time or something. And the drill instructor was yelling at him; he was saying some stuff about my mom. Then he called him "motherfuck-er." Mark was pissed. I was pissed. . . . Later on, within a hour of that—I guess my brother said something. My senior drill instructor [ran] over to Mark and—no lie, this caught us all by surprise—he drop-kicked him. Right in the chest. Ran up, jumped in the air, and [makes sound effect]. Mark fell to the ground. It's just weird to see a senior drill instructor in charlies do this to a recruit. He said, "You know I didn't mean to do that, right?" My brother goes, "Yes, sir." [The DI] didn't hurt him; he just wanted to wake him up and surprise him. It was nothing destructive. The only thing that was bruised was his ego. Finally, the other drill instructor pulled [the senior DI] aside and said, "Hey, they just came off emergency leave because of their mom." And he's like, oh. Of course the drill instruc-tor's not gonna apologize, but he's like, "Okay," and he walked off. But that was the only confrontation that [either of us] had. Our whole platoon woke up after that.

Z: Do you feel it's okay for DIs to hit recruits?

W: As long as they're not being malicious, then it's okay. If they're out to actually beat the hell out of you, to degrade you, that's something else. But an occasional slap is okay.

Z: Has being a Marine made you more masculine?

W: Stereotypically, yes. In actuality, as far as my personal view of what is masculine, no.

Z: What is masculine to you?

W: [Pause.] Opening the door for women, being thoughtful enough to help women out, things like that. It's not necessarily being loud and definite in your demeanor. Caring enough to take responsibility for yourself and your wife and your kids—that to me is being masculine. It has nothing to do with the big, burly man. Or the how-many-women-can-I-have-in-one-night thing. That's not masculine.

Z: Are you different from most Marines in the way you view masculinity?

W: Yeah. [Laughs.] I think I am. The Marine Corps view of masculinity [is] the bodybuilder; to go out in the field and never take a shower; and kill, kill, kill. And that's what they drill in you. That's typical in the Marine Corps, but I don't feel I'm the typical Marine. . . . There's nothing wrong with being gung ho about the Marine Corps as long as you know that it's just a way of life. It's not the only way of life, and eventually you're gonna have to get out and do your own thing.

Marie: Can I say something? A masculine man in the Marine Corps is somebody who's arrogant, egotistical, and ignorant. And Wood is different from that; he's not arrogant, and he has a lot of knowledge that I would say that ninety percent of the male Marines don't have.

Z: How would you describe the attitude among Marines toward "gays in the military?"

W: Really ignorant. Really stereotypical. They feel that all gays are effeminate, or something. It's nothing but fear. They think "I can't be anywhere near them in a combat situation or on a ship or in the field" because they feel they're gonna be sexually molested, when nothing could be further from the truth. All that it would take is for them to be educated, to realize that's not how it is. If people would start to realize that, I think their views would change. But the Marine Corps will be the last [service branch] to change. The Marine Corps is built on tradition and customs and history. For it to change takes a lot of pressure. As a matter of fact, I just [took part in] a big heated discussion. It wasn't even a discussion; it was just a bitch session. It's the level of maturity and it's the level of intelligence that you deal with—I'll try and sit and talk with somebody, the topic will come up at work, and I'll be for gays in the military. And somebody will say, "Fuck those fags." So, here we are, combative already. So you try to overlook that, you try to sidestep some things, try to find out why they feel that way. And a lot of it is just flat-out ignorance. They don't know, but they're sure they know. That this is the way it is and oh my God. . . . I don't understand. Why can't people just be accepting? You don't have to like it! As long as it's not interfering with you, who cares? Most people would say, "I just don't want it around me." Okay, fine, but you can't close your eyes to the fact that it happens. "I don't want to see it." Well, then you better be accepting of the fact that you can't go anywhere; you're gonna stay in your house. I think it'd be safe to assume that a fourth of the Marine Corps is gay. At least a fourth.

Z: What do you base that on?

W: Years of being around Mark, and learning to recognize who is and who isn't, and talking with Mark—right now, in my work section of sixty-eight people, I know five who are gay. And I have suspicions of five others.

Z: There's a stereotype that gays in the military tend to be in certain job fields. Cooks are among them. [Wood is a cook.]

W: You think? Really? I never heard of that.

Z:—And of course admin. As opposed to grunts. On the other hand, I've heard that there's sometimes more what could be called homosexual activity going on among men who don't consider themselves gay, particularly infantry guys out in the field.

W: Uh-huh.

Z: One Marine I interviewed told me about a contest to see who could ejaculate the farthest. Have you heard stories like that?

W: Yeah. [Laughs.] I've heard stories about seeing who can come quicker, and that if you're the quickest you're the stud.

Z: Have you witnessed any of these competitions?

W: No, no.

Z: But you do think that does go on?

W: Well, yeah. That definitely goes on. That's a typical male machismo thing. And the stereotypical Marine, "I can do this and I can do that"—everything's performance. Performance, performance, performance.

Z: What can you tell me about attitudes toward women in the Marine Corps?

W: A lot of male Marines do not like female Marines. Guys look at women Marines like "Why did you come in? Are you a dyke? Are you a slut? Or are you one of those one-third who want to finish their college education, do what you wanna do, and get out?" They categorize women a lot quicker than they do men. And the gay women—they want nothing to do with 'em. I think they think worse than if it was a gay man. In civilian society, it's socially acceptable for two women to be gay, because you can see two women kissin' on each other in a bar, and a guy would think, I want to watch; if it's two men, it's bad. But in the Marine Corps, if they see a gay woman—I don't know why, but I think they take more offense to that.[2]

Z: What is your opinion on the issue of women in combat, and on women in the Marine Corps generally?

W [to Marie]: You really wanna hear it? I got no problem with women bein' in the military. But I think that the standards should be changed somewhat, because . . . You have your female standards and your male standards. Which is fine. Women are not as physically strong as men. But I feel that women should be in combat just like the men because I feel that women should be in the military for the same reason as men. If they're needed for war, they should go to war. It shouldn't be "every woman should free a man to fight." I don't think that's right or fair.

Z: Marie is shaking her head no. Let me ask her some of these questions.

M: I was adopted. I grew up in New England. My father worked in textiles, and my mom was a housewife for a long time. Now she's a special ed[ucation] teacher. I lived with them until I was sixteen. Then I just didn't want to live with them anymore. My mom was hurt because I wanted to find my real mom. I ended up just leaving, not in the best way. It left a lot of scars. But everything's better now and I believe I'm a stronger person for it.

My dad was a Green Beret in special forces in the Army. He used to tell me stories. I remember just knowing that I would be in the military. I didn't know which branch, of course, because I didn't know the difference, but I knew that I was going to be in the military. Because I liked the uniformity and the discipline. That's what attracted me. When I started checking everything out, I didn't like the Army guy because he didn't present himself well. I didn't like the Navy because I didn't want to go on a ship. The Air Force was more technical, and that appealed to me. But the first time I saw the Marine Corps recruiter—he was in his blues, and I thought: wow, he stands tall and proud and he's cocky. He's got confidence.

I joined when I was nineteen. I had already been living on my own since I was sixteen. But I wanted to be able to stand up for myself more. And I liked challenging myself; I always wanted to find out what my limit was. I joined the Marine Corps to see what I could do. It went well. I liked boot camp. It was hard, but it was fun.

W: Hmm. [In a later conversation I asked Wood about this "Hmm." He said: "Boot camp was *funny*, but I don't think that it was *fun*. The worst movie is more fun than boot camp."]

Z: You found boot camp fun?

M: Yes. Because you're competing with everybody. When I was in high school, you had this clique and that clique; you knew popular people, you had the geeks and the people who smoke—I thought it was all baloney and I didn't like it. I liked the uniformity of the military.

Z: How is Marine Corps recruit training different for women?

M: Our training is longer than theirs, because women don't go to MCT. We learn defensive training, stuff like that, where they learn aggressive training. Other than that we do basically everything they do.

Z: Did the DIs yell at you in the same way?

M: Oh yes. And, to be honest, we were struck every once in a while. I didn't mind it because I thought, whatever happens, it's how you take the situation and it will make you a better person in the long run. I figured the more that we encountered in boot camp, the less shocked we would be once we got out in the real world.

Z: What do you do in the Marine Corps?
M: I make movies. I'm a videographer. We tape change of command ceremonies, things like that, for documentation purposes. We do training videos for recruits. It's probably the best job in the Marine Corps.
Z: Apart from your job, how do you like the Marine Corps?
M: It is a lifestyle. If you choose to accept it, then it's good. If you choose not to, then you're going to be unhappy. When I got out of boot camp I thought I was invincible. I thought I was going to be hard core. I was excited; I was looking forward to traveling, to doing things. I was going to become a drill instructor. But now, I've ended up seeing a lot of hypocrisy in the Marine Corps. It's very hard for a woman; there's a lot of men who feel we shouldn't even be in the Marine Corps.
Z: Are women in the Marine Corps always called and thought of as "WMs?" Or are they seen as just Marines?
M: No, we're not seen as just Marines. Actually, I don't think I've ever been looked at as just a Marine. People say it, but they don't mean it.
There's a lot of sexual harassment. The section I work at, I've had gunnies say, "C'mon [Marie's last name], let's go take a shower. Mm, mm, mm, what I could do with you." Stuff like that. Because they are the rank they are, and because they knew that I was a naïve farm girl, they thought that they could do this. It happened the day I went to boot camp. From then on, it's been ongoing. Over time, I've learned to stand up for myself. Now I just say, "Master Guns, I don't like that." I just walk away.
Z: Have they ever touched you?
M: Yes. I've had a gunnery sergeant take me off base against my will and tell me that he wanted to have sex with me. He was married. And this is a crime in the military; you can get put in jail for adultery. The whole time I was like, "Gunny, bring me home. Gunny, bring me home." He was like, "Don't call me gunny, call me Chuck." He ended up bringing me back. And he was NJP'd [given nonjudicial punishment].
Z: So you filed a complaint.
M: Right. To tell you the truth, if I had never come in the military and I had something like this happen, I probably wouldn't know what to do and I probably would have just kept my mouth shut. Being in the Marine Corps teaches you to stand up for yourself.
Wood: You kind of have to. It's a different culture, a different society—
M: And it's male-dominated. If you want to be a female in a male-domi-

nated society like the Marine Corps, you have to be able to stand your ground.

Z: Have you observed that the men who join the Marine Corps are trying to attain a certain kind of masculinity?

M: I think a lot of men come in because they want to go to school or something, but also because they want to seem macho. They want the title "Marine." If you're in the Army, people are like, oh, that's nice. But if you're in the Marine Corps, people are like, wow, you're a Marine! A lot of people want that. I wanted that. Then once you get in, you see how everything really works. At boot camp, the drill instructors paint this wonderful picture of what you're supposed to do. It's really glorious. But once you get out in the field, you realize what these men are like. I've worked with many men who go around and cheat on their wives.

Wood: A good eighty percent of the married straight men in the Marine Corps—

Marie:—think that monogamy is a kind of wood. There was one guy I worked with—he was married—and every day he would come in and brag to his superiors, "I did this with this girl and this with that girl." And my superiors *favor* that; that's what they *like*. Women don't go in and say, "Yeah, I did this guy last night." If they did, they would be viewed as sluts.

Z: Have you experienced the famous camaraderie with other Marines?

Marie: [Pause.] You find it in boot camp. The day that you graduate you feel it. The esprit de corps—officers preach it, but to tell you the truth, I think that it's a figment of the imagination.

Wood: I feel that it's there. Of course it's strongest when you're first starting out. 'Cause that's all you know—

Marie: But then you start to see—

Wood: You start to see, and the rose-colored glasses fade. When I first started, it was esprit de corps and semper fi and all that. Now that I've been in nine and a half years—you go through your phases; one year you want to get out, the next year you're all gung ho. So, it's there, but not as much as people perceive it to be, or would like it to be.

Marie [to Wood]: I don't think it's there as much as you say it is. Where I work, people stab each other in the back.

Wood: You've got to look out for yourself. But I feel it's a more tightly knit bond than in the civilian world.

Z: Living in an all-woman barracks, have you ever felt any sense of sexual tension?

Marie: No.

Wood [to Marie]: You didn't? Really?

Marie: [Shakes head.]

Z: One analysis of the objection to gays in the military is that men who consider themselves straight take a certain pleasure in the bonding, closeness, and sexual tension of living and working with other young men.

Wood: [Nods.] Like in *Lord of the Flies*.

Z: Especially when gays are not supposed to be there, there can be a certain secret erotic pleasure . . .

W: Yeah. Yeah. That's a male thing, though, I think. Because it's accepted. A lot of times when you get a bunch of men together—[like at] CRT, Combat Readiness Training. That's where you go to the field for two weeks and do your rifle training. I guess males look at it as—if we're in the field for two weeks, if I was to go up and pinch somebody on the butt, big deal, so what? Or go walk around and act like a frivolous girl. No one would say anything. The grosser you get and the weirder you get—it's funny, and it's a tension release.

Marie [to Z]: He's the grossest.

Wood: [Laughs.] Yeah. And that's the typical male bonding kind of thing. And then there's that fine line, and it's all personal; someone might take offense if I was to do this or that.

Z: I've heard of sexual acts happening between men where the idea was, since they were Marines, they couldn't be gay—

W: Yeah. "We're married guys. We can't be gay."

Z: And that is part of the opposition to gays. When you have "out" gays there, it casts a suspicion on anything that might possibly be called "gay." Homoerotic bonding is supposed to be crucial because men won't risk their lives for some abstract idea of protecting democracy, but they will for their buddies. And the military leadership has said, you can't have that kind of love between guys if they're afraid of it being "gay."

W: See, I don't understand that. Because it's no different. I'll love a man just as easy as I'll love a woman. I mean, I'm not gonna be sexual with 'em. But I'll still have feelings for the guys. But I can't understand why guys or girls or whoever draw the line on that, to feel that way. . . .

Your whole life you grow up with opposites: heaven and hell, black and white, male and female, masculine and feminine. That's the only way that a lot of people can think. To say that you can be a man and masculine and gay—that's a big turn. People get lost and confused.

Marie: You can't be in a grey area—

Wood: The military has no grey area.

Marie: If you're in a border area, then there's something wrong with you.

Z [to Marie]: Have you met his brother?

M: No. I've talked to him on the phone a few times. [Mark lives overseas.] I like him.

Z: How did you react when he told you that his brother was gay?

Marie: I was like, oh.

Wood: You weren't shocked or anything. You were accepting.

Z: Had you ever met a "gay" person?

Marie: Actually, no, I hadn't. But I read a lot. I've got this big fat book, [Randy Shilts's] *Conduct Unbecoming*. And one of my drill instructors was suspected to be a lesbian. But my parents raised me to be open and accepting.

Wood: My parents didn't raise me to be open and accepting. Well, my dad did. My mom—she wasn't open about anything, really. I would say I'm a lot more like my dad. He was a small guy. Sensitive. He wasn't really macho, but he still liked to go out and have a beer with the guys. I'm the same way. I like to play poker. But I'm weird, I'm not the norm. I'm in the military, but I also like the arts, all the sensitive things. I've got two contradictory sides. And I don't know if that's because of my acceptance of my brother, or because it was instilled in us because of my dad. I would say probably both.

Z: Will you stay in the Marine Corps?

Marie: No, I'm gonna get out. I see a lot of staff NCOs, and they're hypocrites. I don't want to end up that way. And also because I want a family. The Marine Corps is not solid for me.

Wood: I plan on putting in my twenty years then getting out. I'm just staying in for the pension, not for the esprit de corps, semper fi.

And it's an ego thing too. People look at you like, "Oh, he's a Marine." They respond to you differently. I suck that up. I like that.

Z: Do you find that people are intimidated by your being a Marine?

W: Yeah.

Z: And you enjoy that?

W: Yeah. I'm not gonna lie. It's nice.

Part Two: Two Months Later

Wood and I got together for a one-on-one follow-up conversation the day before he left for drill instructor school.

Z: Why are you going to drill instructor school? Doesn't that require you to be more gung ho than you say you are?

W: [Laughs.] To see if I can do it. And to use the Marine Corps to better myself. Sometimes, I have problems being assertive in certain situations. I want to be a teacher when I get out, and being a drill instructor will help me deal with little seventeen- and eighteen-year-olds. And it will help me stay in shape. Plus [if you make a career out of] the Marine Corps, somewhere along the line you have to be either a recruiter, a drill instructor, or [an] MSG, Marine security guard. Drill instructor is the hardest out of the three. But being married, and being on MSG, I'd be moving around too much. I like to move around to different places, but not every three or six months. And a recruiter—I would rather yell at a little seventeen- or eighteen-year-old than try to be his buddy and get him in. Because of their mentality. When I was seventeen, you couldn't tell me anything. And I wouldn't like to have to bullshit and lie to get somebody in the Marine Corps just so I can meet a quota. It's easier for me to be just a total hard-ass.

Z: The drill instructor is such a tremendously powerful figure, as all of the guys I've interviewed, and the few women, made clear to me. It must be a real rush to feel that power over eighty recruits. The Marines I've talked to have said, "You never forget your drill instructors." How forceful of an impression did your drill instructors make on you?

W: [Pause.] At the time, a highly forceful one. Has anything from them carried through until now? I would probably say yes.

On a four-man drill instructor team, you've got a brand new one, "Bob New Hat" they call him; he just got there. All he does is run around and yell and stress everybody out, and there's nothin' that you can do right. Then there's the "Third Hat," they call him; he yells, but he also talks to you one-on-one. He figures out how you are, lets you know what he expects; he gives you reasons why he's yelling at you. Then there's "The Heavy": He's the senior's right-hand man. He's the one that does all the drilling. Then the senior, who's the big daddy. He's the one who comforts all the recruits and says, "It's okay. You're all right. You'll graduate," that kind of thing.

My senior didn't really make much of an impression because we all knew that that was his last cycle, and all he cared about was what would better him. The only one who made an impression on me was Sergeant Smith. He was the Bob. And that was because of his forcefulness. I myself—and this is one of the reasons why I want to be a drill instructor. When stress is shoved down right in you, right down your throat, I tend to fog up a little bit, become a little slower in my reasoning, because I want to think it out. Even though it's only a couple of seconds, I tend to forget some things I would normally remember. I want to try and get rid of that.

Sergeant Smith, he was able to do all that at a moment's notice, and see through all the stuff, and if ten thousand things were happening at once, he could filter out all of them and do the one thing that had to be done. So that was the only drill instructor who made an impression on me. [Pause.] I'd like to see him. I'd like to kick his ass. [Laughs.]

Z: In our previous conversation you said that you understood sexual identity to be the result of conscious and subconscious choices, and that you could imagine having made different choices. Have you ever had any sexual experiences with other males?

W: Just growing up, with my brother. I'm tryin' to think how old we were. Probably about nine. We would touch each other. I think that's normal; I've read that that's normal. And I think at around that point is where we made our decision whether we wanted to be gay or not. I don't mean to make it a simplistic thing, but I think at that point I decided not to because I was tired of [touching Mark], and didn't find any more pleasure or excitement in it, but he kept on goin' that way, and later on had his struggle with comin' out.

So, I tested the waters a little, but I've never actually had sex with a guy. I've been approached a lot. I've been asked, touched, prodded, and all that other stuff.

Z: What do you mean?

W: One instance. Mark hadn't yet told me that he was. This was overseas, my first year in the Corps. I remember the guy's name now. Sergeant N. I didn't suspect that he was. But one night I came back to the barracks; Mark was out. I went to bed, fell asleep. We lived in little cubes in an open squad bay. Sergeant N came in and he starts touchin' me. I woke up, but I just laid there. I didn't know who it was. Then he started touchin' me more, trying to go down on me. So that's when I stopped him. I said, "Hey, I'm sorry. I don't know who you think I am. But no." I wasn't rude to him. And he didn't leave. He said, "Aw, come on." I said, "No!" So then he got up and left. Obviously, he felt weird about it the next day, but I never said nothin' to him. And I didn't perceive him any different. I didn't really think nothin' of it. But that was it.

Z: Did he know it was you?

W: I don't know if he thought I was Mark, or what.

Z: Do you recall what your early sexual fantasies were like?

W: I didn't start masturbating until I was thirteen. I'd cut out little pictures in magazines, nude pictures of girls in *Playboy* and *Penthouse*, trying to imagine what my ideal girl would be. Sometimes, I'd have fantasies about girls in school. Just basic stuff. Maybe doing it in some weird places or something.

Z: How old were you when you first had sex?

W: Nineteen. That was with Helen. It was in the front seat of a car. With Mark in the back with some girl! [Laughs.] I'd look up every once in a while, but as far as I know he was just doing the touchy-feely type thing.

Z: Did Mark ever have sex with women?

W: I think he did. Once or twice. He said it was no big deal. Another interesting correlation—both of us like oral sex. Giving and receiving. Both of us like it a lot more than most guys, I guess. We're alike on that aspect. To be blunt, I guess he just decided that guys do it better than girls. Or that guys know more what they want.

Z: How do you respond when gay guys say that to you?

W: That guys do it better? I can see that being true. [Pause.] A good question would be why I consider [the idea] a turn-off. . . . I think there's guys that are sexy. I do find myself attracted somewhat, sometimes, to a guy because he's got nice eyes, or he's got a nice build, or I like his demeanor. I find that nice, but not in a sexual way. I can't see a guy giving me oral sex, or me doing it to another guy. I'm used to—maybe it's the long hair of women.

Z: How do you feel when other men find you sexually attractive?

W: I like that. I don't feel threatened by it. It's just as much a compliment if a guy says "Hey, nice ass," as a girl saying, "Hey, nice ass."

Z: Has that happened?

W: Yeah. [Waves.] "Thanks, guy." [Laughs.]

Z: In the big national debate on "gays in the military" much was made of the "shower argument." Military guys were quoted saying, "I don't want no fag lookin' at me in the shower."

W: Obviously, they're insecure with themselves.

Z: It wouldn't bother you to have some guy watching you—feeling sexual excitement seeing you naked?

W: No. That wouldn't bother me. 'Cause I know that I would control the situation. If it even became necessary to control it. And I'd kind of take it as a compliment.

Z: You mentioned to me that you were in a gay bar not too long ago.

W: Yeah, I went out there with [a friend]. There were guys there who'd ask me to dance. I'd smile at 'em, "No thanks." But then I thought, well, wait a minute, why don't I? But then the military thing kicked in and I decided I better not, because [the gay dance club is] really close to the base. But if

I was somewhere else . . . I still don't know if I would. I have danced with other guys, but they were friends, drinking buddies.

Z: Have people ever mistaken you for Mark?

W: Oh, yeah.

Z: I picture somebody coming up and putting their hands over your eyes . . .

W: Givin' me a kiss on the back of the neck or something? No, nobody's ever done that. That'd be comical. Most of the time they come runnin' up, "Maaark! Maaark!" Or touch my arm or somethin', and right from the word go I'd say, "Hey, I'm not Mark."

Z: Growing up, did you guys ever play around with that?

W: Oh yeah, in the typical way. Dating each other's girlfriends. Taking each other's tests in high school. We even did that at boot camp.

Z: How would you define what is feminine?

W: Feminine . . . I hate to say this, but . . . somewhat vulnerable? But not completely. I think women should be independent, and not as vulnerable as they used to be, but. . . . Femininity to me would be . . . beauty—No, I wouldn't say that, because I also find beauty in men, too. [Pause.] Where I would see a difference between masculinity and femininity would be . . . It's a hard question.

Z: It is. Every one I've asked—

W: Stumbles.

Z: Are there qualities in you that you think of as feminine?

W: Oh yeah. My open-mindedness. The art that I do. [Wood paints.] Certain feelings that I have I think are feminine. The masculine side is my assertiveness, the Marine Corps, drill instructor, things like that.

Z: Do you think being a drill instructor will make you more masculine?

W: No. No. By this stage in my life, I think I've defined my masculinity. The only thing being a drill instructor is gonna make me do is yell more. [Laughs.]

Major Luke:
Isolated Pain

The Marine Corps has often been compared to a religious sect or cult. In the 1960s, one young officer found the Corps to be "a society unto itself, demanding total commitment to its doctrines and values, rather like one of those quasi-religious military orders of ancient times, the Teutonic Knights or the Theban Band."[1] A reporter who tagged along with the Marines in Somalia in 1993 wrote that Marines "live isolated lives, cloistered in timeless rituals and bent to service like monks of an austere sect."[2] A sign at Parris Island reads "SURRENDER MIND AND SPIRIT TO HARSH INSTRUCTION AND RECEIVE A SOUL."[3]

In his 1994 book *American Samurai*, Craig Cameron, a history professor and a former Marine Corps lieutenant, examines the influence of myth and imagination on the performance of combat by Marines in World War II. He provides some historical background helpful for understanding present-day Marines. Way back in 1911, prescient Marine Corps leaders created a special Recruiting Publicity Bureau to market the service to the U.S. public. "The slogans, recruiting posters, and ad campaigns [of that period] used to draw men into the service created an archetypal public image of the Marines that has persisted in modified form to this day."[4] In 1921, commandant of the Marine Corps John A. Lejeune delivered a Marine Corps birthday message intended to foster a mystical belief in "this high name" of Marine. Lejeune's message, which is read to all Marines annually as part of the November 10 Marine Corps birthday ceremony, speaks of an eternal spirit that animates Marines.[5] Writes Cameron, "For those who truly believe, this message promises Marines immortality for their warrior spirit and assures them that the men of the nation will hold a high regard for their masculine values."[6]

Cameron tells us that in World War II, "the means by which [Marine] identity was spread and so deeply instilled was through the manipulation and fabrication of gender roles." Marines were defined by what they were not. They were not the Army, the Navy, the Japanese, but most important, Marines were not nurturing, life-giving *women.*[7]

Just as masculinity, *Marineness must be mystified because it won't hold up under questioning.* To drill instructors of the World War II era,

> the creation and inculcation of [Marine] identity seemed to depend on an intuitive understanding and acceptance of a remote and abstract ideal of what the term "Marine" should embody. . . . Attempting to articulate this nebulous ideal, the product of film and fiction, "old corps" myth and wartime legend, seemed for some Marines to strip it of symbolic value. . . . The success of the Marine Corps at creating an institutional tradition is in one sense measured by how many Marine authors . . . can offer no definition of a Marine identity but simply assert it as a natural and unconscious fact of their existence.[8]

Gay men have their own mythic images of The Marine. Corporal Alex said that his sex partners expected him to be cold and emotionless. Lieutenant Frank found that because of his size, build, and butchness, some prospective lovers assumed that he must be a top man. Other Marines speak of the pressure exerted on them to conform to the sexual stereotype that "all Marines are bottoms." As Major Luke comments in the following interview, "Sometimes you meet people and they have preconceived notions about you, and they don't give you the chance to explore other options!"

I met Major Luke in the fall of 1992. He impressed me with his gentlemanly refinement, his youthful impishness, and his lonesomeness. At 35, he had not yet tasted the romantic love for which he longed. His prospects for meeting someone at the tiny remote base where he was stationed seemed bleak. He eschewed participation in gay social organizations out of fear of exposure. There was, however, a ray of hope in his life. Bill Clinton had just been voted into office, and Major Luke had written a letter to—had in effect come out to—the new President. It looked as though a bright new day was dawning for military gays.

Part One

Zeeland: You were telling me that you went out one night wearing—which uniform was it?

Major Luke: Evening dress. It's a uniform I had just bought, because you're not required to get it until you become a major. A good reason why is because it costs a thousand dollars. Very fancy uniform. Went to the [Marine Corps] birthday ball and went out afterwards to one of the local "family" bars.

Z: What reception were you accorded?

L: Not much. I think people thought it was a costume I was wearing. If I had done it [in San Diego] there would definitely be a different reaction, because there's more military down here.

Z: How many people are stationed at your base?

L: Couple hundred.

Z: Did you tell me that you've met only one other gay military man there?

L: I haven't met him. I've only seen him. I know where he works, but we haven't talked.

Z: What exactly is your job? You're not a pilot, or are you?

L: [Pause.] One doesn't want to get too specific. I'm an aviator. [Laughs.] That's good enough. I fly in a combat jet. In a squadron you do many other things in addition to that. You have other jobs, other callings, but my primary job is flying.

Z: In eighth grade you taught yourself "The Marines' Hymn."

L: Yeah. I don't remember now why I did it; all I can remember is going to the library and finding it in a book and trying to memorize all the verses. But [growing up] I never talked about the Marine Corps as a career option. People were definitely surprised when I did it.

Z: You come from a military family?

L: My father was in the Navy, my mother was in the Navy.

Z: Both officers?

L: Yeah. My brother is a Coast Guard officer, and my sister is a Navy officer. One brother chose not to pursue that life. He's sort of an antimilitaristic, left-wing, bleeding-heart peacenik type of person—the black sheep of the family. Of course in using that term I don't hold anything against him. The most important thing to me is always—People ask me,

"How can you stand being around people who hold the opposite views?"
I tell them, "That's what America stands for: the right to hold the view-
point and make the choices you want to." And that's why I'm where I am.

Z: What attracted you to the idea of military service?

L: I grew up with it. I don't think I was ever attracted to it as much as I
never thought of doing anything else. It was just always where I thought
I'd end up.

Z: You told me that you did consider one alternative.

L: For a while I considered getting a criminal justice degree and pursuing
a law enforcement career. . . . I have always been best at people traits and
talents. I think I'd be a very good social worker; I think I'd be a very good
psychologist. I'm a very empathetic person, and I tend to gravitate to
situations where I can deal with people on a person-to-person basis. I
didn't look at being a cop like, I-want-to-be-a-cop-so-I-can-bust-heads-
type-thing. I thought of it as: I want to be a police officer to help people.

Z: But Marine and cop are two of the butchest jobs you can hold. It's
interesting that you would choose those jobs to "help people." . . . Growing up, did you think of yourself as conventionally masculine?

L: [Pause.] I don't think I thought of myself either way. I didn't think of
myself as feminine or effeminate. I don't think I walked around gauging
my masculinity against anybody else . . .

I think I knew I was gay, or tended towards that, since about the age of
thirteen. In my high school years, that was always in the back of my mind.
So it dictates how you live. I was pretty much a solitary person. I think the
reason was I knew there were things about me that were different, and I
didn't have anybody to talk to about them. Stayed to myself. Read a lot.

Z: What made you aware of this difference?

L: I don't know. I just was. There wasn't any act or incident that brought
me along one path; there wasn't any defining moment where I said, this is
what I am. That didn't come until a couple years ago. Back then it was just
something that, as you grew through your sexuality, you became aware of.
And I was just aware that I was going in a direction other than everybody
else.

Z: You felt an attraction to other boys.

L: I don't think I was attracted to other boys back then. I just was not
attracted to women. With enough egging on, anybody can be bold, but I
still am a fairly shy person. And I was pretty introverted back then. I had a
speech impediment when I was in first or second grade, and I was always
terrified of speaking in public. Even now, when I have to teach a class—in
fact, I usually get written up as one of the better instructors because I don't
stand up there and talk in monotone; I'm very vocal and I move around a

lot, and it keeps everybody interested. But right before I start, my hands will be dripping sweat. Still. It's like I told you before, I'm afraid of heights. But the way to get through it is just to go full force.

Z: By jumping out of airplanes, you told me.

L: That kind of gets me a little hyper. A lot hyper.

Z: I read a survey somewhere that, given the choice, most Americans say they would rather undergo root canal surgery than speak in public.

L: In flight school they give you a psychological aptitude test. One of the questions they ask you is, which would you rather do: be violently ill on a public bus with all these people around, or slam your hand in a car door? And inevitably, all the Navy guys say they would rather be violently ill on the bus, and all the Marines say they would rather slam their hand in the car door. I would slam my hand in the car door.

Z: Why?

L: Isolated pain. As opposed to public humiliation.

Z: What does that suggest about the differences between Navy men and Marines?

L: It's more the type of people the service attracts rather than the type of person the service creates. People say the Marine Corps has made them that way; but really those types of people are attracted to the service.

What the Marine Corps wants and what the Marine Corps pitches is somebody who is forceful, aggressive, willing-to-walk-into-a-hail-of-bullets-type-thing. I'm obviously none of those. Like I said, the way I get over things I'm afraid of, or things I can't face, is I jump with both feet into it. Maybe that's why I chose the Marine Corps. I'd grown up in the Navy and gone to the Naval Academy so, obviously, going in the Navy would not have presented any more challenges to me. It would have been the status quo. Going in the Marine Corps would be doing something my father wouldn't probably think I was capable of doing. He wrote me a letter the first day I got in school. I got the first piece of mail of anybody. He said, "When you flunk out, you're more than welcome to come home and go to a community college." He might have done that because he knows me, and by doing that—I kept that letter and gave it back to him on graduation day. My parents have always known the quickest way to get me to do something is to tell me I can't do it. But I guess I don't know my parents well enough to say if they're that crafty.

I grew up in a family where nobody was willing to show their emotions. That obviously shapes you as well. My dad couldn't. We got everything; we couldn't want for anything, but as we were growing up I don't think he ever said "I love you." He was—not unloving or uncaring, just very stern and strict. It shows in my family. The kids, we're not too communicative with each other. It's not that we dislike each other, it's just that we don't reach out for each other. All very self-reliant. I'm more than willing to help anybody in anything, but it's almost a physical impossibility for me to turn around and ask somebody to help me. Can't do it. I either do it myself, or—no, I just do it myself.

Z: Have you found that you have certain things in common with other Marine Corps officers, as far as background and outlook?

L: We're all fairly independent. The Marine Corps as a service sure as heck doesn't rely on anyone else. . . .

If you look at the ads—Marine Corps ads are always focused big-time on the warrior, the hard parts, the challenges. I haven't seen a whole lot of Navy ads on TV lately, but they used to emphasize the social aspect, where the Marine Corps has always emphasized the—not that you're a lone individual, but at least the requirements are there to be an independent thinker, self-motivator type-person. If a Marine did a Navy ad, what it would show would be probably a frigate or a destroyer out in the North Atlantic in a force-ten gale, and shots of how hectic, frenzied, and chaotic it can be as you're trying to get some place and things are falling off and the whole ship's bouncing around, with a voice-over that said something to the effect that "We're looking for individuals that can handle this." That's how our ads are. I think one of the earlier recruiting posters said, "We never promised you a rose garden," and showed a boot with a DI yelling at him. The Army pushes only the fact that you can get money for college. "We'll give you twenty-five thousand dollars if you join!" They try and bribe you. The Navy ones I've seen now are all emphasizing the technological aspect, and trying to pitch the skills you'll learn that you can use in later life. And they tell you all the fun you'll have: the port visits, the adventure; they show happy people having a good time. "You'll find a lot of friends in the Navy." [Laughs.] Maybe more than they wanted you to find!

Z: I don't think the public is terribly shocked at the idea of homosexuality among sailors, but Marines are imagined to be virile beyond reproach.

L: The Marine Corps is more of a religion. It really is. Both in the way we push it, and the way you live it. Without sounding heretical, what we have is a faith, a creed, a religious belief. And that probably goes into that same category, that we're beyond or above the temptations of the world, or what the common man has to live with. We're on some higher plane, as the defenders of truth and freedom.

Z: Are you saying that sailors give in to those temptations, but Marines don't?

L: No. We've just got better PR. [Laughs.]

Z: Did you find Joseph Steffan's book *Honor Bound* representative of your experiences at the Naval Academy?

L: [Pause.] Yeah, I guess. Vaguely. My experiences there—I didn't walk around day to day thinking of my sexuality. The Naval Academy is a place where they definitely pile an awful lot on you, so that you have plenty more to think about than your own problems. And you don't have the time to think about them because you're too busy taking twenty to twenty-two credit hours of work. And on top of that you have a sport that you're required to participate in, and you have military duties and functions as well. There isn't a whole lot of free time left to sit there and reflect on minor stuff. . . .

I didn't go to my first gay club until I moved back out to California after flight school. I was twenty-six.

Z: You said that as a teenager you did not feel an attraction to males. At some point though, I assume you found yourself starting to look at other guys in a sexual way.

L: [Pause.] My senior year in high school I had a couple of experiences. They were one-night type of things.

Z: Friends from school?

L: No. People you meet. [Laughs.]

Z: In public places?

L: In public places. I think not ever looking for a relationship had a lot to do with being raised in a stern environment. It really wasn't until mid-twenties when I started thinking of any nesting urges. Religion has a lot to do with that too. When you feel that everything else is a mortal sin, you spend most of your time locking those thoughts out of your mind until obviously they get a little too overwhelming. Then, you go out on the prowl and come back and say your three Our Fathers and two Hail Marys and promise you'll never do it again—until three or four months later when the pressures build up and you go out again.

I'm a spiritual person. And everything from day one from being raised on up told me [that homosexuality is] wrong. I'd love to have kids; I'd love to have a *Leave it to Beaver*-type family and everything else, and that was a role I kept striving for. Even got engaged once, proposed another time. But . . . got smart and chickened out.

Z: Have you ever had sex with a woman?

L: Nope.

Z: You told me that you tried to fantasize about women while masturbating, but that it just didn't work.

L: No, it didn't. And when I was in prep school with the other guys we went to X-rated movies a couple times. Absolutely nothing. "This is it?"

Z: But you also told me that you don't respond to gay porn, either.

L: No. And that's more because I think porno movies or magazines—to me, it's a pretty voyeuristic and shallow entertainment. And I think it actually does more damage. I've always been taught that you treat every person with respect and kindness. And those types of videos and magazines show no respect for people. Whether or not the person wanted to do it, it shows a disregard for people as people.

Obviously, one of the first things that attracts us to someone is the physical, but it's not going to be a lot of fun if you want to talk about Proust [indicates my book shelf] and the other person wants to talk about *The Three Stooges*. Not that watching *The Three Stooges* is a bad thing, because I enjoy that myself, but. . . . A cute guy will turn me on in a second, and I'll say, "I want to know him." But I'm more attracted to an intelligent person who has his act together and has goals than somebody who is cute and has no clue about his life.

Z: Your first visit to a gay bar—

L: It was a disaster.

I'm not even sure how I found it. But, went there, sat outside for probably an hour. Went in and found the nearest dark corner to stand in, and stood there for about an hour. Left and said: "This was worthless, I'll never do that again." But obviously no one was going to come near me because I was standing in the corner all defensive, arms folded, and glaring at anybody who came by. I don't know why I went there originally, if I figured there would be wild sexual orgies, or maybe somebody would try and pick me up, or—I didn't know what I was looking for and, consequently, didn't find anything.

Z: There are gay social organizations, gay churches, other alternative ways of meeting people.

L: I didn't know about any of those organizations. Plus which I probably wouldn't have gotten involved with them anyway. Being in the military, I didn't want my name on any list. I didn't want to have anything that could attach me to the gay life. And that's a shame. Because by being afraid of any contact with gay society, you deny yourself the benefits of meeting "normal" people instead of barflies. Frequent bar devotees are definitely a little bit skewed in their morality and in their viewpoints and in their approach to life.

Z: Bars would seem especially unsuited to you since you don't drink.

L: My not drinking has really never been a hindrance to going a bar. I don't feel inhibited by the fact that people are drinking. Most people don't know that I'm not drinking. I drink club soda, and I guess it looks like a gin and tonic. . . .

I was based with a squadron. Every Friday night is happy hour. You go to the officers' club; everybody does. It's required. Part of your job is to socialize. Important, because of the fact that these are the people you fly with, and the people you may have to die with, or die for. There was another guy in my squadron who didn't drink, who was one of these people who made it known that he did not approve of it; he wouldn't go to the bars, and he looked down on the drinkers. He wasn't in the squadron very long. You tend to get sent elsewhere if you're not bonding. You really need to know each other because you have to trust your life to these people and they have to trust theirs to you. They have to feel that you will come through if it's required. So I used to [participate] like all the other junior officers who would sit there and get drunk, and we'd make lots of noise and have fights and wrestling matches and jump up and down on the tables and just have a good time.

Z: What can you tell me about homoerotic aspects to male bonding among officers?

L: It's different in the aviation community than it is with the Navy surface line officers, or with Marine Corps infantry officers. Particularly infantry officers; they have their own protocol, and I don't think they bond. It's not proper, because if one person gets killed, everybody has to know their place so they can all fill in on up. There cannot be any question about it. They're very strict on their hierarchy.

On the aviation side it's a lot different, because when you're doing things at six hundred miles an hour—it's very intense. You're so completely, totally focused and channeled on one thing and one thing alone that you can't really take time to think: "What's the other guy doing?" You have to *know* what he's going to do. And he has to be the type of person you can trust: You've seen him fly enough, you know his style and technique, and you know what his strengths and weaknesses are. Nobody hides anything from anybody. Our bonding comes from the intensity of the flying. In the workplace we're a very sarcastic bunch. If somebody screws up, everybody's there to jump on their case; if there's any blood spilled, we're all on it right then and there. It's to gauge your reaction to all that extra pressure on you as you fight back. Do you tell them to go take a hike, or do you withdraw and kind of wander away and become less a part of the group?

We're very intense in everything we do. If you're fighting another guy in the air, or you're practicing your bomb deliveries on the ground, you're doing it like everything in the world and your life counts on it. Once you're trained to do that in your job, it kind of carries over into everything else—your personal life, your social life. When your job is a matter of life and death, to release that tremendous tension you go a little overboard on the celebrating. The parties that are held in the officers' clubs are more rambunctious and festive than you're going to see at some happy hour bar that civilians go to. We'll get into fights, but just a lot of horseplay; a lot of pushing around. You're drinking, you're happy, you're with your friends, you're with other guys that risk their lives, and nobody else in the world understands that. Civilians don't understand what it's like to land on a carrier. It's not an easy thing, especially in the rain or at night. So you're with your own kind. You roughhouse. You're one big family. And the club—it's your club, so you don't feel constrained by what would be proper etiquette somewhere else.

Z: How easily are you able to engage in this horseplay as a gay man?

L: Easy. The military teaches you how to role-play very well. And you just take that and apply it to something they maybe didn't expect you to apply it to. [Aside:] (Or maybe they do expect you to.) There are women in the bars, and some of them are "camp followers," but bars are more of a guy thing. And the majority of time is spent just talking shop with your friends.

Z: What do you do when the talk is about women? Do you ever lie, tell stories?

L: No. I never have. I don't like to lie. I think it would be more damaging to put up a facade than to say nothing. And for the first six years of my career, I was dating women, occasionally, and I was engaged, so there wasn't a lot of pretending that I had to do. There were enough instances of seeing me in the company of ladies, and I was serious about them.

Z: You were at [the 1991] Tailhook [convention in Las Vegas].

L: Yeah. [Luke gives me a look that says: What about it?]

It's not nearly the party that the press made it out to be. And unfortunately the military hierarchy has gone along with that, even though they know better.

Z: You're saying that these things these women said happened did not?

L: I am saying that they didn't happen to the extent that they said.

People going to a convention, yeah, they go for the professional aspect, but they go for the fun, too. And you have a floor of the hotel with rooms rented out strictly as party rooms. Each room is sponsored by a squadron, and each room has a bar, so you just go from room to room to see what they've got. You have three to four thousand people trying to fit into a space that probably accommodates two to three hundred. You can't get down the hallway without pushing and shoving your way through. A lot of drinking. And a lot of men because, obviously, Tailhook—only a couple of women can claim that privilege. So it's a fraternity. Very few guys bring their wives. Some do, but they'll bring 'em for a little bit then shuttle 'em off. Just so that they can get a taste of it. There are women aviators there, and there are women who come because they know it's a good party. So you attract camp followers again. You attract various types of people: retired military, students, girls who just want to see if it's fun, girls who are still looking for a husband, and women who are there for professional reasons. To get down the hallway—they called it a "gauntlet," but there was nothing organized; you just had a bunch of drunk guys that were crammed into a hallway that couldn't hold any more people.

Z: But do you question whether some of these guys were groping passing women's bodies?

L: I guarantee you they probably did. But, (A) I don't think to the extent that it was made out to be, and (B) there were women who went down there flashing their breasts. I had one woman come up to me and raise her blouse: she was collecting stickers, and having them put on her breasts. I didn't have a sticker so she went someplace else.

So most women didn't go down that hallway, because they know [that] when men get drunk they act like Neanderthals. "Do I really want to go down that hallway? Probably not." And they'd go outside because there was a pool and patio and people were a little bit more sober there. But if they did go down that hallway I guarantee you they got their fanny patted, and maybe some drunken Romeo coming up to them saying "Hey honey, you wanna see a real fighter pilot?" But I don't think—they've only got twenty-four women who complained of abuse of any sort. Out of that twenty-four, two or three are what I would consider abuse. . . .

The big thing to point out is that, out of three or four thousand participants, what you're talking about is from twenty to fifty guys who are boorish idiots who, when a lady said no, didn't get the idea. But that Tailhook was tamer than ones in previous years! It was a lot more calm. It's just that, at this one, somebody got out of hand and somebody decided to make a complaint, and the Navy attacked the wrong problem. They saw it as a public relations problem instead of a problem of dignity, and they tried to solve the PR problem by saying "We need to hush the press up," instead of realizing "This woman has a problem and we need to solve it." They shot themselves in the foot.

Z: Can you give me some succinct formulation of aviators' attitudes toward women aviators?

L: They shouldn't be there. Is that succinct enough? [Laughs.] Primarily because it's a combat arm, and women are not permitted to go into combat. If you asked most aviators, that's the reason. If it weren't for Tailhook, the issue would probably be on the back burner a long time. Reason number two is physiological. Whether it's true or not, most people believe that women cannot handle the stress and pressures of combat. The human race as a whole believes that women should not be subjected to the horrors of war. Whether or not a woman can do the job, I don't think she should be degraded to that point. That may be very Neanderthal of me, but I don't think women should be subjected to murder and killing. And it's not the "I-am-the-provider-and-you-go-fix-dinner" thing, it's that I think women hold a special role in our society. And gay or not, I still think that as the ones that give life they shouldn't be taking life away.

Z: I notice that in the public debates on "gays in the military" and women in combat, the same people speak out against both. I wonder if you don't see some link there . . . People in the pro-gay, pro-women-in-combat camp say, "The military is run by a bunch of white heterosexual males who don't want to yield power to other groups."

L: No. I think most people, when they think of gays, they classify them in the feminine role: the women, the children, the gays, the sick, the weak, the ones who are not perfect, or the ones who are not strong. The reason most people don't want gays in combat is because they don't think of them as strong and masculine warriors who you can depend your life on. . . .

The only thing I can say to respond to that is that I was there in combat; there were gays in combat and [the fact] that you didn't know, that does not lessen their combat experience. With that knowledge, obviously, the intelligent man sits back and realizes, well, I guess it really doesn't matter because he was there.

Z: Although it usually goes unspoken in the gays-in-the-military debate, in denouncing homosexuality, people are mentally picturing *what we do*. It's generally supposed that a man who plays a passive role in anal sex is relinquishing power; if he's on the bottom then he's not a leader, and other men can't be expected to follow him. If he's on top, then how can another guy be expected to stand next to him in the shower without fearing that he could be looked at and made to feel "feminine"?

L: The problem people have there obviously is their traditional concept of two genders: male and female; if you're not male, you must be female. Well, if you're a guy and you're homosexual, you must be feminine. Whether creating another gender to describe us would solve that problem, I don't know.

Z: But in opposing women in combat it sounds like you want to maintain this rigid distinction between male and female.

L: Me? No. I said that women as lifegivers should not be subjected to the horrors of taking life. I don't see that as forcing them into a feminine lower caste role; it's just that I don't think they should be subjected to something

I don't think anybody should be subjected to. But if anybody should, the actual ones who have the spear in hand, and pull the trigger, I don't think it should be women, just because—it conflicts with them giving life. I think for us, and for our children, in a society like that, life would be cheapened even more. If you think we've got wars now, I think we'd have greater ones if women became involved in all parts of combat.

Z: Marines see themselves as elite, and tougher or harder than sailors. Sailors respond to this by saying that Marines "are just a branch of the Navy."

L: They just say it because they know it pisses us off. Without competition, as the communists have found out, there's no growth and there's no progress. Even if there is no perceived competition, we as human individuals are going to create competition. Because without it you get nothing done. When I was on a ship one time, this other guy and I were taking some correspondence courses. We didn't say "Let's compete" or anything, it just sprung up naturally that he'd walk down the passageway and say "I've finished Chapter Eight." I may have been only on Chapter Six. I'd get all pissed off; I'd go back to my room and I'd work through the night, and I'd do Chapter Seven, Eight, Nine, and Ten, so the next day I could say, "I'm done with Ten." And he'd go back and do the same thing. So we created competition where there shouldn't have been any because we weren't competing with each other for a grade. We did it because it made us get through that course a lot quicker. Anywhere where there is Navy and Marine Corps as a team, everyone wants to stress their uniqueness and importance, and to do that you have to compete with somebody.

Z: An obvious reason why young men who are uncomfortably conscious of a sexual attraction to other men might want to join the Marine Corps would be to refute society's message that that attraction makes them less than completely masculine.

L: Who knows. That may be the reason I did. It never came to mind, and I'm not sure I'll volunteer that, but I've always chosen what I could find as the hardest, most difficult path, just to prove I could do it. . . .

The Marine Corps really is more of a religion. Or if not a religion, a secret order. Or fraternal organization or something. Whatever you want to call it, it's mystical. The Marine Corps has created the image that we are different from everybody else. That attracts those people who feel that they are outsiders. Our ads encourage that. The lone knight, saving the world. That does two things: (A) we trust no one outside of the Marine

Corps, and (B) we rely on our fellow Marine completely. Without hesitation. So it's a self-fulfilling prophecy.

The closeness you feel with a Marine—maybe one way to describe it is [like this]. One time I was sitting in an airport. There was some sort of Hare Krishna guy soliciting money. It was kind of funny, because he was incognito; he was wearing a wig and civilian clothes, but it was a real bad wig and you could tell he was a Hare Krishna. And he was going up to sailors and Air Force guys and getting lots of money out of them. I was sitting back and watching. I actually talked to the guy and asked him about his religion before I concluded he was definitely a few cents short of a dollar. And then I saw him go up to a Marine. I saw him give his pitch, and the Marine start to reach for his wallet, and where I had paid no attention to the Air Force or Navy guys, I got up and walked over to the Marine and said, "Put your wallet back and walk away. I'm a Marine." He said, "Okay." He turned around and walked away. I turned to the Hare Krishna guy and said, "Look, I don't care what you do to the sailors or Air Force, but don't do it to a Marine," then went back and sat down. You see another Marine in trouble or about to get ripped off, you'll do anything to help him, where you may not necessarily do it for the sailor.

Z: But you did spend those years at the Naval Academy. You don't have any loyalty to the Navy?

L: A little. Not to the extent of the Marine Corps. The Navy does not inculcate nearly the camaraderie, pride, tradition that the Marines do.

I chose the Marine Corps based on the examples I saw. Marines impressed me with their bearing, their dignity—their care for other people more than anything else. I saw Marine officers cared about their enlisted, and enlisted respected their officers, and I didn't see that in the Navy. I wanted to be in an organization where people looked out for each other. That's always been a prime concern of mine, that I take care of my people.

The Marine Corps . . . how do you put into words . . . things—some are probably primal feelings, things you can't describe. I love what I do, very much. The tradition, and the respect—it makes you feel like you belong, and that you have worth as a person.

Z: And today, when you hear "The Marine's Hymn"? Does it send chills down your spine?

L: Well, you stand up at attention. That's required. [Pause.] No. The National Anthem, I'll get tears in my eyes. My school song, I'll get tears in my eyes. Marine Corps hymn—I don't. You sing out as loud and as boldly as you can. Different emotion. Much more pride. Fierceness and forcefulness and projecting, as opposed to sentimentality. Maybe when I'm sixty a tear will come up.

Part Two: Two and a Half Years Later

By the time Major Luke and I got together for our second taped conversation, much had changed. President Clinton had failed to deliver on his promise to help military gays. The book for which I had originally interviewed Luke had been published; it received little mainstream notice from a public bored with the topic of gays in the military. But things had changed for Major Luke, too, and for the better. Two duty stations later he was back in San Diego, where his prospects for personal fulfillment were far more promising than they previously had been.

Z: When we last spoke you'd written a letter to Bill Clinton expressing your hopes that he would live up to the expectations of you and the other people who elected him. How do you feel about President Clinton now?
L: Betrayed. I would have had a lot more respect for Clinton if he had done what he had promised and lost, than getting what he and Barney Frank and others say was a half-victory. There are people in the military who came out because they believed his promises. Well, that issue was not the reason I voted for him. But I will vote against him because of that issue.

Z: You said that people have been telling you that you seem to be a happier person these days.
L: Yeah. My friend Tracy Thorne, he's told me on the phone that David Mixner says there's been a big change over me. And some other people, too, said I look a lot happier since I've been out here. Which is probably true.
Z: You've just come back from North Carolina. I'm told there's a big difference between the East Coast Marine Corps and the West Coast Marine Corps. Do you think it's a lot harder for Marines to be gay in North and South Carolina than it is in Southern California?
L: It's different. Before I left, I was starting to meet a few gay enlisted Marines, and they had their own little community. They all went to the beach together, and they'd go out to what local bars there were. I'm sort of a big city person, so it was more frustrating for me; I wanted to participate in more urban gay community things. I wanted to join a gay running club, or a gay scuba diving club, or a gay hiking club. It's not that I feel that I have to be in gay organizations, but I wanted the option. And there were no options out there. There, instead of developing what you'd like to be, you have to accept what's available.

Z: Of course there are more above-ground gay meeting places here in San Diego, but another guy I interviewed who was leaving Camp Pendleton for Lejeune thought that he might find more opportunities for sex there, in underground places that don't tend to exist as much here, where people are more likely to feel forced to either surface as "gay," or not do anything at all.

L: There's a big difference between officers and enlisted. I don't live in a barracks. I don't hang around with a hundred and fifty other guys my age that I can explore possibilities with. I lived out in town, by myself. I worked with mostly other officers, who were all married and have families. As an officer, I was suspect among the enlisted, when I did run into enlisted people out in town, or in the one bar. Unless I was introduced by somebody else. And even when they knew who I was, I was still not let all the way in. When you did go out, half the crowd wanted to go to bed with you because you were an officer, and the other half wanted to stay away from you because you were an officer. There weren't a whole lot of people who wanted to know you as a person.

Z: How does it make you feel when people are sexually attracted to you as a Marine Corps officer?

L: It doesn't make me feel very good. I guess I can understand maybe some of what women complain about, in some ways. Anyone who wanted to be friends with me, I was immediately suspicious of their reasons. I actually stopped going out as much, because, if you did meet somebody, and if you did spend time with them, and afterwards you found out you were right, it was just a one-time notch-on-the-bedpost deal just because you were an officer—it didn't make me feel good.

Z: Did you feel objectified?

L: Yeah. I just . . . I'm an officer in the Marine Corps, and there is the pride, the respect, everything that comes with that. I do my job, and I'm very professional. But as a person, my picture of me is not as an officer in the Marine Corps. It's just like being gay: it's only a part of me, it's not the whole of me. And the problem is, going out some places, that's all you were. You were nothing else. I think it's kind of sad. Because you're a lot of things. You may be a philosopher, a lover, a good runner, great at handicrafts, or whatever.

Z: But I've observed that many Marines, at least the younger ones, seem to want to be looked at, and don't seem to mind so much being reduced to objects. They've built themselves up and they want an audience for it.

L: Yeah, well, probably when I was one or two years in the Marine Corps I was [of that attitude]. Junior enlisted, just like junior officers, probably feel that same way. But after a few years—and I think you see that in the officer corps; the more senior an officer becomes, the more . . . really relaxed an individual he is. I don't know if it's that he's not as concerned about promotion, or if he's just more comfortable with who he is. After thirty or forty or fifty years, you are what you are. There's not much more you can do to change it.

Z: Since coming out, has your view of what is masculine become any less rigid?

L: I think I'm not as concerned about whether or not I'm portraying somebody else's view of masculinity. I'm no longer concerned about projecting a particular image. I'm not gonna deceive. I've even gone as far as—another officer who worked for me made some fairly stupid remarks about gays. In fact, we were out in the field, showering in a tent, and he started spouting off that this was one reason why he would never allow gays in the military, because he would never shower next to a homosexual. After mouthing under my breath, "Too late," I challenged him right there. I said, "Why does it matter to you?" "Huh?" "If you're comfortable in your own sexuality, what should it matter to you if you're showering next to somebody who's gay? You've got a wife and a kid. If you're happy with that, why should it bother you?"

Z: Why do you think it does?

L: [Pause.] Him, I think it actually does bother, but most people I think are usually just saying what they think other people expect to hear. And you can tell that sometimes, when you challenge them and they quickly acquiesce and agree to your point of view. He still wasn't willing to relent. But after a year of me challenging him every time he said anything that was antigay, I have a feeling he probably thinks I'm gay. He's probably pretty certain about it. Which, if his views are really what he feels, must be driving him nuts, because I know he respected me; he worked for and admired and liked me, and we'd go work out together and everything else. It must have driven him crazy, trying to reconcile that with his views. Which is good. Out of conflict comes growth.

Z: But what is there about being looked at in the shower that is so threatening?

L: I don't know. . . . The thought of possibly being put in the position—[laughs] which position I'm not sure!—put in a position where you're not in control. Maybe it's the white man image of being in power, and sex being a way to wield that power; to actually think that somebody is willing to give up that power, or to use that power on you, challenges everything you believe.

Z: Speaking of positions . . .

L: [Laughs.]

Z: "Straight" white males aren't the only ones to have preconceived notions. I expect that over the last couple of years, as you've met gay guys and told them that you're a Marine, you've probably been confronted with certain sexual stereotypes about Marines.

L: [Laughs.] Yeah.

Z: How widespread is that?

L: What, the rumors, or the actuality? I don't know how many people buy into it, but everybody is aware of the popular . . . [Laughs.]

Z: . . . Stereotype that all Marines are bottoms?

L: Pretty much.

Z: Might there be some truth behind that idea?

L: I have absolutely no idea. One thing that I've kind of learned—and maybe for a long time it was because I had my own preconceived notions about life, family, God, country, and everything else—probably about eighty percent of my preconceived notions or ideas or viewpoints got severely challenged, and a lot of them got discarded or changed. So now I don't listen to a whole lot of rumors, and I'm not willing to form an opinion one way or another because I know that so many things are not what I thought they were. I take every person as an individual.

In evading your questions, am I demonstrating any capabilities for public service yet? [Laughs.]

Z: [Laughs.] I think so. But of course you're right that this stereotype is just that. But if there *were* some truth behind it, why do you think that would be? What explanation could there be for violating thousands of years of cross-cultural homosexual military tradition that dictates that the more masculine, senior, and powerful guy always has to be on top?

L: I think a lot of the reason, if it is true that Marines would be all bottoms, or be willing to surrender control of power, and be subjugated, or whatever terms you want to put in there, probably just comes from the fact that their job, their profession, is built upon a hierarchical structure where rank gives you power, and everything is very male dominant, and so focused on that. The way to counter that—surrendering those things allows you probably to reveal yourself to other people, or at least to find balance, or just to work on that part of you that's not developed. I know that, for myself, in the military, everything I do is so strictly regimented, that on my off-time, I'm the opposite. . . . And, you know, as to whether or not the question was going to come up what my preferences might be—which I'm sure is one of the questions that is lurking in there! Or at least you're trying to get me to volunteer that information. [Pause.] Uh, personally . . . as you lean forward as the great secret is about to come out!

Z: Don't say that. Remind me to tell you afterward about one reviewer's fantasy about my interviewing methods.

L: The military life, and my life as a whole, has been very nonemotional and very Spock-like, and so regimented that when I'm with somebody, what I need most is just to be close with them. I don't have, on my side, any preconceived likes or dislikes. There may be things I haven't done yet, but it's not necessarily because I don't want to. I just haven't had the opportunity. Sometimes you meet people and they have preconceived notions about you, and they don't give you the chance to explore other options! [Laughs.]

Z: Some other Marines I've talked to have told me that they view being penetrated as masculine. One guy quoted a DI aphorism that "pain is weakness leaving the body."

L: There really is a difference between officers and enlisted, both in shared experiences, and where they draw their views from. I didn't go through boot camp. I went through six months of officer training, which was equally challenging. But it wasn't necessarily as harsh. You got yelled at—

Z: Were you ever physically struck?

L: No. So, you know, there's—I dislike drawing differences between officers and enlisted because I've met enlisted people who were every bit as good as, and better than, some officers. But we do have different shared experiences. They may draw things from a harsh DI, where I didn't have a DI at all. So I don't have that in my background to pull from. I've been yelled at by generals and colonels, and that's not a pleasant experience either. But it's certainly nothing to fantasize about! [Laughs.]

L: In the Marine Corps, if there's one single theme, or counsel, that goes throughout your career, it's: "Don't disgrace the Corps." No matter what you do. You can get away with a lot, but that's one thing that is just burned into you. And again, whether that comes from people who don't want to tarnish the image, or whether you think you're held to a higher ideal. . . . Marines, we have an image and a reputation we're proud of, and we don't like to do anything tht detracts from that.

Z: And you feel that way just as much as any other Marine.

L: Yeah. That doesn't mean that, pushed into a corner—If they found out I was gay, and they said, "We'll give you an option: you can resign quietly and go on your way, or you can make noise and we'll prosecute you and put you in prison," I would scream my loudest and make it as public as possible, because I know that's what the Marine Corps fears the most, and that's where my safety would lie.

There's very little I've ever been ashamed of. And I will not allow anybody to make me ashamed of being gay.

Z: In our first conversation, you said that women shouldn't be in combat because as lifegivers they shouldn't be subjected to the horrors of taking life. When you talked about the bonding among aviators, you explained it in strictly functional terms. But being a pilot, like being a Marine, is a terribly butch thing. For a man to feel "masculine" is to feel powerful. You said that excluding women from combat did not mean relegating them to a "lower caste." But feminists would say that only by calling women "nurturing lifegivers" can you elevate yourself as "protecting," as powerful lifetaker. They would say that the maintenance of masculinity, and the advantages you glean from it, requires that "asymmetrical binary opposition."

L: [Pause.] My views haven't changed any. And I did express them to some women, and they did express their displeasure with me. But I have since realized that I have to allow people to do whatever they feel they want to do. I was raised to believe that women don't [take life]; that's inherent in me. Some of those feelings will not change. What has changed is, where maybe before I would not allow them the opportunity to be the warrior, now I will not deny them the opportunity. It's still something I'm uncomfortable with.

Z: You told me that the opposition among aviators to women flying in combat is virtually unanimous.

L: Yeah. I don't know that it's threatening to their masculinity. It blurs the differences in sexuality; that's what makes people uncomfortable. It's probably why straight men don't want gay men with them. Because things become a lot more complex. You can't just hug the guy and think nothing of it. Now you're huggin' the guy and thinkin', "maybe he likes this." If there were a female pilot in the squadron, would she be as accepted as everyone else? No. Why? Because now you've got to watch your p's and q's. You can no longer be foul-mouthed, and tell degrading jokes and stories about women, and use derogatory female terms to abuse men good-humoredly. Things become more complex, and we have to become more civil. Maybe the ability to get back to as primal a stage as possible— it's like undoing your belt, and maybe the top button of your pants after having a good dinner: it allows you to relax. You no longer have to suck the stomach in, you're no longer bound by social customs, you can just be a fat slob. Now, with a woman, you're gonna have to shave all the time. Some woman [reading this] is gonna say that that's the most sexist thing she's ever heard! But again, it's the way I was raised and how I was taught to act around women. You can't pat [a woman aviator's] ass. It just makes [all the guys] insecure.

Z: The guys—the pilots—they hug each other and pat each other's asses?

L: Because they can at least pretend there's nothing in it, and there's nothing taken by it.

Z: Do you have any observation on whether they might get some homoerotic kick out of—

L: No.

Z: I'm not talking about them necessarily getting hard, or jacking off fantasizing about it later, but just some erotic charge that would be spoiled by having—

L: No, I've never thought about it that way.

Z: So you don't see any pleasure in the bonding independent of its function, any pleasure at all which that function might sometimes be an excuse for?

L: I think that there's no denying the fact that everybody likes to belong to a club. When we were little kids, we had a boys club where the girls weren't allowed.

Z: In my neighborhood, all the boys had a tree house, and they had regular circle jerks in there. I'd read about homosexuality in Ann Landers' [advice column], and so was too inhibited to participate.

L: [Laughs.]

Z: Have you ever observed anything like *love* among these bonding pilots?

L: [Pause.] I see affection between guys. And you see more of it when they get drunk. More of the civilization goes away, to where you can grab your buddy and give him a big kiss and say, "I love you, man." You're both as drunk as a skunk, you're allowed to do that. But again, I'm not an outside observer, so it's really hard for me to make an objective statement.

Z: Did you ever feel that you wanted to distance yourself from those situations because you were afraid of perceiving them as sexual?

L: Uh, yes. I am more aware, and so aware now—some other guy may feel it's okay to pat another guy on the ass, or to give him a big kiss, but I would never do that for fear of it being interpreted wrong, because I am gay. Just like—On board ship, there was this one Navy pilot; he used to wear a skirt all the time. Every port we went into, he'd get dressed up in a dress at some party, and everybody thought it was a hoot. I would never be caught dead doing that. I don't think I'd look good in a dress! And I'd be afraid of somebody saying, "That looks just a little too comfortable on him."

Z: Did the Navy pilot look good in a dress?

L: [Laughs.] Yeah, he did. He had the legs for it. So, but I don't know how much of my discomfort is because I'm concerned with discovery. I've dealt with that; it's not something I fear. It may be just the way I was raised, in a very strict, traditional religious family. No men wore skirts. [Laughs.] Other than priests!

Corporal Jack:
Smell of Masculine Marine

From notes written on board the southbound Amtrak to San Diego returning from Oceanside after my interview with Corporal Jack:

I hate cars. I love trains. It was in a sleeping car on the U.S. Army duty train to West Berlin one night in the mid-1980s that I met a handsome blond young Checkpoint Charlie MP from Southern California. We were traveling west, me to my home, he to the Frankfurt airport to fly to his stateside fiancée. Falling into conversation, the MP surprised me with vivid anecdotes about his job: the characters who haunted the wall, the Kreuzberg anarchists who dropped flower pots on the Army jeeps, how he would sit atop a hill and stare down into workaday East Berlin. . . . He asked about me and I told him I was in a band. He wanted to know what kind of music. I made to dismiss the question: GIs with their penchant for bloated corporate rock were unlikely to understand my arcane musical tastes. He offered: "My favorite band is Sparks." This astonished me. The quirky Mael brothers had produced one of my all-time favorite albums, the obscure 1974 "Propaganda."

The MP from California and I talked all the way to the border. Finally, eyeing me as he slipped off his pants and turned off the light, he said, "I think you'd like California."

Again and again I had made this mistake, assuming that soldiers were other *from me, had different interests, different desires. . . .*

Before I started to dress and cut my hair like GIs, I tried for a while to dress like a European. One day at the sports store, a black soldier looked me up and down critically, and demanded: "Are you even American?" Affronted by his tone, I answered, "I'm from Grand Rapids, Michigan." He looked askance and muttered, "Oh. I'm from Muskegon." I admitted that I had been born there.

Now, despite having cohabited with Corporal Alex for more than a year, I felt myself thinking—felt myself *wanting to think*—of Marines as mysterious, as outside my life, as *other.* . . .

Jack and I had met at a party only a few nights before. He was due to leave for a distant reassignment a few days after. In our fleeting but spirited acquaintance we established a few surprising commonalities—and some polar oppositions.

The very boyish-looking 30-year-old white Marine punctuated his words with ellipses so sustained they almost threatened to evanesce us both into the pastel Pacific sunset hues that warmed the Carlsbad surfer bar where we shared a parting Sierra Nevada Ale. . . .

Jack: I've lived in Southern California all my life. I was born in Newport Beach. That's pretty close to [Marine Corps Air Station] El Toro, and I can remember, when I was four or five, watching the jets. The Vietnam War was still going on at the time, but being that young you're immune; you don't grasp it. I used to see on TV—they were talking about the guerrillas, and I thought "What the hell are *apes* doing . . . ?" But I had the little GI Joe [points to GI Joe doll with USMC shirt atop his TV set], and I'd see the Marine Corps jets flying overhead. That was my first exposure to the military.

I came from an upper middle-class family. My dad was a commercial real estate developer, and my mom went into residential real estate, which did really well in Southern California. We moved to San Diego, to Del Mar, in '73. And I remember driving up to my grandparents' house in L.A. and passing through Camp Pendleton. You'd see the helicopters . . . the Marines staging assaults and what not. It looked like fun.

In '80, '81, when we were all sixteen, my one friend had a van, and we kind of fancied ourselves [indicates magazine on his coffee table] *Soldier(s) of Fortune.* That was the name of our little club. On the news today, they're talking about paramilitary organizations [following the April 1995 bombing of the Oklahoma City federal building], but we were just kids having fun . . . it was neat.

So, I liked the idea of the military, but it seemed like the defense of this country was left to people who didn't have a choice: the nothings in the world. I was supposed to go to college and become a real estate developer.

Zeeland: Growing up, when were you first conscious of what you later came to see as a gay desire?

J: [Laughs.] [Pause.] It is somewhat telling, I guess. In second grade. We had, as boys will do, little armies. I was a general of my army in elementary school at Newport Beach. I remember this kid named Brian. He was not in my army, and I wanted people that knew him to more or less recruit him. There was something about him that I wanted to associate with. And I can remember as early as first grade feeling that way towards other guys. At the time you don't know what it is, but . . . some sort of feeling.

Z: Did you feel that this was somehow different from what you thought the other boys might be feeling?

J: [Pause.]

Z: Playing army is certainly a conventionally masculine activity for a little boy. Did you feel that you were normal?

J: I remember putting on my mother's lipstick. God, I hope that's normal! Just experimenting. I never felt the supposed power—all men are aware that women have this tremendous power, just by being what they are. I didn't feel that. I wasn't aware that there was that power. I was. . . . I don't know if I was masculine.

Z: Were you ever called a sissy?

J: No. No. But oddly enough, I don't know that I would have cared. I don't think it would have affected me because I wouldn't have known the implications. I didn't know that I was different. . . .

By junior high school, when you go to gym for the first time, you get to see your peers . . .

Z: Naked.

J: Yes. And by that time most people are aware of sexual arousal. Maybe not identity, but it's normal in puberty and—I had no attraction to women whatsoever. And a growing curiosity about men. When I was younger I used to like the way they looked. Now, it was stimulating in other ways.

One of my best friends—in fact the one who drove the van in our high school group—turned out to be gay. And he had movies and magazines. I thought that was pretty neat. I was pretty naïve at the time. I would see a gay porno movie, and think, "Well, I don't know how much they pay these guys, but they're good looking and masculine, so obviously they can't be gay." That was at eighteen and nineteen.

My first actual sexual encounter—he had just gotten out of the army. I know you're gonna draw a parallel there. [Laughs.] He worked at a restaurant that I worked at. It was Halloween, 1983. I was nineteen, he was maybe twenty-four. This guy invited me over to his house, and while I may not have been sexually attracted to him, we had a sort of sex. He was proud of his honorable discharge certificate, and I didn't know what the hell it was. But by that time he had a moustache and long hair, so I didn't really associate him with the military.

In college there was certainly a lot to look at. I had tremendous crushes on baseball players, and would go watch the games. But I never did anything. I had friends who were girls, and even a girlfriend.

Was I ever sexually attracted to women? I would have to say I'm capable.... Ronald Reagan Junior had a talk show, briefly. I think the first show was about being gay. He had Michelangelo Signorelli on there, who said "I've heard stories about you at Yale!" "Oh really? It never happened. I don't care what you call me, but you're insulting my wife." Quentin Crisp was on the panel. He didn't really say a lot, but he did say, "Men are not homosexual or heterosexual. They are sexual." And I think that's very true. I consider myself a hundred percent gay. But I was able to be aroused by having a girlfriend, like I think straight men can be sexually aroused by another man.

Z: After you decided that you would call yourself gay, did you still feel remnants of the idea that gayness was antithetical to masculinity?

J: No. Not at all. It was probably the movies.

Z: The porn?

J: Yeah. Once I saw that [the actors] were attractive, masculine, and gay, I accepted that pretty quickly. My friend who had them was the one who first took me out to the bars. And I saw for myself that [laughs] while [masculine gay men] may not have been the majority, they did exist.

J: When I came out, in late '86, and started experiencing gay men and gay bars, I felt no attraction whatsoever to military personnel. I had an aversion, even a repulsion, to military personnel.

Z: You'd see sailors and Marines in the bars?

J: Oh yeah. Lots.

Z: What was it about them that turned you off?

J: It was my perception that their lot was something I shouldn't associate with.

Z: What kind of men were you attracted to at that point?

J: Oh, probably preppies. Being from Newport Beach. . . .

Z: College boys?

J: Yeah. A friend of mine would tell me he met somebody that was in the Navy; I'd go "Eww." He'd say, "They're the best! They're clean-cut, they have a job, and they get tested for HIV every six months, so they're pretty much clean. And they're masculine." That kind of . . . germinated that thought, I guess. Because I . . . I like masculine men. Definitely.

Z: How did that thought grow into a particular image, or a particular military man?

J: I remember my first experience. It was—do you know what the "Fruit Loop" is? [It's a gay meeting place in] Balboa Park, right under where the planes come in to land at Lindbergh Field. Aviation is a masculine thing. I have a lot of appreciation for military machinery. I love watching big jets. There was a Navy boy sitting there outside of his car with the stereo going. Six months before that day, his occupation would have been enough to disqualify him. (In fact, six months before then, a sailor named Allan came up to me in [a San Diego gay dance club] and handed me a beer. He was a very attractive man. We were talking, and I was courteous, but not interested because he was in the Navy.) By the time I met the sailor in the park, my attitude had changed. . .

It was a whole new experience. He had his initials stencilled on his underwear. Everything that lay ahead was learning. It was a decent experience, but even if it was a bad experience, I probably would have continued. It was a natural point where I was headed.

Z: So that then became part of your fantasies?

J: I don't know that I had a vivid enough imagination to fantasize about—do you mean the whole *Top Gun* locker room male bonding? The fantasy of being part of a group? It took some time to want to become a part of that. But when it happened, I made up my mind, dammit, and no one was gonna talk me out of it. I didn't get recruited. I walked in and knew what I wanted.

It was early 1989, the economy was still going really strong, and I had a management job in a land title insurance company. Made good money, got a new car, went to work Monday through Friday, eight to five. I did well at it. [Laughs.] You know, I was a yuppie. I had a Rolex [watch], I had Armani ties, the whole conspicuous consumption thing.

Z: Fulfilling your family's expectations.

J: Yeah. I guess in most of America joining the military is an accepted thing. In my instance joining the military was an act of rebellion.

You probably want to know why I joined the military, and why I chose the Marine Corps. If I'm going to be honest with myself, there was a certain amount of eroticism. From early '87 to my decision in the summer of '89, in that two-year period—I wasn't exclusively attracted to military men, but it definitely grew. And I would go up to Oceanside on weekends. Never connected. But I would observe—I even got my hair cut shorter to see if I could kind of like, assimilate. (I realize now that's probably a detriment. If you're trying to cruise a Marine, he'll be more wary of a fellow Marine unknown to him.)

One time I had been with my brother in a shooting range, and I was wearing camouflage pants that I bought at a thrift store; they were old faded ones like you see guys with pony tails wearing in the malls. Now, the camouflage utility uniform is not authorized for leave or liberty. And certainly you don't wear it with tennis shoes and a T-shirt. So I was ignorant and I was in Oceanside, and I remember a guy telling me, "Hey devil dog, you're not allowed to wear your cammies out in town!" The lingo in just that small sentence . . . what's a "devil dog," "cammies," and "out in town?" And that was neat. [Laughs.] Because, you know, it was fraudulent, but I felt like I was part of . . . That's a term of affection, "devil dog." I liked it. And then shortly after that, I did join. Which was kind of a shock to my family, and certainly to many of my friends. [Laughs.] What I do is definitely a far cry from what most of my peers do, unless they went to Annapolis or West Point.

Z: So off you went to boot camp. In your own backyard.

J: Right there at the airport. I could identify all the buildings in downtown [San Diego]. I could get up on the rapelling tower and look out over at Point Loma. After the first couple weeks at MCRD, we went to Camp Pendleton, and rode on Interstate 5 right past my house. . . .

You hear taps at ten o'clock at night for the first time: wow. I'm here. I wonder what's gonna happen? They want to strip you, figuratively and literally, of all your civilian ways. And make you talk, and react, and think the way they want you to. That's the purpose of boot camp. I liked it. In a weird way I definitely miss . . . the last week or so, it was so familiar . . . For eighty days it was part of you. In some ways, you're as close to these people as you'll ever be to anyone. It brings you together. You are a unit. You're eighty people working as one.

You go through a week called "receiving." They process you, start your medical records, issue you everything. And then you get assigned to a platoon. And the first day of that, the senior drill instructor came up and asked for me by name out of the eighty people. Uh-oh! He announced to me that, according to some test, I was the smartest in the platoon, and that I would therefore be the secretary, the "scribe." I had a lot of clerical duties, making rosters and whatnot. So having everyone think that I was the smartest, and being seven years older than most of them—I was kind of in the limelight. I would have preferred to be somewhat anonymous.

Z: You enlisted with a probably somewhat different perspective from most of the other recruits. Do you feel that you bonded with them fully despite that?

J: [Pause.] Not really. [Pause.]

Z: Were they as successful in breaking down your identity and building you up as—

J: No. Definitely not. I mean, by twenty-five you're pretty much. . . . I wasn't a scared, naïve eighteen-year-old just out of high school. So it probably didn't have the entire desired effect.

Z: You must have still found it intimidating at times.

J: I don't really know that I was intimidated.

Z: No? Being shouted at constantly. . . .

J: You kind of become immune to it, build a shell or whatever. You don't take it personally.

Z: Were you ever physically struck?

J: No. Like I was talking to you earlier about *Full Metal Jacket*—I kind of wish it was more like that. If someone's doing something really stupid, and you can't get through to them . . . Not that it makes you a man to be able to be hit, but it may stop them from being so stupid.

Z: What happened with your sexuality at boot camp?

J: There's a rumor, which they deny, that they put saltpeter in the food. Some people say it's the shots they give you—they give you so many shots, you don't even know what they all are, you're just a pin cushion. I was able to identify people I was attracted to, but it was never arousal. Never masturbated until we got to the field.

Out in the field, in a shelter half, each individual—everything in boot camp is teamwork. You never think just for yourself, you always consider what ramifications any action you might take will have on everybody else. It's the buddy system throughout. They call it a "shelter half," because each man has half a tent in his possession, half the tent stakes required to put up a tent, half the poles. So when he's coupled with another guy they make the whole. It's a two-man tent. I was in that at night, and felt really horny, and I definitely was needing to take care of myself. And so in that very confined space for two people I—quietly—just kind of rolled over on my side and . . . It's a dirt floor, so.

In the field in boot camp, as part of the ritual, to build trust (it's not titled "today we're gonna learn how to trust someone else," but it's one of those subtle things that builds up to that in the end), you are shaved by and you shave another recruit. And that's a weird thing. I thought it was weird. But most of these guys aren't really experienced with shaving, so maybe it was just because I was older that it seemed weird for me to have someone shave me. . . .

I like being out of doors. It wasn't camping, but it was neat. I liked all of boot camp. And I like the field. Even to this day. In the air wing, I'm looked at as a freak of nature for liking it, because you're always dirty, dusty; you're gonna get dirt in your food; your hands are never clean; you shave with cold water. . . .

Z: So you did think of yourself as being different from other Marines all along?

J: All alone?

Z: All along.

J: Yeah, I suppose. For a number of factors.

When I actually went out into the fleet marine force after my school and everything, I got the job I wanted and discovered that I really didn't want it. The air wing is a lot different from the rest of the Marine Corps. There's weak leadership, there's no attention to grooming standards, appearance. When you work on a thirty million dollar jet, they don't want you to be sweating about insignificant little details that aren't pertinent to safety. And unfortunately—it sounds paradoxical, but when you don't have respect for other people, or it's not enforced—it lowers morale. You basically are just a low-paid, harassed, overworked jet mechanic employed by the Marine Corps. You don't have a lot of esprit de corps. There's a lot of back stabbing. It's unfortunate and I wish I could change it. I don't belong in the air wing, but that's the only thing they'll let me do.

Z: Have there been any times when you have felt the famous brotherhood with other Marines?

J: Yeah, to a limited extent. But never to the extent that the grunts trust each other with their lives. A pilot will come out and I'll strap him in, answer any of his questions. "Is this supposed to be loose?" He'll trust me in that sense. But I don't think we get as close. I also think the air wing has more intelligent people so they're kind of into their own pursuits. Grunts are individuals too, but their job is to be confined with and really know each other. A squad leader in the grunts can tell you about any of his men: their birthdays, their educational background, where they're from, whether they have children. It's part of his job. In the air wing, you get up, take a shower, and go to work; you come back and do whatever you do. I didn't know it at the time, or I really would have chosen something else. I'm almost an outcast because I desire—I'd rather be a grunt. For the closeness.

J: [Indicates photo in a Navy roommate's cruise book depicting a line of men undergoing the "crossing the line" initiation, each man holding the genitals of the man before him.] That's called the "elephant walk." It's also done naked. Very fraternal!

Z: Do Marines ever get to do anything like that?

J: When you pick up rank, they put your new rank on your collar, they don't put the backings on the pins, and with an open palm drive them into your collar bone. A lot of times when you pick up NCO you get "blood stripes," [symbolizing] the red stripe on the trousers of your dress blues. I have a videotape of people in shorts getting their blood stripes: you knee the person in the side of the thigh where the blood stripes would be. So you've just had metal pins driven into your collar bone, then you go through a gauntlet, on either side there's guys and they punch you with their fists, very hard. It's all officially prohibited.

In the air wing, we take—it's called ordnance tape. It's about four inches wide, very sticky stuff that we use to hold stuff together, and if it's someone's birthday, or they're getting out of the Marine Corps, or any number of reasons, we'll grab them, and put them on the bottom of a dog pile; many other individuals jump on top—it's called "stacking." We mummify some people! Pilots' last flights, we grab them as they get out of the aircraft, we tape them into a chair, and put tech-pet, which is technical petrolatum, in their hair. We pour Speedy Dry down the back of their flight suits; it's like cat litter, we use it to clean up oil spills. Take 'em out on the wash rack, where you wash jets, and stick a hose down the front of their shirt. It's great fun. Everyone gathers around and cheers and yells.

Z: When was the first time you had genital sex with another Marine?
J: [Laughs.] [Pause.] It was just over a year after I went to boot camp before I was permanently stationed doing my job in the Marine Corps. I had come from North Carolina back to San Diego, my hometown, and went out to [a gay dance club]. Walked in, and almost immediately saw what looked like a jarhead. I went up and talked to him. He was in fact a Marine. He was, in fact, masculine and very handsome. And he was, in fact, what used to be the sailor who bought me the beer several years earlier. It was Allan. He'd gotten out of the Navy and joined the Marine Corps! In life, you don't get a lot of second chances. So not only was it the first time I had sex after I became a Marine, it was the first time I had sex with a Marine. And that's what I wanted. They were now my brothers.

It turned out he was stationed in my new unit. The next night was the Marine Corps birthday ball. I had been with this unit for one day, and he and I sat at my unit's table next to my commanding officer. It was kind of neat to gloat and think, "If you guys only knew."

This was shortly after the invasion of Kuwait. Within a month Allan left for Saudi Arabia. I was not scheduled to go. I volunteered. I ended up over there. We both got back within a week of each other. We were pretty much just friends after that. Today we're roommates.
Z: Did you meet other gay Marines through him?

J: Through him, and on my own.

Z: Would you say now that you're part of a clique?

J: Yeah. A network. It's always refreshing. There are quite a few out there. And more every day!

Z: Are there "straight" men who are included in this network?

J: Yeah. Some are exclusively heterosexual, not experimenting, and some do so under confused circumstances. They know what's going on, but they deny it to the extent that it's not discussed.

Z: And they would be reluctant to answer my questions on tape about it?

J: [Laughs.] Correct.

Z: I'm guessing that when you joined the Marine Corps, you hoped to have sex with Marines who aren't necessarily "gay."

J: Yeah. When I was a civilian, I thought it would be different if I could somehow infiltrate from the outside. I knew it didn't work very well as a civilian posing as a Marine. It had a backfiring effect. [Laughs.] I would be walking around Oceanside with short hair, looking for other young men with short hair, and I became a target myself. By doing that I would have the old men in Mercedes asking me if I needed a ride.

If it's after two in the morning and there is a lone Marine walking down Hill Street, it would be interesting to observe from a distance exactly how many times he's offered a ride by these predators. And I can't be every-where at once, so I can't say they're not getting those rides.

Z: There must be some awareness among Marines that that goes on.

J: Definitely.

Z: Is it ever talked about?

J: No.

In any Marine's career, at one point or another, they're going to come through here. And if they ever take the bus out in town, and if they ever walk around—I think it would be hard not to notice what's going on. There's a lot of older gentlemen driving around in nicer cars who are very friendly. [Laughs.]

Z: Who you told me you detest.

J: Detest? That's much too pleasant a word. They're only twice my age.

Z: Is it their age that bothers you?

J: Their modus operandi. When I say predators, it's not a euphemism. They are like birds of prey. What they'll do is sit in a parked car across from the bookstore and wait until they see a young Marine walk in, and then they jump out of the car and run across the street. I was in this bookstore Saturday night and saw some salt-and-pepper-haired man walk up to a very large drunk Marine and hand him some of the tokens that are used in the video booths in the back. Which is where [the chaser] can determine whether or not [he] stands a chance, because if [the Marine is] receptive to eye contact, or not protesting the proximity—it's a weeding-out process. This man is so bold—it's incredible. I know that this man has been *shot*. I'm sure they've all been beaten up. And at risk to life and limb, they continue to do it. Oceanside is not a pretty town. It's got one of the highest murder rates anywhere. And they don't care.

I just hate to think that I could ever become that. But obviously, tastes change, or I wouldn't be here. So, I think I have some control over it.

Z: You did tell me that you had two recent successes of your own in meeting straight Marines. Tell me your modus operandi.

J: They're waiting at the bus stop. It's night time. I have a red sticker, a DOD decal, which allows me to get on base, which fortunately none of the predators have. So that's my little advantage that I have over them that doesn't require boldness. I don't even have to roll the window down; I can just pull up. It's also less threatening, I think. I'm obviously a Marine, so that's either good or bad, but I'll go up to the bus stop and ask if they need a ride. Then we just cruise around, look at all the hookers, laugh at 'em. Drive around, talk. Get to be . . . friends. Find out where they're from, what they do. [Laughs.] You can tell if they're nice guys or not. And then—it gets towards two o'clock, you need to buy beer if you're going to buy beer, so you go buy the beer. You need a place to drink it. I have a place. We come here. Maybe talk some more. Drink some more beer. If we've got food, eat the food. Maybe watch a straight porno . . .

[The tape side ends.]

Z: Have you had any close buddy relationships with "straight" Marines?

J: Oh yeah.

The Marine Corps is two hundred and eighteen years old. The Continental Congress in 1775 raised two battalions of Marines. So they're older than the United States. The Marine Corps was founded in a place called The Tun Tavern in Philadelphia. So it was started in a bar! Like these militia they're talking about on the news: a couple guys sitting around drinking, they agree on something. And the first Marines were embarked on ships in the Navy. They were paid with rum. [Laughs.] So you have a long history of the Marine Corps as a drinking organization. And unfortunately now, due to Tailhook and drunk driving and political correctness—it's not p.c. to drink a lot anymore. But it's still an integral part of Marine Corps life and they can never do away with it. You go to a squadron party, there better damn well be a keg of beer! That will never change.

This buddy of mine, Bill—we were drinking buddies. I met him about a month after I got to school. We became really good friends. We were assigned to work on the same type of aircraft, so we went through another six months of school together. He got married. Then we were both stationed [at the same base, in the same squadron] and we got even closer.

Bill had some . . . effeminate traits to him. We went on a six-month deployment. We went to the gym a lot, and we drank a lot. We had . . . a really deep friendship. And—beds in the Marine Corps are not big. Sometimes he would come and get in my bed with me. I don't really know why.

Z: Would he hold you?

J: [Pause.] Well—he would put his arm around me. Yeah. [Laughs.] It's weird.

Z: Did he ever talk about this?

J: No. I remember one time someone knocked on the door to say there was a phone call. It was a Sunday morning, early. I wasn't aware of [laughs] the situation. I remember wondering if they saw us in bed together. It wouldn't have caused any problems if they had . . . But I was pretty much closeted.

Z: You never came out to Bill?

J: No.

Z: You must have wondered how he would respond if you were to . . .

J: One time, to see what it was exactly all about, I went down to his room and got in bed with him. And again, nothing transpired. But it was just close.

He probably knows I'm gay. He was absolutely my closest friend in the Marine Corps. He moved to Oregon after he got out. I still talk to him every once in a while.

J: I'm not an advocate of gay rights, and I'm not going to go out and wear my dress blues to a gay pride parade. At times I've been tempted to [come out to] people. Not necessarily [to] the closest people. I always had— maybe because of my age, and my culture, and my education—some of the traits that make a good officer. But I was sweating it out with the enlisted pukes. They get the short end of the stick every time. They're always getting screwed around with. I always had a lot of—a lot of the younger guys really admired me. So I was kind of torn between telling them and shattering whatever idea they had of what a "fag" was and—I thought if I came out to them, I could really change their perception. "God, I admired him before, and he was gay; it obviously doesn't matter."

Z: But you didn't do that.

J: No.

I had a long discussion with [Lieutenant] Tim [interviewed in *Sailors and Sexual Identity*] about me [staying] in the Marine Corps. And it's hard for him to see my perspective, but one of the questions he asked me was, "Are you reenlisting because the only identity you have is your title 'United States Marine'?" That's a lot to do with it. It's not my only identity, but it's something I've earned. It's respectable. Even though ten years ago I would have not have respected what I now am! It's something that—I feel good about it. I've never been an openly gay person so I've never, I guess, felt good about being gay. But I can feel good about being a Marine. And [laughs] it's a great combination.

Z: This straight man that you were buddies with; you said there were qualities about him that were—
J: Effeminate. It's hard to put a finger on it. He was—masculine. From the Pacific Northwest. Lumberjack type. Physically strong. Very muscular. [Pause.] But something just wasn't—Hard to pinpoint. Hard to define what it was that—I'm not sure. It didn't have anything to do with him getting into bed with me. He just had a certain . . . quality, that—maybe it wasn't so much present, it may have been just lacking. I don't know what it was. He had two kids, so he certainly had proven his virility.
Z: Tell me about your own idea of what is masculine, and what is distinct about Marine masculinity as opposed to other kinds.
J: It's not an intellectual quality. Femininity is possibly part of masculinity in some twisted way. [Pause.] It could be the look of masculinity. The square jaw. The GI Joe doll. He's got a scowl—Marines scowl an awful lot. They really do. Like they're pissed off at something. You may ask them a question, or just observe them, and they look . . . mad. And some of 'em have the biggest dimples and the broadest grins with their sparkling white Wisconsin smiles. The Midwestern ones are, I think, the most attractive, and they tend to be more down to earth. The East Coast—you have a lot of guys from New York, New Jersey; they seem to be a little more intense, as far as—
    I think I'm getting away from the point because it's so difficult to put into words. Masculinity to me means . . . what?
Z: Being attracted to masculinity as you are . . .
J: I should know!
Z: Well, I'm sure you know it when you see it.
J: Maybe I can't define masculinity because . . . maybe that's not even a good title for the quality, but, to me, there's something very attractive about that eighteen-year-old Marine. His cockiness. He's a boy trying to be a killer, a man. And that is—maybe that's what I'm calling masculinity . . .

There's ones even older than me. The captain who signed my orders the other day still had that look. The Marine Corps can age you at an accelerated rate in some ways, but at the same time it keeps you young, by physical fitness.

Z: Are women Marines masculine?

J: Yes.

Z: Is it the same masculinity?

J: It's the same scowl. [Laughs.] I can't, you know—masculinity can't be defined because it's—an aura? Something that's not tangible. You can't see it. You can smell it, maybe. It is a sense. And a scent. There's things you associate with—I don't want to get too Freudian, but as a kid you know what Dad's all about and you know what Mom's all about. And a lot of memories are triggered by senses other than sight. A man doesn't smell like perfume.

Z: But how is the masculine Marine smell different from the sailor or the civilian?

J: That's—[Pause.] It's an image. And there's something extra attractive about a young man trying to exhibit—not that it's a facade, but it's. . . . It's fostered, it's nurtured. In my own instance, definitely.

Z: How masculine are you?

J: I'm not sure. I've been to college, I come from a socioeconomic background that is different, so it's difficult for me to say because I can appreciate a lot of things that might be considered queer. [Pause.] Art, music, food. Those things may not be feminine, but they're certainly not macho.

Z: Are you happy with your own masculinity?

J: [Pause.] I don't think it could hurt to be more masculine. There's things that I could do but they're not me. I don't have any tattoos. I don't have a moustache, which a lot of people think may increase the macho factor. I think it looks too contrived, too obvious. Macho is an image that has little to do with masculinity.

Z: I did notice the other night when I first met you, at that party, that, in talking with the other guys, you could hold your own with campy comebacks.

J: [Looks pained.] Maybe the subject matter was campy, but I inherited my humor and wit from my father. And you can definitely use it every day in the Marine Corps. An odd thing in the Marine Corps is the delight a group of guys take in picking on one guy, especially if he makes it known that it bothers him. It's immature, but it's charming. Where else can you be thirty and act like you're in grade school? [Pause.] Camp is funny. I'm not gonna deny that *Priscilla* [: *Queen of the Desert*] was a hoot, but . . . [Indicates apartment:] I think this place needs to be a little more dirty. I think it needs empty pizza boxes and beer cans!

J: [Poses riddle:] How do you separate the men from the boys in the Italian navy?
Z: I give up.
J: With crowbars!
Z: [Laughs.] Italians have a different idea about what is "gay."
J: They're macho. They may not even be masculine.
Z: For them it may be considered okay for a man to fuck another guy, as long as he's on top and he's masculine. The only people who are identified as queer are men who are effeminate and take the passive position in anal intercourse. What can you tell me about the gay popular stereotype that all Marines are bottoms?
J: That part of my . . . Actual intercourse, either receiving or administering it, is not the most important. . . . Even without intercourse, I could feel very fulfilled sexually. And that doesn't necessarily eliminate a dominant or submissive role. I would say I'm more dominant, but I don't enjoy actually fucking. As close as you can get to it is fine. To an observer it might look like it's taking place.
Z: Between the thighs?
J: Yeah. I feel more in control like that.
Z: Why do you think there is this perception about Marines?
J: Oh, it could be attributed to fantasy . . . maybe it's to say that Marine Corps masculinity is only a facade. "You think you're so butch, but we know the truth." But I don't know. There may be some truth to it . . . You can probably make some generalizations. But Marines are all individuals, and they're all unpredictable.

By actually joining the ranks I figured I would have greater insight into what makes Marines tick, what they're about. And while we have "a common lineage," I'm not any closer to figuring out what they're about! For being as conformist as they appear, and despite the uniformity of their heritage, they are all very much unique. Surprisingly. And I have no idea what makes them tick. [Laughs.] I have no idea.

[The last tape runs out. Jack says: "Sorry to be so elusive."]

Corporal Alex (Coda):
A Parable

Alex: Lance Corporal Matthew was from Los Angeles. Out of the four native Californians in our unit, he was probably the most fucked-up. Everybody always commented on that, because everybody thought that Californians are fucked-up anyway.

Zeeland: What did he look like?

A: Dark eyes, dark hair. He was big. Somewhat attractive. He was pretty stupid. His cammies were never ironed the correct way. They'd tell him the correct way, but he never got it right. He never asked for help. Anyways, he had this iguana. It was a small one, about a foot long. He was keeping it in his room. It was against the rules to have pets in the barracks, but he kept his bed on these extension posts, and stuck the cage under the bed. He draped the bedspread over the end of the rack, so that nobody could see that there was an iguana cage under there.

Matthew had an intimate relationship with the iguana. He was always touching it, and talking to it. He talked sweet to it. "Baby you're so fuckin' beautiful. I wish we could get married." Stuff like that. It struck everybody as odd who overheard him talking sweet to his lizard.

Z: He would promenade with it sometimes?

A: Yeah. Out on the catwalk. It never bit him, but it would bite other people. There was one Marine, and he was from New York City, and he hated the iguana. Just because he didn't like the way it looked. Matthew would set it down and it would run after the guy, and the guy would run away.

Z: And the climax of the story is—

A: I guess Matthew was drunk one night. He came home and he picked her up and she bit him. He was swearing, and crying. "You fucking bitch! You fuckin' betrayed me!" He threw her down, grabbed a broom handle, and proceeded to smash her to pieces. He had left the door open, so everybody heard him. I was just in the next room.

Z: He was weeping?

A: Yeah, afterwards. I think it was just rage at first.

Z: Did you go over and talk to him?

A: No. The MPs came. The duty NCO called them. They took him away. He did love the iguana. But I don't even know how he knew it was a she.

Reference Notes

Prologue

1. *Marine Battle Skills Training (MBST) Handbook, Book 2 PVT-LCPL, Individual Combat Basic Tasks* (Arlington, VA: Marine Corps Institute, 1993), p. 2-21-20.

Introduction

1. See Jonathan Ned Katz, *The Invention of Heterosexuality* (New York: Dutton, 1995). Any use by me of the terms "gay," "heterosexual," etc., in this book should be seen in quotation marks and understood to refer to persons who identify themselves as fitting these categories.

2. America Online [AOL], Military City Online, Active Marine Corps Board/Gays in the Military?, April 15, 1995.

3. Judith Butler, *Gender Trouble: Feminism and the Subversion of Identity* (New York: Routledge, 1990), pp. 24-25.

4. General Robert Barrow, quoted in Chuck Lawliss, *The Marine Book: A Portrait of America's Military Elite* (New York: Thames and Hudson, 1988), p. 86.

5. "Because homosexuality as both desire and behavior rears its head when it shouldn't, the necessity to distinguish the real article from frivolous lapses of locker room playfulness dates back to its earliest conceptions. . . ." But John DeCecco and David Allen Parker point out that *all* human sexual behavior is situational to some extent, "That is, it involves a particular person, and either a fantasized or real partner and it occurs at a particular time and in a specific location and culture. Only if one believes in an innate human sexuality so biologically driven that it demands expression regardless of circumstances and available partners, does the distinction between an innate and an acquired homosexuality have mean-

ing." John P. DeCecco and David Allen Parker, *Sex, Cells, and Same-Sex Desire: The Biology of Sexual Preference* (Binghamton, NY: The Haworth Press, 1995), pp. 12-13.

6. "The communion between [Marines in infantry battalions] is as profound as any between lovers. Actually, it is more so." Phillip Caputo, *A Rumor of War* (New York: Holt, Rinehart and Winston, 1977), p. xv.

"There are few human experiences comparable to the camaraderie and brother-love of a Marine infantry unit in combat." Keith W. Nolan, *Battle for Hue, Tet 1968*, quoted in "No Place for Homosexuals" by Captain Mark E. Cantrell, *Marine Corps Gazette*, April 1993, p. 66.

The need to preserve the putative heterosexual purity of this same-sex love is cited again and again as a reason why gays should not be allowed in the Marine Corps. A Marine Corps sergeant posting to an online message board was vehement: " 'Beloved Marines' is a term of brotherhood. We eat, drink, sleep, bathe, and use the 'head' together. . . . We also die together. . . . Living this commitment 24 hours a day with your fellow Marines takes love. This type of love does not involve any sexual connotations WHATSOEVER! (Pardon my emotional outburst[.])" AOL, November 27, 1994. But a former Marine responded that he had observed "unmistakably homosexual overtones in the Marine Corps. I noticed this most in boot camp, where the drill instructors . . . made countless allusions to homosexual practices, such as 'make the man in front of you smile,' (when we were on line, a __ hole-to-bellybutton; another of their favorite phrases)." AOL, April 15, 1995.

A non-Marine posted a message asking "What would Gunny Hartman (*Full Metal Jacket*) have to say on this subject? I wouldn't want to be the person to call him a 'homophobe'!" AOL, February 23, 1995. But the big screen Sergeant Hartman's one pronouncement on the subject of homosexuality seems a little ambivalent: "I'll bet you're the kind of guy that would fuck a person in the ass and *not even have the goddam common courtesy to give him a reach-around!*" *Full Metal Jacket*, screenplay by Stanley Kubrick, Michael Herr, and Gustav Hasford (New York: Knopf, 1987), p. 8.

7. See Plato, *Symposium* and *Phaedra*; Plutarch, "Dialogue on Love," *Moralia*; K. J. Dover, *Greek Homosexuality* (Cambridge,

MA: Harvard University Press, 1978, 1989); David Halperin, *One Hundred Years of Homosexuality and Other Essays on Greek Love* (New York: Routledge, 1990); Louis Crompton, "An Army of Lovers," *History Today*, November, 1994, p. 23.

8. "In an embarrassing breakdown of communications, the Marine Corps said yesterday that it planned to phase out enlistments of married men and women, only to be reversed hours later by Secretary of Defense Les Aspin. . . . The new edict would have produced the paradoxical situation in which the Marines would have accepted gay recruits—as long as they were quiet about their status—but not married heterosexuals." Clifford Krauss, "Corps Marriage Ban Left Waiting at Altar," *The New York Times* News Service, August 12, 1993.

9. Gore Vidal, Foreword to Katz, p. ix.

10. Plutarch, quoted in David D. Gilmore, *Manhood in the Making: Cultural Concepts of Masculinity* (New Haven, CT: Yale University Press, 1990), p. 155.

11. Ian Buruma, *Behind the Mask: On Sexual Demons, Sacred Mothers, Transvestites, Gangsters, Drifters and Other Japanese Cultural Heroes* (New York: Pantheon, 1984), pp. 127-131, quoted in Gilmore, p. 155. See also Tsumeo Watanbe and Jun'ichi Iwata, trans. D. R. Roberts, *The Love of the Samurai: A Thousand Years of Japanese Homosexuality* (London: Gay Men's Press, 1989).

12. "In the old Norse epics the allegation 'X uses Y as his wife' is an intolerable insult to Y but casts no adverse reflection on the morals of X." Dover, p. 105.

13. Gilmore, p. 155.

14. See for example Joseph Carrier, *De Los Otros: Intimacy and Homosexuality Among Mexican Men* (New York: Columbia University Press, 1995). Carrier writes that a sex partner of Arturo, one of the men he profiles, "was very relaxed about sex and was willing to do anything with Arturo that he would do with a woman. There was plenty of foreplay—kissing and hugging—followed by good anal sex. Arturo had to be careful, however, never to touch the married man's rear end. It was the only thing that would make him angry"; p. 104.

15. See for example my *Sailors and Sexual Identity: Crossing the Line Between "Straight" and "Gay" in the U.S. Navy* (Bingham-

ton, NY: The Haworth Press, 1995) pp. 13-14, 28-34, 36-37, 105-106, 130-132, 141-142, 151, 156-157, 170-171, 258, 295-296.

16. Ibid., pp. 13-14.

17. For example, "In *San Diego Summer* [Seabag Video, 1986], a Marine baits a sailor: 'I've heard that squids like to give head.' The [sailor] replies, 'Yeah? Well, *I* hear that Marines like to take it up the ass.' Whereupon the two set to work testing those hypotheses." Rolf Hardesty, "Reviewing the Troops: A History of the American Military Image in Gay Erotica," (2 parts) *Manshots*, February-March 1990, (March) p. 23.

18. Zeeland, pp. 98-99. A Navy officer told me of meeting a wholesome and virile young Marine on the streets of Oceanside. In bed, the officer was disappointed that the Marine wanted to be penetrated, and he was thoroughly chagrinned when, during the act, the Marine yelled out "Fuck that man-pussy!"

19. Mark Simpson, *Male Impersonators: Men Performing Masculinity* (New York: Routledge, 1994), p. 80.

20. Personal communication via Rolf Hardesty from a Naval lieutenant who keeps a journal of observations on the sexual behavior of sailors and Marines.

21. Marines have a West Coast-East Coast binary, but I am told that visitors to Jacksonville, North Carolina are treated to the same pleasure. Regrettably, my budget for this book did not allow for an inspection of East Coast Marines.

22. Simpson, p. 84. From an article Simpson published in the British gay magazine *Attitude* on cruising in Tijuana: "I came here with the intention of preying upon America's clean-limbed youth while they prey on Mexico. In the sexual food chain I intend to be at the top. But who to choose? Jarheads, squids, or college boys? It only takes a minute to eliminate the college boys (too smug) and the squids (too geeky) and thus decide on the jarheads. There's a certain irresistible poetic justice in the idea of seducing a U.S. Marine, historically the means of projecting U.S. power in Latin America. But, even more persuasively, Marines have a number of classical features which attract them to the homosexual predator. . . . All in all, it's really very thoughtful of the U.S. government to go to the trouble of giving teenage Midwestern boys a decent haircut, making them exercise, depriving them of female company and then sending

them to Southern California—Fagville U.S.A.—where they can bring a little joy into the lives of lonely homosexuals. . . .'"

23. Hardesty, p. 30. "One gay wag went so far as to say, 'If the Corps wants to stop its guys from rolling over, it better change its exercise routine. Doesn't the brass realize that all those deep knee-bends make for itchy prostates?'"

24. Ibid., p. 30. "On a doctor's chart of body types . . . [Athletic Model Guild photographer Robert] Mizer will point to the silhouette labeled 'mesomorph': heavy of frame, powerful of musculature, meaty of ass. He'll point next to a sub-type of mesomorph whose lower limbs show heavier framing than the upper. Then, flipping through a big chunk of his thousands of proof sheets, he'll point out that most of his Marines do in fact fit that sub-type. Thus, in theory, those who have the same body type will be more apt to have a similar sexual response." But of course Mr. Mizer may have sought out, or been delivered, models who represented his ideal Marine type.

Some of Mizer's military models can be seen in *Athletic Model Guild: 160 Young Americans Photographed by Robert Mizer* (Amsterdam: Intermale, 1987), and F. Valentine Hooven, III, *Beefcake: The Muscle Magazines of America 1950-1970* (Cologne: Benedikt Taschen, 1995). For further information, contact AMG, P.O. Box 1732, Alameda, CA 94501.

25. Interview with Scott, April 15, 1995: "There were guys who I met in boot camp who had always known, even when they were in grade school, that they were going to go into the Marine Corps. There were guys in my platoon who already had USMC tattoos before coming to boot camp! And they probably got the most shit from the drill instructors. They would tell this one guy, 'We're gonna kick your ass outta boot camp. You're gonna have to walk around for the rest of your life with a USMC tattoo and you didn't make it through boot camp!'"

26. I worked at MCRD as a civilian employee, briefly.

27. "According to their own publicists, the Marine Corps managed to attract 'a particularly virile strain of young American manhood.'" Craig M. Cameron, *American Samurai: Myth, Imagination, and the Conduct of Battle in the First Marine Division, 1941-1951* (New York: Cambridge University Press, 1994), pp. 25-26. Hollywood images of Marine toughness "were not simply a reflection of an existing reality;

they were a source and a condition of that reality. . . . With the First World War a close liaison began [between Hollywood filmmakers and the Marine Corps] that has lasted up to the present. . . . By providing actual Marines as extras, access to bases and training facilities, and technical advisors, the Marine Corps helped ensure that in movies like *Star Spangled Banner* (1917) and *The Unbeliever* (1918), the service was depicted as an elite organization, combat-ready and professional. Lon Chaney, in the role of a tough drill instructor in *Tell it to the Marines* (1926), served as a prototype illustrating how the Marine Corps turned raw recruit-boys into mature, courageous men"; p. 45. Other film titles of the period include *Leathernecking, Come on Marines,* and *The Marines are Coming.*

28. For a mid-1990s update on these long-standing recruiting strategies, see John F. Harris, "Military Recruiters Find the Enemy is Apathy," *Washington Post,* July 4, 1994, p. A-1.

29. John Calendo, "Down in Oceanside," *In Touch,* September 1982, p. 64.

30. Zeeland, pp. 105-106.

31. "Sexual euphemisms such as 'freaking' and 'frigging' are about as profane as [a 1995 drill instructor] ever becomes. Once notoriously foul-mouthed, Parris Island's drill instructors today are forbidden to use obscenities. At the same time, their recruits arrive steeped in casual vulgarity from pop music, cable TV, and everyday conversation. So it is all the more unnerving to face a DI who appears to be insanely angry—but who never swears. Indeed, physical abuses of the past have resulted in limits on corporal punishment that DIs can mete out; now they lean heavily toward cultural indoctrination." Thomas E. Ricks, "'New' Marines Illustrate Growing Gap Between Military and Society: Corps Instills 'Family Values' And Beavis Finds Himself Critical of Civilian Culture—A 'Disgusting' Trip Home," *The Wall Street Journal,* July 27, 1995, p. 1.

Daniel Da Cruz, *Boot* (New York: St. Martin's, 1987), p. 18: "Recruits are shocked to discover that their drill instructors . . . are never—at least hardly ever—profane. . . . Indeed, as early as the second day, the drill instructor asks the assembled platoon: 'Since you've come aboard, has anybody verbally abused you—called you an s.o.b., or a slimebag, or a maggot or faggot, or addressed you in any other degrading terms? . . .' Silence. 'Has anybody abused you physically—hit, pushed, shoved, slapped, kicked, beat, tripped, kneed, elbowed or punched you?' Silence. 'Very well. If you feel you were abused, physically or verbally, you are to inform your Senior Drill Instructor at once.' "

But it is obvious that both verbal and physical abuse persist and are not reported for the reasons stated in H. Paul Jeffers and Dick Levitan, *See Parris and Die: Brutality in the U.S. Marines* (New York: Hawthorn, 1971), p. 6: "Fear of reprisal for what they may tell about cases of maltreatment or brutality often keeps young Marines from speaking out. . . . We came across numerous instances in which Marines told us that they had been warned that Drill Instructors are a tightly knit group who will stick together. The thrust of this threat is that no matter where a man goes, he will always find another Marine who has been a Drill Instructor and who will feel obligated to settle the score for a DI who was punished because of someone's testimony."

And abuse is not reported because many recruits expect violent punishment and believe it is appropriate.

32. Zeeland, p. 19.

33. Jeffers and Levitan, pp. 34-35. The authors gratuitously cite former Marine Lee Harvey Oswald as an example of the dangers of *in*appropriately focused sexual drives.

34. "Elders teach that semen is absolutely vital: it should be consumed daily since the creation of biological maleness and the maintenance of masculinity depend on it. . . . Although homosexual practices emerge from ritual trauma, abundant evidence indicates that most youths also experience them as pleasurable and erotically exciting. . . . With fatherhood, however, homosexuality should cease; thereafter men should engage only in heterosexual activities. Soon enough, the cycle starts over as men steer their young sons, too, along the traditional way into the cult." Gilbert Herdt, *Guardians of the Flutes: Idioms of Masculinity* (New York: McGraw-Hill, 1981), pp. 2-3. The Sambia practice ritual fellatio; in other tribes, such as the Keraki Trans-Fly River people, boys are inseminated anally; pp. 15, 319. See also Gilbert Herdt, ed., *Rituals of Manhood: Male Initiation in Papua New Guinea* (Berkeley, CA: University of California Press, 1982); and Gilbert Herdt, *Ritualized Homosexuality in Melanesia* (Berkeley, CA: University of California Press,

1984). Especially useful as an introduction to this topic is Gilbert Herdt, *The Sambia: Ritual and Gender in New Guinea* (New York: Holt, Rinehart and Winston, 1987).

35. "Stiff, sharp grasses are thrust up" the Sambia boys' noses; their skin is flayed open with "sticks, switches, or bristly objects." Herdt, *Guardians of the Flutes*, pp. 222-234. In the Awa tribe, "the glans penis of each initiate is cut. . . . The foreskin is held back with a split stick, and an incision is made on each side of the glans with a bamboo knife." In a later "severe-penis-cutting ritual," "instruments used for bleeding the nose are not simply jabbed into the nostrils, but are driven in deeply with a stone or wooden pounder to cause very profuse bleeding. Similarly, the glans penis is not simply incised, but small wedges of flesh are removed from either side, producing deep, half-inch-long gashes that occasionally penetrate the urethra. The lacerated glans then is struck sharply and repeatedly with the blade of the bamboo knife used in the cutting and also is rubbed vigorously with salt or nettles." Philip L. Newman and David J. Boyd, "The Making of Men: Ritual and Meaning in Awa Male Initiation" in Herdt, ed., *Rituals of Manhood*, p. 254.

36. Reporting on the "sado-sexual rite of passage," Sam Donaldson intoned: "Watch as this team leader . . . paints a tar-like military shoe dressing called 'edge dressing' on the most sensitive area of [an initiate's] body."

In 1995, the media reported on the court martial case of a chief warrant officer charged with training abuses at Camp Lejeune. One witness, a first lieutenant, "told the court he saw an incident where a Marine was held down by a number of other Marines and threatened with sodomy. He said one of the interrogators rubbed a mini-flashlight across the Marine's rectum. [The first lieutenant] said he informed [the chief warrant officer] of this and other incidents, but the Marines continued to train." "Marine Tells of Camp That Feels Out of Control," Associated Press, August 22, 1995. A four-officer military jury found the warrant officer innocent of all charges, including that he poured Tabasco sauce on a Marine's genitals. "Warrant Officer Cleared of Abuse Charges," *Navy Times*, September 4, 1995, p. 2.

37. Like sailors, seagoing Marines may experience cross-dressing, sadomasochistic play, and simulated anal and oral male-male sex as part of the "crossing the line" ceremony.

38. Roger M. Keesing, Herdt, ed., *Rituals of Manhood*, p. 8.

39. Leo Bersani, *Homos* (Cambridge, MA: Harvard University Press, 1995) p. 96.

40. Leo Bersani, "Is the Rectum a Grave?" in Jonathon Goldberg, ed., *Reclaiming Sodom* (New York: Routledge, 1994), p. 252.

41. Ibid., p. 256.

In *Sailors and Sexual Identity*, Anthony, describing his first experience with a Marine who wanted to be anally penetrated, recalls his surprise: "I expected that Marines were tops. They seem so masculine when you see them, you'd think that would translate when they go to bed. But I've found . . . Marines to be quite the opposite. Every single solitary time with no exception at all." He then adds, "I did let him fuck me too." In answer to my protest that he couldn't then call the Marine a bottom, Anthony says "But he didn't initiate the fucking of me. I jumped up and sat down on him. I was on top the whole time"; p. 31.

42. Bersani, *Homos*, p. 28. See also Frank Browning, "Spirit and Transgression: Looking for Ecstasy in the Penetrated Man," *The Culture of Desire: Paradox and Perversity in Gay Lives Today* (New York: Crown, 1993), pp. 74-105.

43. Kate Bornstein, *Gender Outlaw* (New York: Routledge, 1994) pp. 10-11.

44. Bersani, *Homos*, p. 63. I have met more than a few Marines (and several Army men, but, interestingly, so far no sailors) who made known to me a special attraction to Nazi uniforms, and in some cases a sympathy for fascist politics.

45. Ibid., p. 18.

46. Zeeland, see Figure 2.

47. Viewers of the 1994 movie *Ed Wood* learned the true story that beneath his World War II Marine Corps uniform the (only too serious) filmmaker wore women's undergarments. See Rudolf Grey, *Nightmare of Ecstasy* (Portland, Oregon: Feral House, 1992). "JOE ROBERTSON. We were both in the Marine Corps, [Ed Wood] was in the invasion of Tarawa. 4,000 Marines went in . . . 400 came out. He was one of the 400. He was wearing pink panties and a pink bra

underneath his battle fatigues. And he said to me, 'Thank God Joe I got out, because I wanted to be killed, I didn't want to be wounded, because I could never explain my pink panties and pink bra' "; p. 20.

48. Susan Faludi, "The Naked Citadel," *The New Yorker*, September 5, 1994, p. 81.

49. "The picture of a movie star hooker in mesh stockings ending up happily ever after with her customer makes for good cinema, but it has nothing to do with reality on the streets of Oceanside, young Marines headed for their first liberty were told yesterday. Oceanside Police Sergeant Bob Olson told about 400 students in the School of Infantry [that] 'Seven out of ten of the prostitutes the Marines find on Hill Street and other popular spots are males—transvestites. Do not mess with these people. . . . Stay together, take care of each other. Travel in groups—two or more.' Why does prostitution flourish in Oceanside and elsewhere on the circuit, Olson asked? Because men have a problem with what he called sperm poisoning, which forces them to think with their hormones, he said." The sergeant urged Marines to amuse themselves instead at the El Camino Real shopping mall (where security guards wearing drill instructor-style "smokey" hats are on hand to keep Marines in line). "A veteran street cop prepares young Marines for first liberty," *San Diego Union-Tribune*, March 27, 1993, p. B-1.

An Oceanside drag queen prostitute killed in 1991 by two Marines reportedly dissatisfied with his sexual performance and his refusal to refund $18—but not dissatisfied with his maleness—"belonged to a group of 20 or more transvestite prostitutes who work the streets of downtown Oceanside, according to police." "Pair Face Trial in Transvestite's Slaying," *North County Blade-Citizen*, June 22, 1991, p. B-1.

In 1992, in an effort to reduce prostitution, the Oceanside City Council proposed that all Marines be banned from the downtown area. Business persons, Camp Pendleton officials, and Oceanside police spoke out against the proposal. A police lieutenant argued that "Marines constitute just 30 percent of the 'johns' for prostitutes." "Leaders Pan Marine Ban Plan," *North County Blade-Citizen*, October 21, 1992, p. B-1.

By the summer of 1995, a newspaper reporter found that ". . . the prostitutes, at least the heavily sequined variety, have moved south.

Many of the Marines appear to have departed altogether." "What's in a name? Ask Oceanside," *San Diego Union-Tribune*, June 2, 1995, p. B-1. In the same year, Oceanside public officials renamed the town's main drag, Hill Street, to Coast Highway, in an effort to cleanse the street of its sex/crime/Marine associations. Years of this kind of sanitization hysteria have robbed Oceanside of what grotty charm it once possessed, and the hoped-for tourists remain a chamber of commerce fantasy.

50. Susan Sontag, "Notes on Camp," *Against Interpretation* (New York: Anchor, 1990), p. 279.

51. Butler, pp. 24-25.

52. See Judith Butler, *Bodies That Matter: On the Discursive Limits of "Sex"* (New York: Routledge, 1993); and Monique Wittig, *The Straight Mind and Other Essays* (Boston: Beacon Press, 1992).

53. Physical intimacy among male Marines is alluded to in David Bowne Wood, *A Sense of Values: American Marines in an Uncertain World* (Kansas City, MO: Andrews and McMeel, 1994), p. 46. Wood writes that for the deprivations of Marine Corps life in cramped quarters overseas "there are compensations. One is the physical closeness. On a crowded subway back in the civilian world, these men would shrink from having their knee touch a seatmate's thigh. Here, those inhibitions are absent. Exhausted, lonely . . . they welcome the touch of another human being. . . . Marines say this is something few civilians can understand. It is an important part of their resistance to having openly gay Marines in their ranks. In the stress of combat operations, Major Dick explains, 'somebody puts his hand on your shoulder and it's tremendously comforting, reassuring. To throw a sexual aspect in there, whether it's women Marines or gays, it just screws with that formula.'" But six anonymous comments Wood quotes are evenly split on the issue of whether "gays should be allowed to serve openly in the Marine Corps." So while a first lieutenant says "All the arguments have been heard before but I guess my reason is the thought of fags in my platoon just makes me want to puke," a lance corporal counters "The gays are not the problem, it's the society we have that won't accept them. They are already in, they shouldn't have to hide what they are. We should accept them"; p. 52.

54. As meat is always something more than just meat. Ecofeminist theories link militarism, sexism, homophobia, racism, and the exploitation of animals. See Carol Adams, *The Sexual Politics of Meat: A Feminist Vegetarian Critical Theory* (New York: Continuum, 1990); Josephine Donovan, "Animal Rights and Feminist Theory," *Signs* (15, 1990): 250-375; and Lawrence Finsen and Susan Finsen, *The Animal Rights Movement in America: From Compassion to Respect* (New York: Twayne, 1994). The prevalence of animal metaphors in military life (e.g., "devil dogs," "dogfaces," "airedales," "sea dogs," "SEALS," "squids," "maggots") and in military sexual culture (e.g., "sea bitch," "wog," "wog dog," "powder monkey") may be an area worthy of study.

In the Navy "crossing the line" ceremony, the novitiates, known as "polliwogs," are made to dress like *women*, ape *queer* sex, and crawl around like *animals*—all so that in the end they can stand up as honorable *men*. When women, or queers, are not even symbolically available for men to dominate, animals may be conscripted, as this book's horrific closing parable may show.

55. Katz, p. 14.

56. Gore Vidal, "Someone to Laugh at the Squares With" [Tennessee Williams], *New York Review of Books*, June 13, 1985; reprinted in *At Home: Essays, 1982-1988* (NY: Random House, 1988), p. 48, quoted in Katz, p. 99. In a 1995 interview with the *Advocate*, Vidal answered a question about his being a homosexual: "But I'm not an adjective; I'm a noun, a male with all sorts of sexual possibilities, which should be of no more interest to the state—or anyone else—than a liking say, for rice, not potatoes. . . . To be categorized is simply to be enslaved. Watch out." Judy Wieder, "Vidal on Vidal," *The Advocate*, October 31, 1995, p. 38.

57. Katz, p. 104.

58. Ibid.

59. "Sex is not a thing. It can't be numbered. Sex slithers: It is fluid, aerial, protean and wholly fantastic." D. Keith Mano, "What's a survey of our bedroom habits [the "Sex in America" survey] worth if it isn't any fun?," *Los Angeles Times* Book Review, January 8, 1995, p. 1.

60. DeCecco and Parker, p. 18.

Corporal Keith

1. Judith Butler, *Gender Trouble* (New York: Routledge, 1990) p. 31.
2. From an interview with a gay-identified corporal, Scott:

> Z: I expressed some doubt to you about Keith's story about the "over-the-line" contest, and you said—
>
> S: Yes, I'm sure that story's true, because stuff like that is pretty common. There was one time when there were these two guys sitting on the top rack in their cube in Okinawa with probably twenty people lookin' on, beatin' off to see who could shoot their load the farthest. Both of these guys were big and buff bodybuilders. Everyone knew they were on steroids; you could tell, just by the side effects. It was pretty hot.
>
> Z: What were they saying while they were doing this?
>
> S: They were just giving each other shit. "I'm gonna beat you." "No way man, I got what it takes to kick your ass." Stuff like that. I mean, one of 'em had aspirations to be in a porno movie, so he was practicing.
>
> Z: What were the reactions and comments of the onlookers?
>
> S: Disbelief, for the most part. "Man, I can't believe they're doing that." "Shit, man, look at that!" "You guys are fuckin' crazy, man!" But nobody left. [Laughs.] Everybody stayed.
>
> Z: Were they staring?
>
> S: Yeah. "Dude, man, check it out!" And more and more people came. "Hey man, so-and-so's down there havin' a jack-off contest!" "What? What the fuck, man!" And people would come running down and look.
>
> Z: So who won?
>
> S: To tell you the truth, the hottest one didn't. The other guy did.

David, a sergeant I interviewed, recalled how, overseas, "a lot of guys would get together in the barracks and they would rent pornos. They would sit there and jack off together. Being a cook, I work in the mess hall: I know everybody, and I hear everybody. I would hear guys go, 'Yeah, he comes like a fuckin' horse.' They would never say that they did anything sexually, but to me, watchin' another guy come—you gotta be interested in something."

See David Bowne Wood, *A Sense of Values: American Marines in An Uncertain World* (Kansas City, MO: Andrews and McMeel, 1994), p. 105: Out at sea and bored, a Marine unit's "youngest officers, its lieutenants, have organized a competition to see who can go the longest without spanking the monkey (masturbating). A renegade group has started a countercompetition: who can record the greatest number of successful spankings within a twenty-four-hour period."

See Zeeland, *Sailors and Sexual Identity* (Binghamton, NY: The Haworth Press, 1995) p. 251. According to a Navy chaplain candidate who counseled Marine recruits at MCRD, "Marines are all the time jerking off in front of each other. They'll just stand there and do it. And jerk each other off, too. That's very common from what I have seen."

Mutual masturbation among Marines was also very common in the 1840s and 1850s. See B. R. Burg, *An American Seafarer in the Age of Sail: The Erotic Diaries of Philip C. Van Buskirk*, 1851-1870 (New Haven, CT: Yale University Press, 1994), pp. 24-25.

3. See Figure 2 in *Sailors and Sexual Identity.*

Lance Corporal Ted

1. Most servicemen I interviewed told me that they did not masturbate at boot camp; many claimed that during those three months they never even had erections. (Some cited the hoary myth that, to dampen their libidos, the armed services feed recruits potassium nitrate.) But "RJ," a 22-year-old bisexual Marine Corps infantryman, told me that:

> R: In boot camp I took showers with seventy-five other men. Caught many of them masturbating. It was no big deal.
> Z: Were they embarrassed at getting caught?
> R: Actually, no. They didn't miss a beat.

And Christine, a 30-year-old Marine Corps sergeant, recalled how in boot camp, she:

> watched this one female rub herself up and masturbate in the shower. I thought it was interesting. I don't think I enjoyed it, though. She

was under the shower and the water was beating on her, and I think she just was lonely. I did, however, have this one girl hit on me in boot camp. She was comin' on really strong. She kept wantin' to know what my favorite food was, my favorite colors—my favorite song, because she'll *sing* me a song. In fact, any of the songs that she just got done singing, did I like 'em? And she was singing them for me. . . . She'd walk past me with a broom and start hitting my buttocks with it. One time she pulled my pants up, because I guess my underwear was showing. I mean, it might have been okay if she was attractive, but she was ugly.

2. I had no such qualms in the almost mirror case of an Army infantryman I knew in Frankfurt who, one night, brought his straight buddy (cute, virginal, and so butch that, as a result of a farming accident, on one foot he only had two toes) out to the gay bars with him. The gay soldier, who was supposed to baby-sit the straight soldier and protect him from predators, met up with an old trick and asked if they could sleep in my foyer. Farm Boy (by now very drunk) agreed to bunk down with me in my twin bed—reluctantly, he wanted it to be known. But as I scratched his bristles, he asked me: "If I pass out, do you want me to lay on my stomach, or on my back?"

3. In bed with Ted I only got to sleep with the aid of sedatives, which always leave me feeling somewhat *feminine*. I think of the late rock critic Lester Bangs—an early literary influence—who, in a piece on Lou Reed, wrote that "All humans are the same sex, except albinos. It is the drugs, obviously, that determine the gender of the being. . . . Downs are feminine. Speed is masculine." Lester Bangs, "The Greatest Album Ever Made" [Lou Reed's "Metal Machine Music," RCA, 1976] *Psychotic Reactions and Carburetor Dung* (New York: Vintage, 1988), p. 199.

Corporal Alex

1. "Wilhelm Reich tried to explain the practice among soldiers, cadets, and others of visiting brothels together, on the basis of a hidden goal, which was finding one's comrade, the other man, in the person of the prostitute and having intercourse with him through her. See *Die Funktion der Orgasmus* [Frankfurt, 1972], p. 167." Klaus Theweleit, *Male Fantasies, Volume 1: Women, Floods, Bod-*

ies, History, trans. S. Conway (Minneapolis, MN: University of Minnesota Press, 1987), p. 124.

Captain Eric

1. Michael Granberry, "Inquiry Links Marines to Gay Pornography," *Los Angeles Times*, August 19, 1993, p. A-3. The story was also reported by Connie Chung on the CBS Evening News, August 18, 1993, and on NBC on the following morning's *Today Show*.

2. The tapes are sold mail-order by The Frat House Boys, a Los Angeles-based video distributor.

3. Tony Perry, "10 Pendleton Marines Posed Nude, Probe Finds," *Los Angeles Times*, October 29, 1993, p. B-4.

4. "In May [1988], [Oceanside] police and military officials began investigating Thomas Francis McGrath Jr. [a 48-year-old retired Coast Guardsman; the newspaper published his home address] . . . for paying [as many as 25] Marines up to $60 for two-hour pornographic modelling sessions in his Oceanside condominium. After finding in McGrath's home 33 videos and hundreds of pictures of men masturbating or engaging in homosexual acts—some in partial military uniform—police arrested McGrath on charges of pimping, pandering and running a house of prostitution. He was released last week on $10,500 bail. 'I am certain this is a first,' said Lt. Col. Fred Peck, who heads the public affairs division of the Marine Corps headquarters in Washington, D.C." Dana Steckbauer, *San Diego Tribune*, "Pendleton Marine discharged in wake of porn-ring probe," June 23, 1988, B-3. "'For the purposes of this case, we consider the models to be prostitutes,' said Mike Goldsmith, an investigator with the Oceanside Police Department. . . . '[McGrath] had a regular camcorder, like the ones you'd use to film your kids.'" Tom Burgess, "Marines in Sex Videos Facing Charges," *San Diego Union* June 23, 1988, B-1. Ultimately, police dropped the charges against McGrath, but five Marines were discharged as a result of the investigation. McGrath's Kly-Max Studio remained closed, but his tapes, originally released under such titles as *Real Marines* (4 vols., 1989) and *Every Day is the Fourth of July* (1991), keep resurfacing through new distributors.

"Late in 1976 . . . a Marine sergeant went roaming through an adult book store in Oceanside, and happened upon an incriminating picture from the film [*Hot Day in L.A.* (Brentwood, 1975)]. His reaction shook the store: 'Those cocksuckers are in *my* unit!'" Hardesty (February 1990), p. 72. Other 1970s Brentwood films that feature active-duty Marines include *Marine Furlough* (1976), *Small Town Boy* (1976), *Mark* (1977), and *Truck Stop* (1977). According to Hardesty, "The fallout from the scandal helped to sink the Brentwood studio and threatened many Marine careers. But . . . decision-makers at the Pentagon proved as anxious as the pornographers to limit bad publicity and to let the dust settle."

5. From 1945 until his death in 1992, Robert Mizer photographed more than 5,000 models for his Athletic Model Guild (AMG), including many Marines and sailors. See Introduction endnote 24 and Figures 13-18.

6. Interview with Rolf Hardesty, August 30, 1995. Between 1969 and 1975, Hardesty says he manned the San Diego County end of an "underground railway" that shuttled sailors and Marines from San Diego, Oceanside, and San Clemente to the Hollywood male escort and porn industries. He told the author that, throughout the Vietnam years, desperate AWOL servicemen were an easy and attractive mark for filmmakers and pimps. Some active-duty sailors and Marines continued to supplement their paychecks this way in the mid-1990s.

7. According to Bobby's statement to the *Los Angeles Times*, he was inspired to make his videos by the 1989 movie *sex, lies, and videotape*. "What transpired, he said, were stories of 'heartbreak and sadness,' as dozens of men in their early 20s spoke of the loneliness and desperation of growing up poor in small towns across America. Much of that emotion, he said, involved confusion over women and 'changing sex roles.'" Such conversations are not represented in the commercially available tapes, in which Bobby's most trenchant questions are "When was the last time you had pussy?" and "Do you like to fuck a girl in the ass?"

8. In a videotape recorded after his release from prison, Bobby coyly boasts to one young Marine, "I'm very famous." He asks if the Marine would like to see a sample of his handiwork. Watching Bobby fellate another Marine on video, the masturbating Marine is unable to keep from ejaculating. Bobby asks: "[Was it] because you see me in action?"

The Marine answers, "That too."

"*Ahhhhh!*" Bobby shrieks scathingly.

The Marine stutters "But of course—I will admit—Granted, I don't like—I'll admit, I'm the kind of guy that actually prefers— But sometimes—"

Sergeant Wood and Corporal Marie

1. John Preston, ed., *A Member of the Family: Gay Men Write About Their Families* (New York: Dutton, 1992), pp. 6-10.

2. A lesbian Marine I interviewed told me that women in the Marine Corps do not bond like male Marines bond. Christine, a 30-year-old sergeant, said that "because we don't go to war, [the bonding is] just not there. . . . I always thought, dammit, they can do it, why can't we? I can't ever recall any females being together like the men are. Hangin' out, touchin'. One of my [gay Marine] friends was able to kiss numerous straight Marines at this one party. And it was okay for him to do it. It's okay for the guys to touch and be close, but it's not okay for the women."

Major Luke

1. Phillip Caputo, *A Rumor of War* (New York: Holt, Rinehart and Winston, 1977), quoted in Craig M. Cameron, *American Samurai* (New York: Cambridge University Press, 1994), p. 52.

2. David Bowne Wood, *A Sense of Values* (Kansas City, MO: Andrews and McMeel, 1994), p. 2.

3. Ibid., p. 16.

4. Cameron, p. 25.

5. John A. Lejuene, quoted in Cameron, p. 28. Cameron notes that "the entire birthday ceremony is carefully staged, heightening the emotional atmosphere in which this message is read. One of the other passages most frequently quoted at the annual ball has always been King Henry's 'band of brothers' speech to his troops from Shakespeare's *Henry V*." See Keith's interview for mention of an alternative gay Marine ball.

6. Cameron, p. 28.

7. Ibid., p. 64.

8. Ibid., p. 63.

Shakespeare's *Henry V*." See Keith's interview for mention of an alternative gay Marine ball.

6. Cameron, p. 28.
7. Ibid., p. 64.
8. Ibid., p. 63.